WHERE TO WATCH WILDLIFE IN BRITAIN

BY LOW-CARBON TRANSPORT

WHERE TO WATCH WILDLIFE IN BRITAIN BY LOW-CARBON TRANSPORT

Megan Shersby, Heather Devey,
Rebecca Gibson and Dan Rouse

BLOOMSBURY

BLOOMSBURY WILDLIFE
Bloomsbury Publishing Plc
50 Bedford Square, London, WC1B 3DP, UK
Bloomsbury Publishing Ireland Limited,
29 Earlsfort Terrace, Dublin 2, D02 AY28, Ireland

BLOOMSBURY, BLOOMSBURY WILDLIFE and the Diana logo are trademarks of
Bloomsbury Publishing Plc

First published in the United Kingdom 2026

Copyright © Megan Shersby, Heather Devey, Rebecca Gibson and Dan Rouse 2026

Megan Shersby, Heather Devey, Rebecca Gibson and Dan Rouse have asserted their rights under
the Copyright, Designs and Patents Act, 1988, to be identified as Authors of this work

For legal purposes the Credits on p. 236
constitute an extension of this copyright page

All rights reserved. No part of this publication may be: i) reproduced or transmitted in any form, electronic or mechanical, including photocopying, recording or by means of any information storage or retrieval system without prior permission in writing from the publishers; or ii) used or reproduced in any way for the training, development or operation of artificial intelligence (AI) technologies, including generative AI technologies. The rights holders expressly reserve this publication from the text and data mining exception as per Article 4(3) of the Digital Single Market Directive (EU) 2019/790

Bloomsbury Publishing Plc does not have any control over, or responsibility for, any third-party websites referred to or in this book. All internet addresses given in this book were correct at the time of going to press. The author and publisher regret any inconvenience caused if addresses have changed or sites have ceased to exist, but can accept no responsibility for any such changes

A catalogue record for this book is available from the British Library

Library of Congress Cataloguing-in-Publication data has been applied for

ISBN: PB: 978-1-3994-1265-0; ePub: 978-1-3994-1267-4; ePDF: 978-1-3994-1268-1

2 4 6 8 10 9 7 5 3 1

Design by Big Orange Door
Maps by L Wright Design
Printed and bound in China by C&C Offset Printing Co., Ltd.

To find out more about our authors and books visit www.bloomsbury.com
and sign up for our newsletters
For product safety related questions contact productsafety@bloomsbury.com

CONTENTS

How to use this book 6
Map of the regions 8

SOUTHERN ENGLAND AND MIDLANDS 9
London 10
Norwich 23
Birmingham 33
Bristol 44
Exeter 55

NORTHERN ENGLAND 66
Carlisle 67
Hull 78
Leeds 89
Liverpool 100
Newcastle 111

WALES 122
St Davids 123
Swansea 134
Llandudno 145
Bangor 156
Wrexham 166

SCOTLAND 176
Edinburgh 177
Dundee 190
Dumfries 203
Oban 214
Elgin 224

Useful resources 234
Glossary and abbreviations 235
Photo credits 236
Index 237

HOW TO USE THIS BOOK

Where to Watch Wildlife: By Low-carbon Transport is your guide to discovering the rich natural heritage and captivating wildlife found in and around 20 cities and towns across England, Scotland and Wales – all accessible without the need for a car. Whether nestled within urban boundaries, or a short train or bus journey away, we've carefully selected 103 nature reserves and green spaces waiting to be explored. Each site offers opportunities to observe a diverse array of wildlife, with some home to species that are rare or particularly special.

At a time when the realities of climate change are becoming ever more pressing, finding ways to reduce our carbon footprint has never felt more vital. In writing this book, we wanted to celebrate exploring nature without a car and show that some of the richest wildlife experiences can be found close to our cities. Travelling slowly and lightly not only lessens our impact on the natural world, but also deepens our connection to it, inviting us to notice more, linger longer, and rediscover the quiet joy of wildlife on our doorstep.

Knot.

Green-veined white.

Common toad.

The book is designed around 20 urban hubs from which to visit five or six sites. Each author has aimed to cover a range of habitats and species available in a hub, though it was a challenge to limit each city's reserves to just a handful of the standout sites. Every single one can be reached from the city centre by walking, cycling or public transport – and in fact, some can only be reached this way. Although there are a few which are a little more challenging, they are worth the effort and time required to reach them.

Each city hub begins with an overview of the different sites, habitat types and species that can be found in the area, as well as a reference map to help you plan your visits. For every featured site, you will find detailed directions from a central location – typically the main bus or railway station – as well as full addresses, postcodes, grid references, OS map references and What3Words co-ordinates for key entrances or locations. Most of these sites are open throughout the year during daylight hours, and the majority are free to enter. Where opening hours or entry fees apply, these are clearly noted. Every effort has been made to ensure that the information provided is accurate and up to date at the time of printing; however, these may change. For the latest information regarding opening times and prices, we recommend checking the websites of the relevant organisations.

Information on accessibility, including ground conditions and available facilities on site or nearby, has been given wherever possible, though individual needs vary and access may change since printing. Additional resources are listed in the Resources section on page 234, including websites specialising in accessibility that already cover some of the reserves and continue to grow with their listings. You'll also find a glossary of terms and abbreviations used in the book on page 235.

It is important to remember that these reserves are natural ecosystems, lovingly cared for by staff, volunteers and local communities. Please take your litter home with you, remain on designated paths, and where dogs are permitted, keep them on a lead to protect the animals, plants and fungi that call these spaces home.

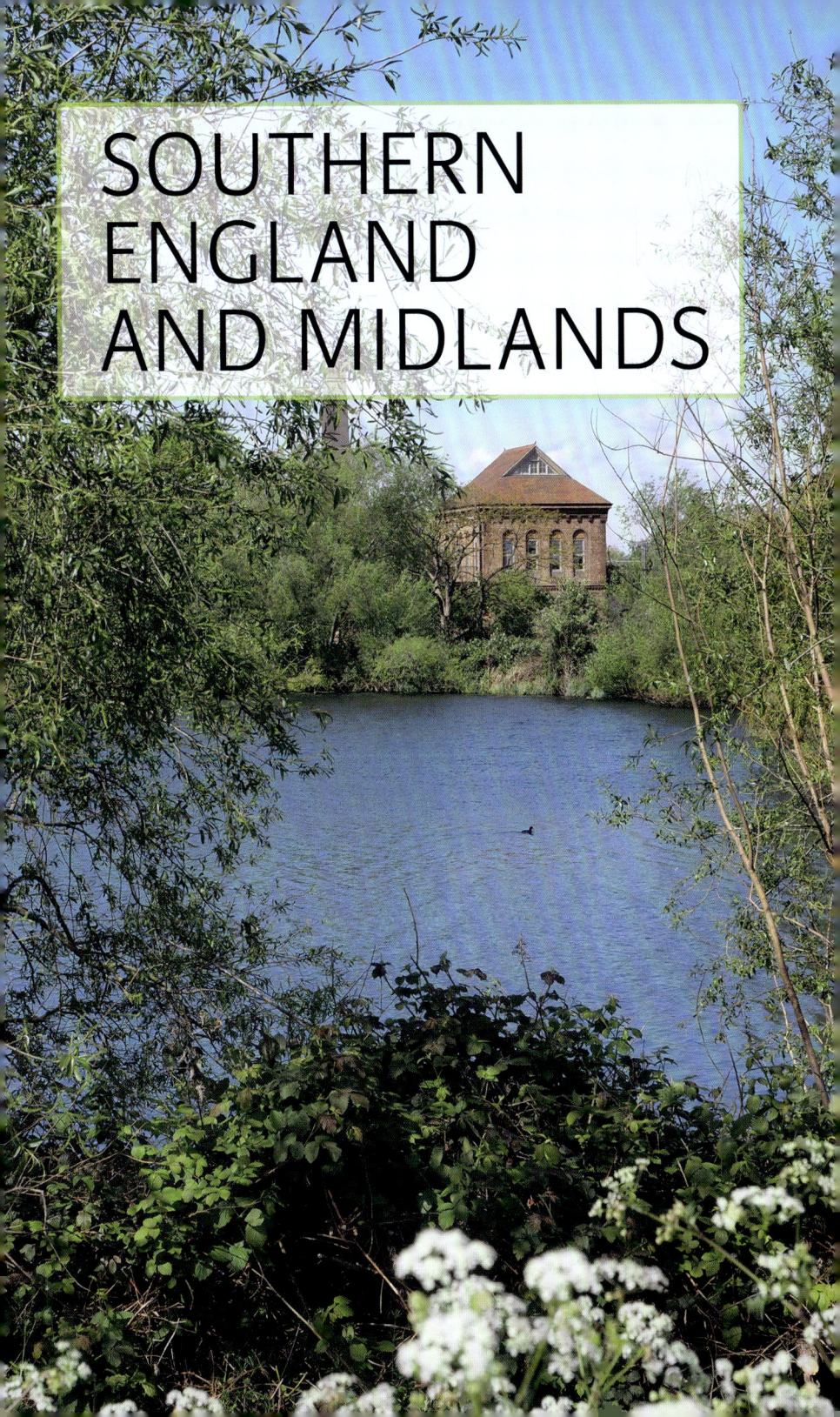

SOUTHERN ENGLAND AND MIDLANDS

LONDON

Home to almost nine million people, and visited by huge numbers of regular commuters and tourists, London's towering buildings, busy roads and the constant presence of other people can make it feel like there's no wildlife to be found here. However, this city has an amazing array of green and blue spaces to explore.

At its heart, running through the city like a life-giving artery, is the River Thames. The river is tidal eastwards from Teddington in west London, and while you may only see birds on the surface, it is full of other wildlife below, including 125 species of fish, crustaceans, molluscs and other invertebrates. The river is even used by mammals such as grey and common seals, and harbour porpoises.

Outside of the River Thames, there are ancient woodlands, wetlands, wildflower meadows and more. London is considered to be the world's largest urban forest with 8.4 million trees – more than a fifth of the capital has tree cover. In July 2019, London also became the world's first National Park City. An impressive 49.7 per cent of the city is made up of green or blue spaces, and 15,000 different species have been recorded.

As the capital, London is very well served by public transport, although there is a notable north–south divide for the distribution of London Underground stations, due to a mix of factors including land size, history and geology.

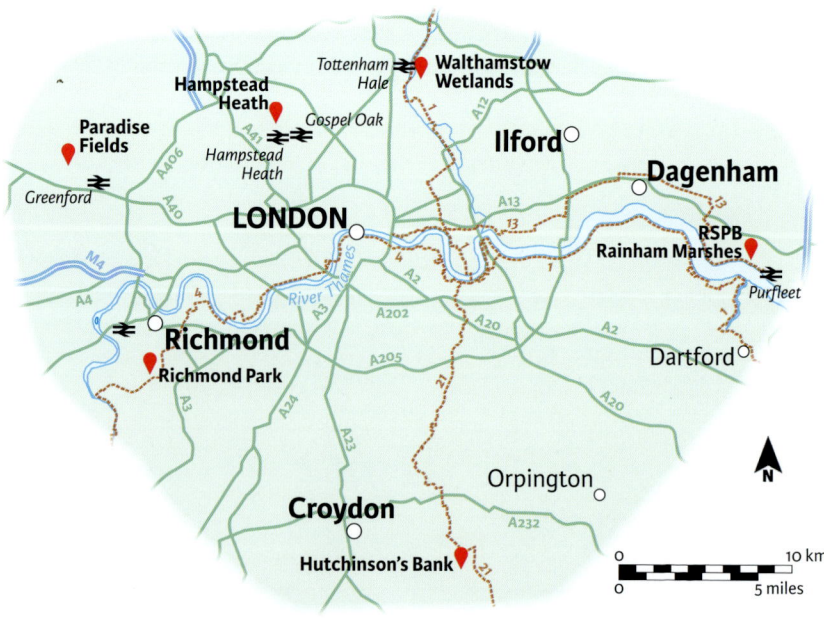

Previous page: Walthamstow Wetlands, London.

HAMPSTEAD HEATH

Hampstead Heath, Gordon House Rd, London NW5 1LT • OS Explorer Map 173
• Grid refs TQ283857 (entrance near Gospel Oak station), TQ254870 (entrance near Golders Green station), TQ262863 (Whitestone Pond, where North End Road and Spaniards Road meet, north of Hampstead station), TQ270874 (Kenwood House)
• What3Words: hill.script.quick (entrance near Gospel Oak station)

How to get there: The vastness of Hampstead Heath means there is a wide variety of public transport options taking you to different points around the park. Along the southern edge of the park, the main railway and Tube options are Hampstead station (Northern line), Hampstead Heath station (Mildmay Overground line), and Gospel Oak station (Mildmay and Suffragette Overground lines). In the northeast, there is Golders Green station (Northern line). • Along Spaniards Road and Hampstead Lane, which run along the north and between the main Heath and the northeastern sections, there are bus stops visited by 210, 310 and 603 buses. Along Highgate West Hill, running almost parallel and then alongside the eastern edge of the park, there are bus stops visited by the 214 bus. • There are a number of cycling paths within Hampstead Heath, as well as cycling stands for personal and hired (Lime and Forest) bicycles spaced around the edges of the park. The Camden Cyclists website has detailed information.

Access and conditions: There are accessible toilets and baby-changing facilities around the heath. The surfaced paths are suitable for wheelchairs, mobility scooters and prams. Mobility scooters are available to borrow free of charge from the Parliament Hill Lido. The Heath Hands charity runs accessible events. • Dogs are welcome in the park; however, only assistance dogs are allowed in some areas, such as the swimming ponds and Kenwood House. • Golders Hill Park opens at 07:00 and closes between 16:30 and 21:00 depending on the season. The Hill Garden and Pergola opens at 08:30 and closes between 15:30 and 20:00 depending on the season. Kenwood Estate has varying opening hours.

•• Stretching across much of northern Camden, and extending into southern Barnet, Hampstead Heath is an extensive public park featuring grasslands, heathland, ponds and formal gardens, as well as historic buildings and leisure facilities. The heath is beautiful to visit all year round, whether in glorious summer warmth or when peacefully frozen in winter, a magical scene that inspired C. S. Lewis's *The Lion, the Witch and the Wardrobe*.

With a variety of habitats across a large area, more than 180 species of birds have been recorded. It is a great spot for seeing birds of prey, in particular kestrels, buzzards and hobbies. Kestrels have bred in the park for years, buzzards on the Kenwood Estate since 2020 and hobbies are summer visitors. Tawny owls are seen regularly and are known to breed. In summer 2024 a barn owl was seen for the first time since the 1940s.

Additional exciting birds include woodcock on autumn migration, common crossbills during irruption years, spotted

Brimstone.

and pied flycatchers, and ring ouzel. A Dartford warbler, the first in 30 years, was seen in November 2024.

The park is a stronghold for the capital's hedgehogs, holding the largest population in London. A large-scale camera trap survey in 2018 produced 376 sightings (of around 100 individuals) across a two-week period.

Hampstead Heath is famous for being one of the best spots in London for outdoor swimming, with three natural ponds and an outdoor chlorinated pool at Parliament Hill Lido. The ponds have deep, opaque and untreated water and are suitable for competent swimmers only. They provide a great opportunity to get closer to nature at a different level, but are very popular in summer – so book ahead.

Taking up part of Hampstead Heath is the stunning Kenwood House, first built in 1616 and now managed by English Heritage. The house, along with its gardens and wider estate, are free to visit, though advance booking for the house is advised during busy periods. The estate has various seasonal highlights, including carpets of snowdrops in winter, bluebells in spring, hay meadows alive with flowers and insects in summer, and impressive veteran trees, such as the 350-year-old sweet chestnut near Elms Gate. One third of Kenwood's 45 hectares is a Site of Special Scientific Interest (SSSI) thanks to the standing deadwood, which is ideal habitat for a range of wildlife. The SSSI also contains a sphagnum bog.

HUTCHINSON'S BANK

Featherbed Lane, New Addington, Croydon CR0 0JT (website address), North Downs Road, New Addington, Croydon CR0 0LB (public transport entrance point) • OS Explorer Map 161 • Grid refs TQ379621 (entrance to reserve from footpath by waste facility), TQ381616 (middle of the reserve) • What3Words: exile.active.dawn (entrance to reserve from footpath by waste facility), frozen.purely.brush (middle of reserve)

How to get there: Take the tram to the New Addington stop, or the 64/130/314/664 bus to the New Addington Tram Stop. Follow one of the footpaths west to North Downs Road, then walk south to the household waste recycling centre. On the south side of the centre's entrance, there is a path to the reserve entrance. Threecorner Grove Reserve can be accessed via the southern part of Hutchinson's Bank. Chapel Bank can be accessed via a footpath running through Threecorner Grove, then crossing Featherbed Lane. • Hutchinson's Bank is close to National Cycle Network Route 21, which goes through New Addington, where there are cycle racks.

Access and conditions: The reserve is located on one side of a valley, with relatively steep sides. There is a tarmac path running from North Downs Road to the reserve entrance and through the woodland down to the meadows, after which there are some small non-tarmac paths criss-crossing the reserve. There are benches in the reserve. Access via a gate for wheelchairs or other mobility devices can be arranged from Farleigh Dean Crescent, but the path down from North Down Road to Farleigh Dean Crescent is unsuitable. Access to Chapel Bank is via a relatively narrow road – cross with care.

•• A pleasant place to visit all year round, Hutchinson's Bank and its neighbouring reserves shine particularly brightly in spring and summer, when orchids bloom and butterflies dance in the wildflower meadows. Combined, the three reserves make up 28 hectares of mixed habitats. Hutchinson's Bank came under London Wildlife Trust's management in 1987, following Chapel Bank in 1984, and has become a hotspot for insects, with 28 species of butterflies recorded here and more than 100 species of moths. As a chalkland site, it is fantastic for butterflies such as the chalkhill blue, small blue, brown and green hairstreaks, and five of the UK's eight skipper species. The site is notorious as an illegal reintroduction site for locally extinct butterflies and made the news in recent years for the appearance of black-veined white and Glanville fritillary butterflies.

Sheep grazing was brought back into the management plan of the site in 1995 in order to prevent the reserve being dominated by grasses, scrub and trees. The Trust has also created chalk scrapes, planted foodplants for specific butterflies (such as kidney vetch for the small blue), and encouraged yellow-rattle, a hemi-parasite which prevents grasses from completely taking over. The wildflowers have thrived, including pyramidal and bee orchids.

For those interested in geology, it is possible to find fossils of sea urchins in the chalk rocks, an amazing reminder of how the land has changed over millions of years.

Close to Hutchinson's Bank are two other nature reserves also owned by London Wildlife Trust. Threecorner Grove is a 2-hectare triangular-shaped reserve of ancient chalk woodland, particularly well known for its wild cherry trees, which bloom in spring. It is also an excellent spot for bluebells and wild garlic.

Further south and across the road lies the 13-hectare reserve of Chapel Bank, which is a good site for orchids, including the rare and amusingly shaped man orchid, and insects. Over 20 species of butterfly can be seen here, including the Glanville fritillary, Duke of Burgundy, green hairstreak and small blue. Conservation work has been undertaken to get rid of invasive scrub and to open it up again for the wildflowers and grassland.

Green hairstreak.

PARADISE FIELDS

Perivale, Greenford UB6 0AD • OS Explorer Map 173 • Grid refs TQ150840 (entrance to the reserve at the underpass), TQ153841 (entrance to the reserve at the canal) • What3Words: funny.cares.final (entrance to the reserve at the underpass), thanks.healthier.wasp (entrance to the reserve at the canal)

How to get there: Take the Central line train or 92/105 buses to Greenford Underground and National Rail station. Walk north along Oldfield Lane North, then east along Rockware Avenue. Cross Greenford Road A4127 and take the footpath between the road and McDonald's to access the underpass leading into the reserve. Alternatively, take the 395 bus to the Westway Cross Retail Park, and access the underpass from the footpath. • The main path through is part of the Capital Ring Walk, a 78-mile (126km) circular walk through London divided into 15 sections. The walk from Greenford station through Paradise Fields is the first part of Section 9. • There are no cycle racks at Paradise Fields, but there are some available at the nearby shopping centre.

Access and conditions: There is a tarmac path running through Paradise Fields from the underpass to the Grand Union Canal. Dogs are allowed, but must be kept on a lead. There are no facilities or dedicated Blue Badge parking on the reserve. There is a small car park next to the retail park, separate to the retail park's own parking, with dedicated Blue Badge parking. Some shops have accessible toilets and baby-changing facilities for customers.

•• Although it is part of the large Horsenden Hill Nature Reserve, Paradise Fields itself is only 8 hectares in size and is separated from the larger reserve by the Grand Union Canal. Unusually, you can actually walk through the beaver enclosure, stepping inside the tall metal fences that run along the boundaries of the reserve and through the double heavy-duty gates – all installed to prevent the beavers escaping.

Introduced to the reserve in October 2023, the family of five beavers welcomed its first two kits in the spring of 2024, hailed as the first beavers to be born in urban London in more than 400 years. As the beaver family grows further, the offspring may be the foundations for new reintroductions elsewhere.

It is hard to spot the reintroduced beavers, and timing is key. Beavers typically leave their lodges at dawn and dusk, and can be spooked by unusual noises and smells, especially by dogs. However, it is still worth visiting the reserve to see the signs of beaver presence – which includes three lodges and nine functional dams across the site – and to look out for other wildlife. Since the reintroduction, ecologists and volunteers working on the project have seen an improvement in water quality and clarity, with an increase in invertebrates including dragonflies and the appearance of cased caddisflies and freshwater shrimp. Kingfishers have been seen more often, hunting for prey on the brook, whilst water rail and snipe have been sighted for

Beaver dam.

the first time. Two new bat species have been recorded, Leisler's and Daubenton's, both of which are indicator species for a healthy ecosystem. Paradise Fields is also home to brown hairstreak butterflies, a relatively rare species that is gradually making a comeback in London. The Ealing Wildlife Group's butterfly team believe that the coppicing work of the beavers is helping to create good habitat for blackthorn, on which the brown hairstreaks lay their eggs.

Alongside improving the reserve's biodiversity, the beavers have also had an important impact in holding back water. Previously, there had been flooding downstream of Paradise Fields and the site had been identified for further engineering works. The beaver reintroduction seems to have helped, increasing the water-holding capacity at the site, and the areas downstream remain unflooded, despite high rainfall events.

The urban location of the Ealing project – and the accessibility of its enclosure – means that this is a unique site, and could inspire further urban reintroductions in the future. It is an unusual feeling to hear the roar of the busy traffic and see the high-rise flats nearby and know that you are so close to such special wild animals.

In addition to the now-famous beavers, harvest mice have also been reintroduced to the site, and it may become a receptor site for water vole reintroductions as part of a wider recovery plan.

RICHMOND PARK

Richmond Gate Lodge, Richmond TW10 5HU • OS Explorer Map 161 • Grid refs TQ185736 (Richmond Gate entrance), TQ199728 (Pen Ponds) • What3Words: piper.frogs.gloves (Richmond Gate entrance), slip.smile.dice (Pen Ponds)

How to get there: There are multiple entrances to Richmond Park, and a variety of train, Underground and bus routes which go near it. Richmond station, to the north of the park and just over a 1-mile (1.6km) walk from one of the main entrances at Richmond Gate Lodge, is serviced by the Mildmay Overground line, District line and South Western Railway. • National Cycle Network Route 4 runs through the middle of Richmond Park. Cycling within the park is permitted on some of the larger roads where stated and off-road on the Tamsin Trail. There are cycling racks at various points around the outside of the park.

Access and conditions: Richmond Park has numerous tarmac paths that are suitable for wheelchairs, and seven disabled toilets (mostly around the edge of park, though there are some by the disabled parking bays at the Isabella Plantation). Within the park, there is a free minibus service with disabled access which operates every Monday, Wednesday and Friday between late March and late November (and sometimes later in the year). • The pedestrian gates are open 24/7 (with the exception of during the deer culls), and the vehicle gates are open 07:30–16:00. • If visiting with a dog, it is a legal requirement that you keep it under close control, and on the lead around the ponds and lakes and between May and July during the deer birthing season.

•• Richmond Park is famous for its herds of red deer and fallow deer, which have freely roamed the park since 1637. Created by Charles I, the park was enclosed and used for hunting deer.

The largest park in London, it has a number of wildlife and conservation designations: National Nature Reserve, Site of Special Scientific Interest (SSSI), Special Area of Conservation (SAC) and Conservation Area. One of the reasons for the SSSI designation is the lowland acid grassland (the largest area in Greater London) which benefits from the deer grazing and is home to plants that thrive in areas of low fertility, such as sheep's sorrel, mouse-ear hawkweed and harebell. In autumn, the grassland can be a good location for finding colourful waxcap fungi, including the green parrot, scarlet and golden waxcaps.

There are more than 1,000 ancient and veteran trees in the park, the most famous of which is the Royal Oak. Thought to be around 750 years old, it has a large split down one side and is hollow in the centre.

Almost 30 species of butterflies are breeding or regularly seen here. Purple emperor butterflies are sometimes spotted, though it is unknown if they breed in the park. In September 2024, there was even a sighting of a pair of long-tailed blue butterflies, a species that is not yet resident in the UK, but may become so as a result of climate change. The park is also a stronghold for the double-line moth, a red-brown species that feeds on grasses as a caterpillar. Mostly found in southwest England and southern Wales, this moth is a UK BAP priority species.

One of the park's conservation designations comes from a different insect resident – the stag beetle. This is the UK's largest beetle species, growing up to 10cm in length. Males are particularly impressive with their large antler-like jaws, which they use to battle other males – a bit like the deer rut, but on a much smaller scale. London is a hotspot for this declining species, which can spend up to four years as a larva within deadwood. Look out for the adults between mid-May and late July, and if you spot one, submit a sighting to the park or to Greenspace Information for Greater London (GiGL).

Richmond Park is managed by the Royal Parks. The Friends of Richmond Park is a charity that funds conservation projects, undertakes volunteering work such as litter picking and operates the park visitor centre.

The park undertakes humane culling of deer in February and November for a period of up to six weeks in order to manage the population and prevent overgrazing. The park is closed overnight during these times. The venison is sold, and the money raised is used for deer feed and to employ Wildlife Officers.

RSPB RAINHAM MARSHES

Rainham Marshes, New Tank Hill Rd, Purfleet, Thurrock RM19 1SZ • OS Explorer Map 162 • Grid ref TQ547787 (visitor centre) • What3Words: safely.hotels.value

How to get there: Take the c2c train to Purfleet, then walk west along London Road, then down the footpath along the Royal Hotel until you reach the river. Walk northwest along the riverbank, past the Purfleet Heritage and Military Centre, then across the bridge over the Mardyke. Either take the metal bridge to go into the RSPB building and the nature reserve (around 0.7 miles or just over 1km in total), or stay on the path to continue walking along the riverbank. • Alternatively, there is a longer walking route (around 3.5 miles or 5.6km) from Rainham station to Purfleet station. This route makes up section 24 of the London Loop, and a step-by-step guide can be found on the Inner London Ramblers website. • There are bus stops for the 22 and 44 buses on Tank Hill Road, both south of the car entrance to the reserve. • Route 13 of the National Cycle Network passes between Rainham and Purfleet, and includes the riverside path on the outside of the reserve. There are cycle racks available at the reserve.

Access and conditions: Upon leaving the visitor centre to enter the reserve, there is a metal non-slip grill with a short steep section. On the reserve, there is a mix of gravel paths and boardwalks. There are accessible toilets in the visitor centre. Assistance dogs are welcome. • The RSPB reserve has seasonal opening hours, and is closed on some days – check the website before visiting.

•• Located on the northern bank of the River Thames, RSPB Rainham Marshes is known as one of the best birding sites in London thanks to its variety of habitats, spreading across 411 hectares of reedbeds and saltmarshes – as well as the Thames foreshore just outside the reserve boundaries.

For more than 100 years, the marshes belonged to the military and were used as firing ranges. There are still some remnants of this time, such as the shooting butts. The RSPB purchased 352 hectares of the reserve in 2000, and manages more of the SSSI land outside of the reserve's boundaries. The reserve has been described as the RSPB's 'flagship reserve in London'.

There are three main walking routes, which vary in distance between 0.5 miles (0.8km) on the shorter circular woodland walk and 2.4 miles (3.9km) on the circular walk around the reserve. The former will let you see typical woodland birds, whereas the latter will give you both wetland and woodland species, since it comes back through the woodland.

The river walk, alongside the reserve but not part of it, allows you to look over the Thames on one side and the reserve on the other. Looking to the Thames, keep an eye out for gulls. On the mudflats, there are various waders such as black-tailed godwits and redshanks. In autumn, you might even see a gannet that has ventured up along the river. The vegetation along the river walk can be home to stonechats and Dartford warblers. You can make the river walk a circular 1.5-mile (2.4km) route by walking along the path inside the reserve and leaving by the one-way turnstile gate to access the river walk.

The reserve team has created scrapes and marshes, and connected the ditches to control where the water goes. These ditches are great for water voles and marsh frogs. There are a number of hides dotted around the reserve that provide excellent views over the scrapes and pools. The reedbed habitat is perfect for bearded tits and Cetti's warblers. In 2024, an otter was spotted on the reserve for the first time, and further sightings suggest that the species is now living on the reserve.

The visitor centre won a number of awards for its sustainable design and provides a cosy spot to watch wildlife during bad weather.

WALTHAMSTOW WETLANDS

2 Forest Road, Walthamstow, London N17 9NH • OS Explorer Map 173 • Grid refs TQ348892 (Engine House), TQ350883 (Coppermill Tower) • What3Words: palms.hidden.memory (Engine House), nodded.damage.unions (Coppermill Tower)

How to get there: There are a couple of rail and Underground stations within walking distance of the reserve's entrances. Take the West Anglia rail or Victoria line to Tottenham Hale, then walk east along Ferry Lane, which crosses over the River Lea. The main entrance is on the south of the road, whilst the Maynard entrance provides access to the northern part of the reserve (on the north side of the road, after The Paddock). Alternatively, take the Victoria line or Suffragette Overground line to Blackhorse Road, and walk west along Ferry Lane. A third option is to take the Weaver Overground line to St James Street station, head north on St James Street, then west on Coppermill Lane to the Coppermill Lane entrance. • The local area is served by a number of buses, with Ferry Lane served by the 123, 230 and W4 buses. If travelling from the west, alight at the Mill Mead Road stop and then walk west along Ferry Lane (and follow directions above). If travelling from the east, alight at the Walthamstow Wetlands bus stop, and continue walking east to access the Maynard entrance on the same side of the road. • National Cycle Network Route 1 passes around the eastern and southern edges of the reserve, and some of the paths within the reserve can be used for cycling too. There are cycling stands at various points in the reserve, including by the Engine House.

Access and conditions: There are tarmac paths within the reserve. The Engine House is accessible to wheelchair users and prams, with platform lifts, accessible toilets and baby-changing facilities. Assistance dogs are allowed on the reserve. • Opening times are 09:30–16:00 (October–March) or 17:00 (April–September), plus some seasonal hours. Permit holders are able to access the site outside of these hours.

•• One of Europe's largest urban wetlands, Walthamstow Wetlands is a nature reserve in northeast London managed by London Wildlife Trust, as well as a working reservoir owned by Thames Water. The 10 reservoirs, first built between 1863 and 1904, provide drinking water to 3.5 million people in London.

The reservoirs and the habitats around them provide opportunities for feeding, breeding and resting animals and their importance is recognised through a variety of designations including SSSI, Ramsar site (a Wetland of International Importance) and part of the Lea Valley Special Protection Area. Alongside the 100-plus species of birds, the reserve is home to mammals, such as water voles and hedgehogs, and insects – particularly dragonflies.

If you visit in late winter or early spring, you should look out for the dazzling courtship display of great crested grebes. Terns are a common sight during summer, with common terns breeding on artificial tern rafts, and passage of Arctic terns and sometimes Sandwich and black terns. Swifts, swallows and house martins can be

Common tern.

seen feeding during the summer. Not all will breed at the reserve, with some travelling in from nearby. Cloudy and chilly days can be a great time for spotting swifts as the poor weather means that the reservoirs are the best site for feeding. Up to a thousand birds can be seen swooping over the water, feeding on midges and other flying insects.

The site is also occasionally visited by rarer birds, with some stopping for a fleeting visit – such as a hen harrier seen in 2024 – and others remaining on the reserve for days, weeks or months at a time, including whimbrels, curlews and black-necked grebes.

The reservoirs make up London's largest fishery and are home to brown and rainbow trout, bream and perch. Both local and visiting anglers can fish, with day tickets available on arrival.

The Engine House, located near the main entrance on Ferry Lane, was built in 1894 and remained operational until the 1980s. Nowadays it hosts the visitor centre, including a shop stocking eco-friendly products, a café and an event space. During the development of the site into a nature reserve, the 30m high brick chimney was rebuilt and hosts a number of bird boxes.

The other main building on site is the Grade II listed Coppermill Tower, located near the Coppermill Lane entrance. Originally built in 1806, it now has a fantastic viewing platform and is also home to nesting swifts and roosting bats.

NORWICH

The largest city in East Anglia, Norwich is the county town of Norfolk and claims to be the most complete medieval city in the UK – including an impressive cathedral in the centre of the city, which began life as a Benedictine monastery and has stood in Norwich for more than 900 years.

To the east of the city lies the Broads National Park, a fantastic network of rivers, broads, fens, marshes, meadows and more. Whilst the River Wensum runs through the city, the River Yare skirts around the southern edge before joining up with the Wensum at Whitlington and entering the National Park. Although the Wensum is actually larger and longer, it is considered a tributary of the Yare, and after their confluence, the downstream section is referred to as the River Yare.

The Broads National Park is home to a wide variety of wildlife. It is famous for its birdlife but also the endemic subspecies of the swallowtail butterfly, which is found nowhere else in the UK – or the world. It can be tricky to use public transport to access some of the beautiful reserves; fortunately one of the train routes north of the River Yare between Norwich and Great Yarmouth has stops close to, and sometimes within, RSPB reserves including Strumpshaw Fen (page 29) and Berney Marshes (page 31). South of the river, however, there are no train lines, so you will need to use buses to visit the reserves.

SWEET BRIAR MARSHES

Hellesdon Rd, Norwich NR6 5EE • OS Explorer Map 737 • Grid ref TG210099 (eastern entrance by Marriott's Way) • What3Words: bridge.risen.decay

How to get there: Access the reserve via Marriott's Way, a footpath, cycle route and bridleway, which has a few entry points. The start of the Way at the Barn Road and Barker Street roundabout is a little under a 2-mile (3.2km) walk to the reserve. • Alternatively, take the 30 or 30A bus from Norwich Castle Meadow and alight at the Higham Street stop, cross the road and turn right into the field, following the path up to the Marriott's Way and then turn left. Alternatively, cross the river when you alight, turn left and walk along the Riverside Walk which will bring you to the south of the reserve. • Another route is to take the 23, 28, 29, X29, 30 or 30A buses from Norwich Castle Meadow to Drayton Road and alight at either the Parr Road or Whiffler Road stops, and walk south through Sloughbottom Park to join the Marriott's Way from the north. • The National Cycle Network Route 1 passes along the Marriott's Way at the north of the reserve, and there are cycle racks at both the eastern and western entrances of the reserve.

Access and conditions: The Marriott's Way has a hard surface between central Norwich and Sweet Briar Marshes, and there is good accessibility onto and within the reserve. There are no facilities. Assistance dogs are welcome. • At the time of writing, there are plans to create accessible parking and toilets, and more footpaths within the reserve and joining to local reserves and walking routes. Further facilities are planned for the future, including outdoor classrooms, an information hub, and a new bridge over the river.

•• Opened to the public in May 2024, Sweet Briar Marshes is the newest nature reserve in Norfolk Wildlife Trust's (NWT) portfolio, consisting of 36 hectares of mixed habitats alongside the River Wensum, a spring-fed chalk river, just a couple of miles from the city centre. The land was arable farmland until the late 1990s, despite being increasingly surrounded by development of housing and industrial estates. In early 2022, after being approached by members of the local

community, NWT ran an appeal to purchase the land at Sweet Briar Marshes when it was being sold and was at risk of being lost as a wild space. It was the fastest successful campaign in the charity's history.

The reserve is a Site of Special Scientific Interest (SSSI) and is home to a variety of wildlife, with the meadows filled with butterflies, dragonflies, damselflies and flowers during summer, whilst swallows and swifts hunt for insects overhead. Listen out for sedge and willow warblers, song thrushes, reed buntings and common whitethroats. It has even had a nightingale visiting.

One of the key roles of the reserve, alongside preserving the area as a wild place and improving its biodiversity, is to provide a space for local people to connect with the wildlife on their doorstep. The long-term ambition is to create 'A Wilder Norwich for All', with Sweet Briar Marshes acting as a key green hub for both wildlife and communities.

Southern marsh orchid.

Travelling into Sweet Briar Meadows from either Sloughbottom Park or east along the Marriott's Way also provides the opportunity to visit Wensum Local Nature Reserve, which has Mile Cross Marsh on the north side of the river and Sycamore Crescent Wood on the south side of the river.

WHEATFEN NATURE RESERVE

The Covey, Surlingham, Norwich NR14 7AL • OS Explorer Map OL40 • Grid ref TG324056 (entrance) • What3Words: prowling.comply.animate

How to get there: Take the 85 bus from Norwich bus station to Surlingham, alighting at the School Lane bus stop (around a 1-hour journey). Walk east along Walnut Hill, School Lane and The Green, turn right onto The Covey and continue until you reach the entrance to the reserve. Alternatively, alight at the Surlingham Lane stop in Rockland St Mary, walk east along The Street, turn north into Green Lane and follow the Wherryman's Way route until you reach the entrance to the reserve. • The National Cycle Network Route 1 runs along Mill Road, and cycling along the Green and then south along The Covey will bring you to the reserve, where there are cycle racks by the car park.

Access and conditions: The boardwalk is suitable for wheelchairs, but it doesn't go all the way around the reserve. The remaining paths are flat and may be suitable for some wheelchairs, but can be wet and muddy. There is an accessible toilet by the car park. No dogs, including assistance dogs, are allowed on the reserve. • Open from sunrise to sunset. The path to the River Yare is only open in summer. The reserve may be closed if flooded.

Swallowtail butterfly.

•• Wheatfen Nature Reserve is a delightful 52-hectare reserve on the southern side of the River Yare, partially opposite RSPB Strumpshaw Fen on the other side. In fact, when staring out over the water, you will be looking directly at Strumpshaw. Like Strumpshaw, it is an excellent site for seeing the Norfolk-restricted swallowtail butterfly, but it is not as well known a site and is harder to access.

More than 10,000 species have been recorded at Wheatfen, thanks to the hard work of expert naturalists. Alongside the famous swallowtail, it is known as a good site for seeing Norfolk hawker and scarce chaser dragonflies, as well as the willow emerald damselfly, which was first seen in Britain in 2007 in Felixstowe. In 2024, the reserve joined some other Norfolk wetland reserves to become a reintroduction site for the large marsh grasshopper. The largest grasshopper species in the UK, this impressive insect had become restricted to just a few locations in the New Forest, Dorset and Somerset, until a partnership project led by Citizen Zoo began to reintroduce it to Norfolk.

Keen naturalists will be excited by the presence of a particular small brown beetle. Lacking a common English name, *Galeruca laticollis* is a leaf beetle measuring just 6–9mm. It was thought to be extinct in the UK since 1919, but was rediscovered in the mid-1990s at Wheatfen, where it has been consistently seen since. Wheatfen remains the only known UK site for the species. The larvae feed on common meadow-rue and the adults on creeping thistle, and the reserve is managed to allow these two plants – and thus the beetle – to thrive. The site is also the only known UK home for Indian feather moss (*Timmia megapolitana*), first found here in 2000.

The reserve is managed by the Ted Ellis Trust, who employ a Reserve Warden and a Trainee Warden, and have a dedicated group of trustees and volunteers to manage the reserve. The trust is named for the dedicated local naturalist and writer Ted Ellis, who purchased Wheatfen with his wife Phyllis. It is one of the best-recorded sites in the UK and new species are still being found on a regular basis. Recent additions include the sprawler moth, yellow-legged clearwing moth and a couple of harvestman species.

When Ted died in 1986, the charitable trust was set up to run Wheatfen as a nature reserve open to the public. The trust runs frequent events for visitors to enjoy, including guided walks, wildlife safaris for families and a celebration of the swallowtail butterfly on World Swallowtail Day (on or around the second Sunday in June).

To the south of Wheatfen lies an even lesser known reserve, RSPB Rockland Marshes. It can be easily reached from Wheatfen by following the Wherryman's Way path from Wheatfen's entrance, down to the edge of Rockland St Mary, and back towards the River Yare. This small reserve overlooks Rockland Broad, a stretch of calm water connected to the River Yare by two dykes, which has a healthy population of water lilies. There is a bird hide overlooking the broad and the marshes. Look out for great crested grebes and terns on the water and marsh harriers over the marshes.

RSPB SURLINGHAM CHURCH MARSH

Church Ln, Surlingham, Norwich NR14 7DF • OS Explorer Map OL40 • Grid ref TG304066 (entrance by church) • What3Words: uplifting.school.exposes

How to get there: Take the 85 bus from Norwich bus station to Surlingham, alighting at the School Lane bus stop (around a 20-minute journey). Walk west along Walnut Hill, turn left onto Bramerton Road, right onto Church Lane and continue straight onto the Wherryman's Way towards the river until you reach the reserve (less than 1-mile/1.6km walk). Take care as there are limited pavements and grass verges. • The National Cycle Network Route 1 runs along Bramerton Road; turn north into Church Lane to reach the reserve entrance. There are no cycle racks.
Access and conditions: Paths are mostly flat, but are not surfaced and can be muddy and flooded. There are no facilities. Assistance dogs are welcome.

•• On the southern side of the River Yare, ensconced between the village of Surlingham and the river, is a small RSPB reserve called Surlingham Church Marsh. Until the 1960s, this was a grazing marsh for cattle, and in 1986 it was taken on by the RSPB, who still use grazing Highland cattle as part of the conservation management plan.

The 28-hectare reserve has a circular walk around the edge of the reserve boundary, with the Wherryman's Way route allowing you to look in over the marsh and out over the River Yare. It's worth noting that the riverside footpath can get flooded by the River Yare, so wellies are recommended.

Small in size it may be, but it has Site of Special Scientific Interest (SSSI) designation and there's certainly plenty of wildlife to be seen. Look out for birds of prey including sparrowhawk, hobby, marsh harriers and barn owls, and listen out for birds in the reedbeds such as bearded tits and Cetti's, reed, sedge and even grasshopper warblers. If you're lucky, you might spot the bright blue of a kingfisher, or spy the subtle camouflage of a common or jack snipe, or a bittern.

After following the loop of the river, the

path brings you to a bird hide, although it is more like a bus shelter. This allows you to look out over the pools, used by great crested grebes, ducks and waders.

After the bird hide, you can choose to turn inland and follow the footpath along the dyke – where you might hear or see water voles – until you turn right to head back towards St Mary's church. Alternatively, you can continue following the Wherryman's Way route along the river, and walk along to the Ferry Inn. This is a nice spot for a cuppa and a bite to eat partway through your walk. You can either return to the reserve back along the river, or follow the Wherryman's Way up the road a short distance, and then take the footpath on the right, which will lead back to the reserve.

Both circular walks lead you back alongside the range at the Gun Club, where shooting takes place on Thursdays and Sundays. Further along, a little path away from the main route leads up to the ruins of a small Norman church. The

surrounding land is partially managed, but is an excellent site for elderflower trees and for wildflowers.

If you turn left at St Mary's car park instead of heading straight to the river, the Wherryman's Way will take you west towards Bramerton and past Postwick Marshes, where geese and waders might be spotted. Bramerton Pits is also a SSSI, noted for its geological interest and as a site for fossils of marine invertebrates and now-extinct mammals including species of otters and voles from the Pleistocene.

RSPB STRUMPSHAW FEN

Low Rd, Strumpshaw, Norwich NR13 4HS • OS Explorer Map OL40 • Grid ref TG341065 (Strumpshaw entrance) • What3Words: upstarts.blues.objecting

How to get there: Take the Green Line 16 bus from central Norwich to the Stone Road stop, then follow the directions down Stone Road and Low Road to the reserve. • Alternatively, take the train from Norwich to Brundall station. Follow the footpath along the edge of the station car park, which comes out on Strumpshaw Road where you can either walk (turn right and follow the road east to Stone Road) or take the Green Line 16 bus for one stop. • There are no set cycling routes to get to Strumpshaw, but the Yare Valley route on The Broads by Bike website goes to the entrance.

Access and conditions: Whilst Strumpshaw's three trails are mostly flat, they can be bumpy and uneven. Paths can get very wet and muddy, and are sometimes partially closed if the River Yare breaks its banks and floods. The Woodland trail has two short steep slopes, and the Meadow trail has 11 steps. All three trails are available to view in advance via a downloadable map on the reserve's website. There are benches on all three. The toilet block does not have specified accessible toilets, but there are larger cubicles. There are also baby-changing facilities. Assistance dogs are welcome on the reserve. There are two designated Blue Badge spaces at Strumpshaw. • Access to the reserve requires crossing a railway line. There are phones to speak to a signal operator, and red lights and an alarm to indicate when a train is approaching. • The reserve is open dawn to dusk, with the visitor centre and toilets open 09:30–17:00 (April–October) or 10:00–16:00 (November–March). Entrance charges apply for non-RSPB members.

•• The most famous residents of RSPB Strumpshaw Fen are the swallowtail butterflies; this is one of the best sites to see this geographically restricted species (along with Wheatfen Nature Reserve; see page 25). The adults can be seen between mid-May and July, with the peak usually taking place in mid-June. However, it is worth keeping an eye on social media and butterfly websites for reports of sightings. Sometimes a second brood is seen at the end of August to mid-September. The swallowtail is also one of the easiest butterflies to identify in its caterpillar stage, with its relatively large size and distinctive patterning. Look out for caterpillars feeding on milk-parsley in June and July, and sometimes August and September. Staff and volunteers in the visitor centre will be able to share the latest location sightings, though if you're lucky, you might spot a butterfly at the entrance, visiting the planted flowers in the raised beds for nectar.

As this is such a well-known reserve for the species, it can get quite busy during peak swallowtail season, so do bear this in mind if planning a visit. Whilst the crowds are a good indication of where to see one of the butterflies, there may be polite battles to get the best spot for photography.

A visit in June would also be good timing for spotting the Norfolk hawker

Norfolk hawker.

dragonfly. The species has now spread well beyond the Broads' borders and breeds in counties including Cambridgeshire, Kent and Suffolk, with sightings as far away as Yorkshire and Lancashire. However, Norfolk – and Strumpshaw Fen – remains a hotspot for the species.

Another of the reserve's famous invertebrate residents is the fen raft spider. This semi-aquatic spider nearly became extinct in the UK, but was reintroduced to a number of sites, including Strumpshaw, and has increased to almost 4,000 females (larger than the males, they are easily counted as they create distinctive nursery webs).

Of course, the reserve is also brilliant for watching – and hearing – birds. From booming bitterns and calling cuckoos to the 'pinging' calls of bearded tits and the ceaseless songs of sedge, reed and grasshopper warblers amongst the reedbeds, the reserve is bustling with birds. Whilst you listen out for them, keep an eye to the skies for hunting marsh harriers and hobbies, and an eye on the water for mammals such as water voles and otters, while Chinese water deer feed in marshy vegetation.

Strumpshaw Fen also has woodlands and meadows to explore, including an adventure trail for children – or you can hire a kit from the visitor centre for pond dipping. In summer, the meadows are rich with dragonflies (including Norfolk hawker) and damselflies, as well as orchids and other interesting plants – look out for southern marsh orchid and bogbean.

A little way down the road another RSPB reserve, Buckenham Marshes, attracts wintering birds such as white-fronted geese, wigeons, golden plovers and lapwings. The fen raft spider has also been reintroduced here.

RSPB BERNEY MARSHES

Burgh Castle, Great Yarmouth NR31 9PZ • OS Explorer Map OL40 • Grid refs TG460053 (by train station), TG465049 (by river and windmill) • What3Words: reference.headlight.dabbled (by train station), jogged.branch.depths (by river and windmill)

How to get there: Take a Greater Anglia train from Norwich railway station heading to Great Yarmouth via one of the Wherry Lines routes. Stops at Berney Arms (around a 25-minute journey) are very limited, with increased service during summer (check the Greater Anglia website). Cross the tracks at the crossing and head south along the footpath to reach the river and the reserve (less than a 10-minute walk for most). • For a longer walk (over 2 hours), get off the train at Acle, or get the X1, X11 Coastlink or 7 Coastal Reds bus from Norwich bus station to Acle. Then follow the Weavers' Way route down to Berney Arms station.

Access and conditions: The path from the station to the river involves crossing the tracks and an uneven non-tarmacked path, and is unsuitable for most wheelchairs. Dogs are welcome on the reserve. There are no facilities.

•• You can only reach this reserve by train, walking or by boat! It makes for a fun adventure to what feels like the middle of nowhere, even though you are not that far from Norwich.

Once you have alighted at Berney Arms station, you can either walk down to the river, or away from the river, deeper in the marshes, making sure you are back in time for the return train to Norwich. Otherwise, lace up your hiking shoes and walk to another train station to catch a train back to Norwich. Heading downriver, Great Yarmouth station is a 5.5-mile (8.9km) walk. A similar distance back upriver is Reedham station. Both routes will take you along the bank of the River Yare, allowing for plenty of birdwatching opportunities.

As you wander down to the river, watch for waders and wildfowl on the marshland on either side. Aside from the wildlife, the main point of interest is the Berney Arms Windmill, which towers over the marshy landscape. Built in 1865, it is a scheduled monument and managed by English Heritage. Eleven families once lived in the little hamlet, earning a living from grazing cattle or at the mill. The last family left in 1988, and the farmhouse was sold to the RSPB. The pub survived for a couple more decades before closing in 2015. There will often be boats moored up along the stretch of river by the mill and pub, waiting for the tide to be right to enter Breydon Water further downstream.

Parts of two local long-distance walking routes run through Berney Marshes and the wider Halvergate Marshes. The Weavers' Way is a 61-mile (98km) walk between Cromer and Great Yarmouth, with a 12-mile (19.3km) section from Acle, down to Berney Arms station and the river, and then east to Great Yarmouth. The Wherryman's Way is a 37.5-mile (60.4km) walk between Norwich and Great Yarmouth, with the riverside walk between Reedham and Great Yarmouth covered. More details on these two routes can be found on the Norfolk County Council website.

Walking east and downstream along the river, you will go past the old pub, come alongside the railway line again, and see Lockgate Mill – a Grade II listed building built in the early 1800s. At Lockgate Mill, there is an option to turn north and head to Halvergate and then head back down to Berney Arms.

The estuary section of the River Yare (joined by the River Waveney near Berney Arms, and then by the River Bure at Great Yarmouth) is the RSPB Breydon Water reserve, which has a suite of designations including Site of Special Scientific Interest (SSSI), a Ramsar site, and a Special Protection Area (SPA). Low tide exposes the mudflats, but does mean that the birds can be further away and harder to see clearly. The best time is the couple of hours before high tide. The mudflats and marshes are particularly good for seeing wintering waders and wildfowl, and can have interesting visitors during the migration seasons. In summer, look out for terns using the tern roosting platforms, which are located by the viewing hide (in the northeastern corner of the estuary, close to the road). Breydon can also be an excellent site for seeing European spoonbills, a species that has begun breeding in the county in recent years.

BIRMINGHAM

As the UK's second-largest city, Birmingham is referred to as the UK's 'second city', although this honour is also sometimes claimed by Manchester.

It is home to one of the world's largest urban parks, Sutton Park (page 35), which is also a National Nature Reserve. The UK's first urban Wildlife Trust was formed here, out of which has grown the current Wildlife Trust for Birmingham and the Black Country. Birmingham is also the original home of the International Dawn Chorus Day, which was first held in 1984 at Moseley Bog (page 34). In recent years, the Trust lost possession of a 40-hectare nature reserve, consisting of ancient woodlands and wetland habitats, to the HS2 rail project.

Birmingham has relatively small rivers, compared to the great River Thames flowing through London for example. The River Tame and its tributaries run through the city and connect to the River Trent further north. However, it does have a series of well-connected canals, which join up to those in Wolverhampton and part of the Black Country, and together make up 100 miles (161km) of canals, referred to collectively as the Birmingham Canal Navigations.

Its location in the West Midlands means that Birmingham is well connected to other cities by train lines, and there are good bus services within the city.

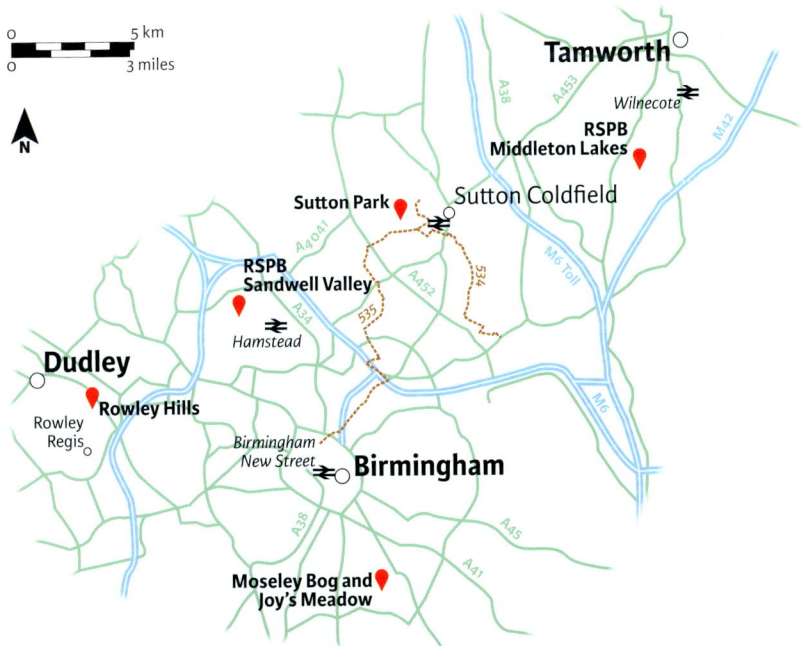

MOSELEY BOG AND JOY'S MEADOW

Yardley Wood Road, Birmingham B13 9JX • OS Explorer Map 220 • Grid ref SP090820 (main entrance) • What3Words: shaky.list.comical

How to get there: From central Birmingham, take the 2 or 3 bus and alight at the Linkswood Close/Windermere Road bus stop (around a 35-minute journey from New Street station), which is by the main entrance to the reserve.

Access and conditions: There is a mixture of surfaced, boardwalk and unsurfaced (sometimes muddy) paths through the reserve. There are no facilities. Assistance dogs are welcome. The small car park at the Yardley Wood entrance is primarily for visitors with limited mobility.

Scarlet elf cup fungus.

Common spotted orchid.

•• Located in south Birmingham, this little reserve covers only 11 hectares but has an impressive variety of habitats within it and an extensive history behind it. Its most famous connection is to J. R. R. Tolkien, the author of *The Hobbit* and *The Lord of the Rings*. Tolkien grew up locally, and spent his childhood playing in the reserve. Moseley Bog is said to be the inspiration for the 'old forest' of Middle Earth, and visitors from across the world come to the reserve to see it for themselves.

'The Bog', as it is known locally, is actually fen habitat. Much of the local fen habitat has been lost to development, and the Birmingham and Black Country Wildlife Trust (BBC WT) regularly remove colonising trees. The reserve is a delight for fungi enthusiasts, with scarlet and green elf cups, birch polypores, beefsteaks and fly agaric among the many species you may find.

The area next to the bog was threatened with the construction of 22 houses in the 1980s, resulting in the successful 'Save Our Bog' campaign by local resident Joy Fifer. Waste material had previously been dumped here, then capped and a school playing field created on top of it. The steep slope in the reserve marks the edge of this dumping area. After the campaign, the old school playing field was planted to form woodland, and this woodland and a meadow were named in honour of Joy in the late 1990s. The campaign inspired the formation of the Urban Wildlife Group, which later became the Wildlife Trust for Birmingham and the Black Country, and Moseley Bog became a Wildlife Trust reserve in 2010. The meadow is now a brilliant site for wildflowers, particularly common spotted orchids.

Also on the reserve are two 'burnt mounds' from the Bronze Age by Coldbath Brook, which are Scheduled Ancient Monuments and date from around 3,000 years ago. The stones here would have been covered with a structure, heated with fire and had water poured on them to make steam and create a sweat lodge.

You can listen to a podcast tour of the reserve presented by the late poet and author Benjamin Zephaniah, who was born locally and spent time in the reserve. All episodes are available on the BBC WT website.

SUTTON PARK

Park Rd, The Royal Town of Sutton Coldfield, Birmingham, Sutton Coldfield B74 2YT
• OS Explorer Map 220 • Grid ref SP113961 (visitor centre)
• What3Words: fork.lately.moss

How to get there: Take the West Midlands Railway train to Sutton Coldfield (around a 23-minute journey). If you leave the station from platform 1, turn left onto Railway Road, then right onto Park Road, which will take you to the Town Gate of Sutton Park. • Alternatively, Sutton Coldfield is served by a variety of bus routes from central Birmingham, including 66, 907, 1100, X3, X4 and X5. Alight at the Manor Hill stop, then head west on Manor Hill and continue onto Wyndley Lane, and enter the park by Wyndley Pool (head north to reach the visitor centre). • National Cycle Network routes 534 and 535 both go through Sutton Park; 535 is a route directly from central Birmingham to Sutton Park, whilst 534 joins onto 535 at the Birmingham and Fazeley Canal. Cycling within the park is only allowed on the bridleways. There are various cycle stands available in the park, including by the visitor centre, and entrances at Boldmere and Banners Gates.
Access and conditions: There is a mix of footpath surfaces throughout the park, and some slight and steep slopes. A railway line runs through the park (freight trains only) with various points for crossing. There are multiple car parks with designated bays for Blue Badge holders (charge for parking between Easter and September). Two electric Trampers are available for hire from the visitor centre. Accessible toilets and baby-changing facilities are available. • Dogs are welcome but must be kept under control, and on a lead in some areas seasonally. The park opens at 09:00, with closing time changing seasonally.

•• Just 6 miles (9.7km) north/northeast from central Birmingham, Sutton Park is located in the western side of the Royal Town of Sutton Coldfield. It is Birmingham's largest park, and one of the largest urban nature parks in Europe. At 971 hectares, it features a wide range of habitats and is a National Nature Reserve (NNR), with various sections of it designated as a Site of Special Scientific Interest (SSSI), a Site of Local Importance to Nature Conservation (SLINC), and a Scheduled Ancient Monument. With all these designations, it is a well-visited site by local wildlife watchers, and thanks to its wide-open spaces and additional attractions, it is popular with everyone else too, receiving more than two million visitors each year. However, it is still easy to wander off into quiet, wilder areas.

There are plenty of wildlife species to be seen. Look out for resident ravens, which returned to the park in the early 2000s and have continued to breed since. On the heathland, the stonechats are part of a long-term study by the West Midlands Bird Ringing Group. The various pools are home to mute swans, and if you visit in spring, you may spot the beautiful courtship dance of great crested grebes.

Alongside the common butterfly species, Sutton Park is home to a huge variety of invertebrates. If you can follow its fast flight, you might be able to enjoy the sight of a stunning jewelled predator,

Green tiger beetle.

the green tiger beetle. Other notable beetles include the lesser stag beetle and rhinoceros beetle.

The flora is so vast and interesting that a whole book (*The Flora of Sutton Park National Nature Reserve*) has been published on the subject by the Nature Bureau. Some of the botanical highlights include bee orchids in Mere Green and green-winged orchids in the recently created hay meadow, as well as hare's-tail cotton-grass, bluebells, trailing St John's-wort, grass-of-parnassus and wild daffodils. The park is also one of only four locations for the round-leaved whitebeam, a species endemic to the UK.

Fungi enthusiasts are well served with plenty of species to look out for, including amethyst deceiver, fly agaric, green elf cup, dead man's fingers, dryad's saddle, collared earthstar and yellow swamp russula – which was identified as new to science in 1888 during a survey of the park.

A herd of Exmoor ponies live in the park, used as conservation grazers. Cattle also graze there over the summer. The wild mammals include hedgehogs, foxes, and nine species of bats, including Brandt's and Leisler's.

The rangers run a yearly bioblitz event, where the aim is to conduct a variety of wildlife surveys over two days. The event is typically held in the summer and is open to the public, with experts on hand to point out and identify species, and includes a variety of activities such as bird, bat and reptile walks, stream and pond dipping, moth trapping and habitat-specific bug hunts. The event has regularly discovered species that are new records for the site, including beetles, flies and sawflies. New species are often recorded outside of the bioblitz too, with the full species count rapidly approaching 6,000.

ROWLEY HILLS

St Brades Close, Rowley Regis B69 1NX • OS Explorer Map 220 • Grid ref SO977890 (meadow) • What3Words: clap.deny.chew

How to get there: Take the 12, 12A or 126 National Express West Midlands bus towards Dudley and alight at the Bury Hill Road stop (around a 40-minute journey). Head back along the road and enter Rowley Hills via the entrance to the Bury Hill Park section of Rowley Hills.
Access and conditions: There are no facilities or dedicated parking at this reserve, and the reserve has mainly grass paths and some steep slopes.

•• Although it is a small reserve, Rowley has an impressive diversity of species recorded. This includes 24 species of butterflies, including small, large and Essex skippers, small copper, and green hairstreak. The most notable is the marbled white butterfly, an uncommon species in Birmingham and the Black Country for which Rowley is a key site. Despite the name, the marbled white is actually a member of the 'brown' butterflies of the subfamily Satyrinae, and is more closely related to the speckled wood and meadow brown than to the large white or orange-tip. Look out for the flutter of its chequered white and black wings amongst the wildflowers in late June and July. There are also plenty of day-flying moths to be seen, such as the distinctive cinnabar, both six-spot and narrow-bordered five-spot burnets, six-belted clearwing, and burnet companion.

The reserve continues to provide exciting new species records. In early 2024, the weevil species *Otiorhynchus ligustici* was seen there, which produced much excitement — it was only the 12th UK record for this species since 1835, and the first since 1993.

Commoner bird species such as buzzard, sparrowhawk, chiffchaff and green woodpecker are present, but as a high green space within the West Midlands, it can also be a resting point for migratory species on their way to breed elsewhere, such as ring ouzel.

The Rowley Hills have more than 200 plant species recorded, and this diversity may be attributed to the way in which the former quarry was treated at the end of its

Marbled white.

life. The quarry was used as landfill, and then covered with topsoil. This topsoil is quite shallow, which was ideal for grasses and wildflowers, but less so for shrubs and trees, allowing a diversity of other plants to thrive. Look out for the pretty blue-purple blooms of harebells, the swaying heads of ox-eye daisies, swathes of common knapweeds and field scabious, and the pretty little hare's-foot clover. There are bee orchids on site, and pyramidal orchid was found for the first time in 2022.

For fungi species, records include jelly ear and yellow brain growing on dead and decaying branches, scarlet, butter and parrot waxcaps in the grasslands, and verdigris agaric, wood blewit and parasol.

A 1-hectare section of the Rowley Hills is a small reserve called Portway Hill, owned and managed by the Birmingham and Black Country Wildlife Trust.

The underlying dolerite (olivine microgabbro) rock of Rowley Hills is of particular interest to geologists, and is known locally as Rowley Rag. It has spheroid shapes and the texture is known as onion skin as it peels off in layers. The exposed rock face in the former Blue Rock Quarry within Portway Hill is one of the best places to see Rowley Rag. A new cairn and seating were created from dolerite rock in 2014 in front of the exposed rock face. Due to their geological importance, the Blue Rock Quarry and the Rowley Hills are geosites within the Black Country Global Geopark.

RSPB SANDWELL VALLEY

Tanhouse Avenue, Great Barr, Birmingham B43 5AG • OS Explorer Map 220 • Grid ref SP034928 (RSPB visitor centre) • What3Words: logo.exchanges.owner

How to get there: Take a West Midlands train from Birmingham New Street towards Walsall or Rugeley Trent Valley and alight at Hamstead (around a 17-minute journey). Walk or cycle north along Old Walsall Road, turn west and continue along Hamstead Road, turn south onto Tanhouse Avenue, then walk along until you reach the signposted entrance of the reserve. • Alternatively, take the number 16 or 16A National Express West Midlands bus towards either Great Barr or West Bromich, and alight at the James Road stop. Walk northwest along Hamstead Road, then turn south onto Tanhouse Avenue. • Route 5 of the National Cycle Network comes up to the nature reserve from the south, through Sandwell Valley Country Park, crossing the River Tame, and then up along the eastern edge of the reserve. There are cycle racks available outside the visitor centre.
Access and conditions: The visitor centre is closed on Mondays, and open 10:00–16:30 Tuesday–Sunday. The hide closes at 16:00, and the car park at 17:00. • There are two designated bays for Blue Badge holders. Assistance dogs are welcome on the reserve. There are accessible toilets and baby-changing facilities in the visitor centre when open. Binoculars are available to hire from the visitor centre.

•• Located within the Forge Mill Lake Local Nature Reserve, RSPB Sandwell Valley is a lovely nature reserve made up of different habitats. In spring and summer, it is home to nesting lapwings, little ringed plovers, oystercatchers and common terns, as well as a variety of warbler species such as sedge, reed and willow warblers, common whitethroats and chiffchaffs. The hide is a good location for watching waterfowl including snipe, little egrets and a range of duck species, and perhaps a hunting peregrine falcon. If you walk around the path through the woodland in spring, you'll see a display of bluebells.

The lake was dug out in 1981 as part of the flood management for the adjacent meandering River Tame, and has been modified since to increase its capacity.

The River Tame encloses the lake and the reserve in a horseshoe-shaped loop. If you walk along the river, look out for otter spraint on the exposed rocks. If you're lucky you might see a kingfisher. In spring, the grass slope is a good site for seeing female orange-tip butterflies laying eggs on the pretty pink blooms of the cuckooflower.

The RSPB host a variety of events on the reserve, including beginners' birdwatching sessions, bird ringing demonstrations and family events.

Forge Mill Lake and the RSPB Sandwell Valley nature reserve are both part of the larger Sandwell Valley Country Park, which has been awarded a Green Flag Award. The RSPB reserve sits in the northeast corner of the park, and provides a handy access point to explore more of the park's green areas.

The Priory Woods Local Nature Reserve is also contained within the country park, consisting of 21 hectares of woodlands and grasslands, plus a couple of pools, and the ruins of the medieval Benedictine monastery Sandwell Priory. On the western edge of the country park is Sot's Hole Local Nature Reserve, featuring over 5 hectares of woodland, with marshy areas that are good for marsh thistle and water horsetail. The drier areas of the woodland are a wonderful sight in spring when they are covered with carpets of bluebells.

RSPB MIDDLETON LAKES

Tamworth, Staffordshire B78 2BB • OS Explorer Map 232 • Grid refs SP200989 (crossing the canal), SP195983 (visitor welcome) • What3Words: under.slick.funny (crossing the canal), slurs.vegans.sprains (visitor welcome)

How to get there: Take the CrossCountry train from Birmingham New Street towards Nottingham, and alight at Wilnecote station (around a 15-minute journey). Walk or cycle west on Watling Street, crossing the River Tame, and then Atherstone Street and Lichfield Street until you reach the steps on the northern side of the street going down to the canal towpath. To reach the same spot by bus, take the 110 Arriva bus service from Birmingham towards Tamworth and alight at Fazeley Broomfield Avenue. Walk or cycle west until you reach the steps down to the canal path. Cross under the bridge and head south on the towpath until you reach the reserve. The walk is around 3.5 miles (5.6km) from the station to the RSPB welcome centre, or just over 2 miles (3.2km) to enter from the north along the canal. • The towpath along the canal from Fazeley down to the lakes is suitable for bicycles, and there are cycle racks at the RSPB visitor hub.

Access and conditions: There are no toilet facilities at the RSPB visitor hub, but there are public toilets in the neighbouring Middleton Hall's courtyard and accessible toilets and baby-changing facilities on the ground floor of Middleton Hall (limited opening hours). There are three designated bays for Blue Badge holders and the gravel-surfaced car park is open 08:30–16:00 (Nov–Feb) or 08:00–17:00 (Mar–Oct). The footpaths on the reserve are generally flat, with a variety of surfaces. Assistance dogs are welcome.

- Lying only a few miles northeast of Birmingham, RSPB Middleton Lakes is a former gravel quarry, spanning 162 hectares.

The woodlands near the Welcome Hub are home to the largest heronry in Warwickshire (around 35 pairs of grey herons and between six to eight pairs of little egrets), a rookery, and the smallest and rarest of the UK woodpecker species – the lesser spotted woodpecker. This species' UK population has been plummeting, with poor breeding seasons in recent years, and there are concerns about the future of the species nationally. February and March are the best times to listen out for the calling and drumming of this elusive little bird.

Bitterns are returning to Middleton Lakes; a male was heard booming for the first time ever on the reserve in March 2021, and two females raised five chicks through to fledging, the first time in more than 100 years that the species has successfully bred in the West Midlands. In 2024, the site had two booming males on site. Bitterns almost became extinct in the UK, but concentrated conservation work has brought the species back from the brink. At Middleton Lakes, a key factor in the bitterns' return was the creation of a 6-hectare reedbed. It can be hard to see bitterns, since they are so well camouflaged, but if you want to hear a booming male, the loudest bird in the UK, the best time is in spring at dawn or dusk.

Avocets also breed at Middleton Lakes, nesting there for the first time in 2015. Look out for a range of waders and ducks, as well as marsh harriers, barn and, in winter, short-eared owls. If you visit during spring and early summer, you may hear the distinctive call of a male cuckoo or the songs of as many as 10 warbler species: grasshopper, Cetti's, willow, garden, sedge and reed warblers, and chiffchaffs, common whitethroats, lesser whitethroats, and blackcaps. Admire the herds of English Longhorn cattle and Konik ponies, which are used as a conservation grazing tool.

The River Tame flows south through the nature reserve and the Birmingham and Fazeley Canal runs through the middle. If you are walking along the canal towpath southwards from Fazeley, you'll see a fabulous Gothic-style footbridge, which was built in the 1830s.

The RSPB hold a range of events, including beginners' birdwatching sessions, bird ringing demonstrations, dawn chorus experiences for International Dawn Chorus Day and guided fungi walks. There is also a children's play meadow.

Next to the reserve's car park is Middleton Hall and Gardens, a Grade II listed manor house. The grounds include a Georgian walled garden, a lake and a nature trail.

BRISTOL

Situated in southwest England, Bristol is a lively city, filled with character and proud of its green credentials – in 2015, it held the status of European Green Capital, and it is also a Fairtrade City.

Alongside nature reserves and parks, Bristol's green spaces include the wildlife-friendly Arnos Vale Cemetery (page 49), and large estates open to the public such as Ashton Court (page 45). The River Avon and the River Frome both run through the city, and are home to a variety of wildlife – including wild beavers! After one family were discovered living on one of the tributaries, a full-scale survey revealed a number of beaver families in the Avon catchment.

In 2018 alongside London, Bristol (jointly with Bath) was one of the first UK cities to take part in the global City Nature Challenge – and came first out of the 10 European cities taking part, with more than 9,000 observations.

Bristol has great public transport links both within the city and to surrounding areas, and was named as the UK's first cycling city in 2008. In fact, it is actually home to the charity Sustrans, which focuses on walking, wheeling and cycling, and is the custodian of the National Cycle Network.

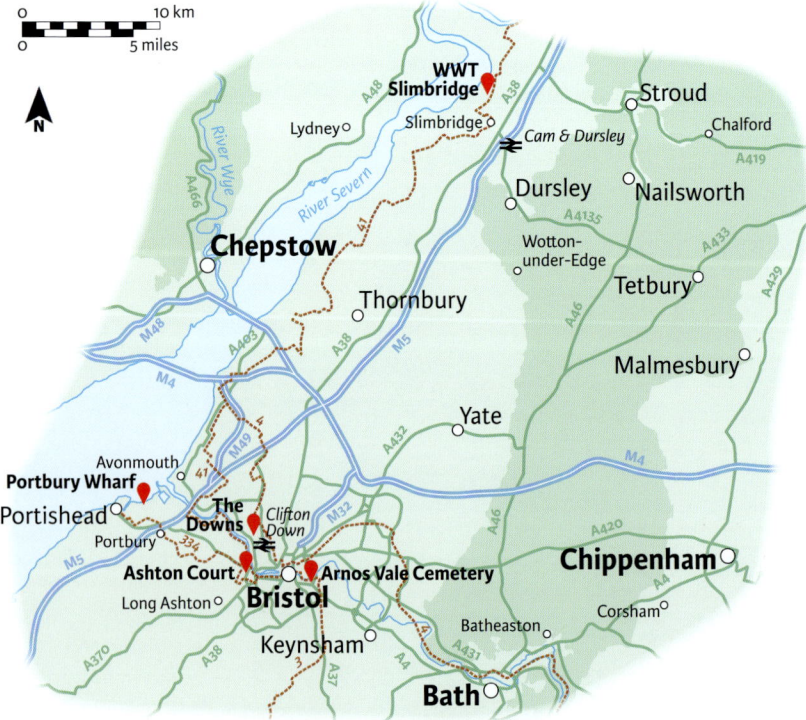

ASHTON COURT

> Long Ashton, Bristol BS41 9JN • OS Explorer Map 154 or 155 • Grid refs ST558726 (Clifton Lodge entrance), ST557718 (Ashton Court building) • What3Words: marble.faster.sooner (Clifton Lodge entrance), edge.intend.fired (Ashton Court building)
>
> **How to get there:** There are multiple entrances to Ashton Court, with two located on the Bristol side of the park. • Take the X4 towards Portishead, and alight at Clanage Road stop. Walk back south down Clanage Road and turn right into Kennel Lodge Road, which will take you up to Mansion House car park (with footpaths available across the fields off to the left below the car park). • Alternatively, take the X6 towards Clevedon or X9 towards Nailsea, and alight at the David Lloyd Centre bus stop. Continue up the road and cross at the traffic lights. Turn right and follow Ashton Road to enter the Church Lodge car park. • National Cycle Network Route 334 passes through Ashton Court, joining onto the 'Festival Way' part of route 33 at Kennel Lodge Road. Alternatively, you can cycle across the Clifton Suspension Bridge and down Bridge Road to the Clifton Lodge entrance. There are cycle racks in the car parks.
>
> **Access and conditions:** There are some hard-surfaced paths around the park, notably the loop between Ashton Court Mansion and Clifton Lodge (some of this is a road used to access the golf club). There are designated bays for Blue Badge holders in the car parks and accessible toilets in the stables courtyard – the courtyard is cobbled – and in the golf café. • The site is open from 08:00; closing times vary through the year.

•• Lying just across the River Avon from Bristol, Ashton Court Estate has 300 hectares of green space to explore and enjoy, including woodlands, wildflower meadows and ponds.

Three species of deer can be found in the estate, including free-ranging wild roe deer. However, the two species that draw the most attention are the red deer and the fallow deer, which are kept in separate fenced enclosures. The Ashton Court deer parks are amongst the oldest in the country, created in 1393. It is possible to walk through some parts of these enclosures, but dogs must be kept on leads, and it is advised not to enter during the rutting season.

The estate is designated as a Site of Special Scientific Interest (SSSI) due to ancient and veteran trees, as well as rare woodland beetles – including the Nationally Scarce cobweb beetle, which favours ancient trees and steals prey remains from spider webs.

The most famous of Ashton Court's ancient trees is the Domesday Oak, so-called because Ashton Court was listed in the Domesday Book commissioned by William the Conqueror in 1085. It is designated as a Tree of National Special Interest (TNSI) and is located northeast of the Keeper's Cottage, on the opposite side of the main tarmac path that runs around the estate. In recent years, it has struggled and may not survive much longer. However, dying and dead wood is still an important part of a tree's life cycle, and it can still provide shelter and food for other wildlife.

It is said that an oak spends 300 years growing, 300 years living and 300 years dying, and the Domesday Oak's current age fits with its gradually decaying status.

More veteran trees and the narrow-leaved helleborine orchid can be found in Clarken Coombe Wood in the southwestern part of the estate, whilst the nearby Cattle Pond and Clarken Coombe Lodge are home to great crested newts and lesser horseshoe bats. Although bluebells are found in many of the estate's woodlands, one of the best views is in Church Wood, by Clarken Coombe Lodge.

The plateau area of the estate, southwest of the golf club, is managed as a hay meadow and is brilliant for common spotted orchids in summer and green-winged orchids in late spring and early summer. Look out for singing skylarks performing. They nest in the plateau, and the area is usually cordoned off to protect them.

Ashton Court Estate is a popular location with a range of features and events, making it an ideal compromise location if you want to head out to see wildlife with a non-wildlife-lover. The Ashton Court Mansion is a Grade I listed building.

THE DOWNS

> Stoke Rd, Bristol BS9 1FG • OS Explorer Map 154 or 155 • Grid refs ST571749 (for near Water Tower on Stoke Road), ST564746 (for entrance to Goat Gully from The Downs), ST565732 (for Clifton Observatory) • What3Words: impact.shades.poster (café by the Water Tower), rail.fast.kicks (entrance to Goat Gulley), expert.margin.pays (Clifton Observatory)
>
> **How to get there:** The Downs is well served by a variety of bus routes, including 505 Stagecoach, B2, 1, 2, 2a, 3, 77 and U1. • Alternatively, take the Great Western Railway train from Bristol Temple Meads towards Severn Beach and alight at Clifton Down (around a 20-minute journey). Walk north up Whiteladies Road, and you will reach the edge of the The Downs by Stoke Road. • National Cycle Network Route 4 passes through The Downs along Stoke Road. There are cycle racks at various points around the edge of The Downs, and by the Water Tower.
>
> **Access and conditions:** There are some flat surfaced paths on The Downs, and some flat grassy paths, which can become wet and muddy. The footpath through the Gully is steep and unsurfaced, making it very unsuitable for wheelchairs. There are limited facilities on The Downs. There are three sets of public toilets at the Clifton Hub, by the Water Tower and at the Sea Walls on the western side of The Downs. All three have accessible toilets; the Clifton Hub and Sea Walls have baby-changing facilities. All three toilets have limited opening hours.

North of the city centre, there are two green spaces – Clifton Downs and Durdham Downs – collectively known as 'The Downs'. The 14 hectares of Site of Nature Conservation Interest (SNCI) are limestone grasslands managed as beautiful wildflower meadows, with species including bird's-foot trefoil and orchids such as bee orchids and autumn lady's tresses. The meadow is left for much of the summer and then cut back after the wildflowers have set seed. These wildflower meadows are particularly good for butterflies, with 27 species seen across The Downs.

Avon Gorge (one side of which is part of The Downs) is well known among botanists as a fantastic site for rare plants. It is designated as a UK Important Plant Area by the conservation charity Plantlife, as well as a Site of Special Scientific Interest (SSSI). More than 30 plants that are considered rare or scarce are found here, including the honewort and autumn squill. For some, such as the Bristol onion and the Bristol rock-cress, this is their only wild UK location, though they are found in Europe – the onion in southern Europe, and the rock-cress in the French Alps and Pyrenees. There are even endemic species found here, growing nowhere else in the world, including multiple species of whitebeam.

Some of the rare plants grow on the cliffs and are out of reach for the general public. Others grow in the Gully, and if you're particularly interested in seeing any of these, it's best to book onto a guided event run by the Avon Gorge and Downs Wildlife Project where an expert botanist will be able to point them out. Avon Gorge's common rock-rose, itself not a rare species nationally, is the foodplant for the silky wave caterpillar, which is found in only three UK sites.

The Gully has become known locally as Goat Gully, thanks to the introduction of these four-legged mammals which have been nicknamed the 'hairy conservationists'. They graze on woody vegetation, rather than on the grasses or wildflowers, and make the management of this steep-sloped area much easier. The goat flock is made up of feral Kashmir goats brought down from North Wales, and an old British breed called the Bagot goat. Unfortunately, there have been fatal incidents involving dogs chasing goats off the cliffs, and therefore dogs must be kept on a lead in the Gully. If you get to the bottom of the Gully, it is best to return back up the same path.

In the southernmost section of Clifton Down, close to the Clifton Suspension Bridge and right next to the public toilets, a section of rocks is home to a rather unusual species, the wall lizard. This colony of non-native lizards was discovered in 2006. It is not known how they came to be there, but they seem to be thriving. Some patience can be required to see them, as they disappear into the rock crevices if they feel threatened.

Wall lizard.

A little walk over Isambard Kingdom Brunel's Clifton Suspension Bridge gives fantastic views of the Avon Gorge, and if you're lucky, you might spot the resident peregrine falcons. It gives a good opportunity to admire the exposed Carboniferous limestone of the gorge, upon which some of the rare plants grow.

ARNOS VALE CEMETERY

Bath Rd, Arnos Vale, Bristol BS4 3EW • OS Explorer Map 155 • Grid refs ST608716 (Bath Road entrance), ST604713 (Cemetery Road entrance) • What3Words: zeal.belly.kings (Bath Road), pure.bunks.scars (Cemetery Road)

How to get there: There are three entrances to Arnos Vale Cemetery; travelling from the city centre will take you to either the main entrance on Bath Road, or the Cemetery Road entrance. *Bath Road entrance:* The Paintworks bus stop on Bath Road is served by a number of bus routes: 1, 39, 349, 522 and X39. After alighting at this bus stop, continue walking along the road, passing the cemetery on the opposite side of the road in order to reach the crossing, then return back to the entrance. Alternatively, the main entrance is around a 1-mile (1.6km) walk from Temple Meads, following the Bath Road (A4) south. *Cemetery Road entrance:* The Brecknock Road bus stop on Wells Road is served by a number of bus routes: 172, 374, 375, 376 Mendip Xplorer, and 376a. After alighting at this bus stop, walk uphill and take the first left onto Cemetery Road, which will take you to the entrance. • National Cycle Network Route 3 passes close to Arnos Vale Cemetery, cutting through Arnos Court Park. Cycle racks are available by the East Lodge and the Spielman Centre.
Access and conditions: Dogs kept on a lead are welcome. There are Blue Badge parking spaces at each chapel and an accessible toilet in the Spielman Centre (with lift access). Some paths are flat, surfaced and suitable for wheelchair users, but some are steep, unsurfaced or otherwise unsuitable.

•• Located roughly 1 mile (1.6km) southwest of Temple Meads station, Arnos Vale Cemetery is a historic site full of fascinating stories of the people buried there. It is also an excellent green space for seeing wildlife, as it is managed with biodiversity in mind. First created in 1837, the site was not originally part of urban Bristol and was instead surrounded by fields. Over the last two centuries, the city has rapidly grown and now surrounds the cemetery.

More than 300,000 people are remembered in the cemetery, and it is still a working cemetery today. A number of important Bristol figures have been laid to rest here, as well as more than 530 servicemen and women. The cemetery also includes the grave of Rajah Rammohun Roy, the 'Father of Modern India', who fell ill and died during a visit to Bristol in 1833. There is a remembrance service for him every year, and his grave has many visitors from around the world.

The 18-hectare site is a Site of Nature Conservation Interest (SNCI), and is managed with that in mind. The grassland is cut once a year, after the wildflowers have set seed, and plants are allowed to grow and flower between many of the tombstones. Look out for butterflies such as holly blue, ringlet and marbled white. There is selective thinning within the woodland, which is home to a variety of bird species including tawny owls, nuthatches and goldcrests, and there are boxes provided for nesting birds and roosting bats. Roe deer, foxes and badgers are present on site, as are slow worms and grass snakes. The ivy of the cemetery hosts a rare plant, the ivy broomrape. This is a parasitic plant, which is lacking in chlorophyll and thus green pigment, and it steals nutrients from the roots of ivy.

The cemetery runs a variety of events on site, including guided tours every Saturday and regular online history talks. There are outdoor events aimed at families, such as story walks, leaf printing and fire lighting workshops, and wildlife and nature events for adults, such as flower arranging and tree identification. The cemetery also takes part in the annual Bristol and Bath Festival of Nature.

WWT SLIMBRIDGE WETLAND CENTRE

Slimbridge, Gloucestershire GL2 7BT • OS Explorer Map OL14 • Grid ref SO722048 (entrance) • What3Words: bleaker.nozzles.plump (entrance)

How to get there: Take the train from Bristol Temple Meads, Stapleton Road, Ashley Down, Filton Abbey Wood or Bristol Parkway stations towards Gloucester, and alight at the Cam and Dursley station (around a 40-minute journey). Take the Robin bus from the station to WWT Slimbridge; this is a request-only bus that must be booked in advance. Alternatively, from the station, walk southwest along Box Road and catch a number 65 Stagecoach bus towards Gloucester. Alight at the Crossroads stop, just after turning onto the A38. Walk 2.1 miles (3.4km) through Slimbridge village and along Kingston Road and Newgrounds Lane. Please note there are no pavements beyond the village, although some footpaths through the fields from Slimbridge village rejoin the route just before the Gloucester and Sharpness Canal. • National Cycle Network Route 41 passes close to WWT Slimbridge; continue down Newgrounds Lane to reach the car park, where there are cycle racks.

Access and conditions: WWT Slimbridge is a Gold Award winner (South West Tourism Awards) for accessibility and inclusion. There are level, hard-surfaced paths, and the majority of the hides are wheelchair accessible, with manual wheelchairs and mobility scooters available for hire (book in advance). There are accessible toilets and designated parking spaces for Blue Badge holders. • Open every day except Christmas Day, with seasonal opening hours. Check the website for current ticket prices.

•• The Wildfowl and Wetlands Trust's (WWT) Slimbridge Wetland Centre is one of the best known nature reserves in the country, thanks to its founder Sir Peter Scott and to both its wild visitors and captive animals.

Slimbridge and the WWT charity were founded in 1946 by Peter Scott, who opened the site to the public and set up a captive breeding programme that saved the endangered nēnē, or Hawaiian goose, from extinction. WWT has been a leader in captive breeding programmes for wild birds since, including spoon-billed sandpipers, common cranes, black-tailed godwits and curlews. The nēnē is one of the captive species kept at Slimbridge, with an area dedicated to the species and information on the work being done to save it.

Outside of the fox-proof fence, the nature reserve covers more than 325 hectares of wetlands, grasslands and the shores of the Severn Estuary, teeming with wildlife all year round. Wildlife designations include Site of Special Scientific Interest (SSSI), Ramsar site and Special Protection Area. There are 13 hides around the reserve, some of which are heated and have 'Guides in the Hides' volunteers to help with identification.

With resident otters and kingfishers on the reserve to spot all year round, each season brings additional star species to look out for. In spring and summer, listen out for the call of cuckoos, the song of chiffchaffs and reed and sedge warblers, and look out for the brilliant swooping flights of house and sand martins, swallows and swifts. Breeding waders can be found on the reserve, including avocets and lapwings. In recent years, common cranes have also begun breeding.

Autumn brings wintering birds, with up to 35,000 wildfowl using the reserve during the cold months including barnacle, Russian white-fronted and greylag geese, whooper swans, ducks such as pintails, pochards and wigeons, and waders including curlews, up to 4,000 golden plovers, and lapwings. Plus, look out for visiting thrush species such as fieldfare and redwing.

The most famous wintering residents, whose arrival is much anticipated every year, are the beautiful Bewick's swans, which migrate to the UK from remote Arctic Russia, and are the smallest swan species found in the UK. Conservation work is undertaken by WWT along the birds' migration route to raise awareness of the declining population.

Slimbridge hosts a variety of events throughout the year, including evenings with the Bewick's swans, bird identification and photography sessions and activities during the school holidays. There are also play areas including an unstructured nature play space.

Bewick's swan.

PORTBURY WHARF NATURE RESERVE

Wharf Ln, Portbury, Portishead, Bristol BS20 7TD • OS Explorer Map 154 • Grid refs ST485760 (entrance off Sheepway), ST484772 (footpath and saltmarsh junction) • What3Words: closes.majors.darling (Sheepway), casual.restless.character (footpath)

How to get there: Take the X4 bus from central Bristol or Hotwells, or the X10 bus from northern Bristol, and alight at the Portishead Ecology Park bus stop on the Sheepway. Cross the road, and enter the reserve through the entrance on the lefthand side of the car park. • The Sheepway entrance is also on the National Cycle Network Route 334, running through Abbots Leigh. Alternatively, you can follow Route 41 along the River Avon and join Route 26, which then joins Route 334 on the Sheepway. Some of the paths within the reserve are open for cycling. There are no cycle racks.

Access and conditions: The reserve's footpaths are flat, and some are surfaced. The seasonal track can be muddy and closed off if unsuitable for visitors to use. There are no facilities on the reserve. Dogs are welcome but must be kept under control (ideally on the lead and staying on paths). The small car parks on the Sheepway and Wharf Lane do not have designated spots for Blue Badge holders.

•• Located 7 miles (11.3km) west of Bristol, Portbury Wharf Nature Reserve is 60 hectares in size and looks out over a protected saltmarsh and the Severn Estuary.

It was created as a nature reserve in the early 2000s and was initially managed by Avon Wildlife Trust. In recent years the ownership and management was taken on by North Somerset Council. The reserve is made up of a number of freshwater ponds and ditches (known locally as rhynes), as well as wildflower meadows and hedgerows. Winter sees the arrival of avian visitors such as snipe and wigeons, as well as the population of resident birds, such as gadwalls, added to. When high tide on the estuary causes the saltmarsh to flood, more birds are pushed inland onto the reserve, including curlews, redshanks and dunlins.

Roe deer are a common sight on the reserve year-round, and water voles are also resident – though much harder to spot. If you're lucky, you might see one or hear the characteristic 'plop' of one entering the water. Even harder to see, and protected from disturbance, are the great crested newts. The reserve is also home to barn owls, which can be spotted hunting for their prey.

There are insects aplenty on the reserve, with more than 20 species of dragonflies and damselflies recorded, including emperor, migrant hawker and black-tailed skimmer.

The saltmarsh is not part of the reserve, but near the Tower Hide there is an access point out of the reserve. This joins up to the footpath that runs along the top of the marsh, which is now part of the South West section of the King Charles III England Coast Path. The saltmarsh is a Site of Special Scientific Interest (SSSI), and part of the Special Protection Area (SPA), Special Area of Conservation (SAC) and Ramsar site designations of the Severn Estuary. It is regularly flooded by the tides on the Severn Estuary, though the higher parts of the saltmarsh are usually only flooded in very high tides. On very rare occasions, strong winds will push the water of the high tides over the sea wall into the Portbury Wharf Nature Reserve.

The mudflats in front of the saltmarsh are full of small invertebrates, which are fed on by wading birds all year round, but particularly in winter. The plants of the saltmarsh are well adapted to living in these salty conditions, particularly down in the lower part of the marsh. Look out for the pretty flowers of sea aster and sea lavender. The vegetation provides feeding and resting areas for a variety of animals. Flocks of small birds such as goldfinches and linnets can be seen, as can grazing roe deer. Smaller mammals such as field voles and mice will live amongst the vegetation, attracting kestrels and barn owls. It is thought that skylarks breed in the saltmarsh as they have been seen flying and singing above it.

There is an active Friends of Portbury Wharf Nature Reserve group, which increases awareness of the reserve and its wildlife and works with the council to safeguard the reserve. The Friends also runs guided walks, provides talks and monitors the reserve's wildlife. The website is very informative and has a month-by-month guide of species to look out for.

EXETER

The southernmost city covered in this book, Exeter is the county town (and sometimes referred to as the capital) of Devon, and is bisected by the River Exe. To the west and southwest of the city lies the beautiful Dartmoor National Park, the only place in England where it is legal to wild camp (although this has been legally disputed in recent years). To the east, is the East Devon National Landscape, stretching between Exmouth southeast of Exeter all the way through to Lyme Regis and the Dorset border (though it excludes some of the coastal towns).

As well as its existing nature reserves, the local Wildlife Trust took on the six Valley Parks from Exeter City Council in May 2019. These Valley Parks are located around the city, with community involvement and continual work to make them more accessible as green spaces to the city's residents and visitors. Ludwell and Riverside (page 56) in the southwest part of the city are particularly close to each other and are easy to visit by public transport.

Exeter St David's and Exeter Central railway stations have good connections to Bristol and London, as well as to Plymouth to the south. The Exeter to Plymouth line shares its tracks with local service the Riviera Line, which passes along the southern bank of the River Exe and stops off at Dawlish, providing easy access to Dawlish Warren Nature Reserve (page 61). On the northern side of the river, another local line, the Avocet Line, passes through Topsham and ends in Exmouth.

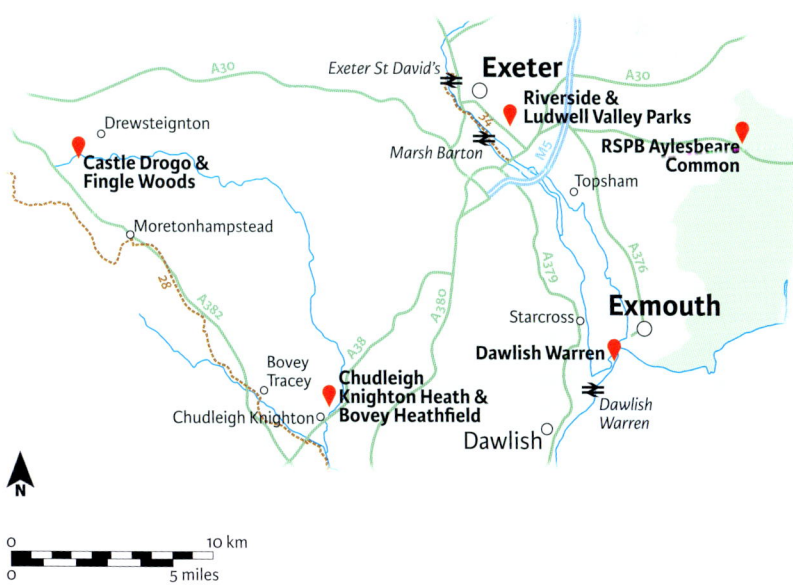

RIVERSIDE AND LUDWELL VALLEY PARKS

Riverside: Exeter EX2 6LT; Ludwell Exeter EX2 6HP • OS Explorer Map 114 • Grid refs SX927907 (Riverside near Marsh Barton station), SX949910 (Ludwell entrance off Pynes Hill), SX940905 (Ludwell entrance off Topsham Road) • What3Words: update.player.pretty (Riverside), roofs.palm.grabs (Pynes Hill), spout.ally.gear (Topsham Road)

How to get there: The 12-mile (16.1km) Exeter Green Circle walking route passes through both Valley Parks.
Riverside: Walk south along the footpaths on either side of the river, following signs for the Riverside Valley Park. Take the Great Western Railway train from Exeter St David's towards Paignton and alight at Marsh Barton station; on exiting turn right and head along Clapperbrook Lane. After crossing over the little bridge, turn right on the footpath to enter the reserve. • National Cycle Network Route 34 passes through the reserve, connecting with Route 2 just to the south, which extends down to Dawlish Warren on the south side of the river or to Exmouth on the north side. There are cycle stands at Marsh Barton station.
Ludwell: A number of bus routes stop at the Crematorium bus stop on Topsham Road at the south of the reserve, from where there are footpaths onto the reserve, including buses 2 (towards Newton Abbot), 7 (towards Totnes), 38 (towards Ivybridge), 39 (towards Newton Abbot), 52 (towards Seaton) and 57 (towards Exmouth). • There are no Sustrans-suggested routes to Ludwell; the footpath along Topsham Road can be cycled along.
Access and conditions: At Riverside, there are some small car parks, but they do not have dedicated bays for Blue Badge holders. Riverside Valley Park has a mixture of flat surfaced, stony and grassy paths. • There is no parking at Ludwell Valley Park, though there is some residential parking. The cycle path between Pynes Hill and Wendover Way is the main accessible path. Other paths are dirt tracks or grassy paths, which can be muddy and steep. Many of the entrances to the park have been widened to improve access for mobility scooters. • There are no facilities at either reserve. Dogs are welcome at both reserves.

•• The six Valley Parks of Exeter are located all around the city, providing green spaces for its residents to enjoy. Once managed by Exeter City Council, they are now looked after by Devon Wildlife Trust and are managed with both wildlife and people in mind. Riverside and Ludwell Valley Parks are located close together in the southeast of the city, and are linked by the small Northbrook Park.

Located just 1 mile (1.6km) down the river from Exeter's Historic Quayside, Riverside Valley Park is a 40-hectare reserve stretching across two of the islands in the River Exe and the Exeter Ship Canal. The cycle path and footpaths are popular routes for commuters heading into Exeter, and the wider park is great for exploring the habitats alongside the River Exe, including wildflower meadows filled

Riverside Valley Park.

with buttercups and ox-eye daisies, and small woodlands. Look out for kingfishers, cormorants and grey herons on the river, and in summer, nesting sand martins. On sunny days, butterflies flutter and bees buzz amongst the flowers of the meadow, and you may spot the warning colours of the harmless wasp beetle on the white flower heads of umbellifers. Dragonflies, such as the emperor dragonfly, and damselflies can be seen flying above the water surface, and the buzz of whirligig beetles can be heard in the small pools within the islands. The shallow water of the River Exe is a good place for seeing pike, and if you are very lucky, you might see a water shrew amongst the riverside vegetation.

To the northeast of Riverside is the 80-hectare Ludwell Valley Park, reached by crossing the River Exe and following a choice of a couple of footpaths. The park is a working farm, with both grazing cattle and arable fields, and provides a variety of habitats for wildlife. Recent conservation

Ludwell Valley Park.

work has included reseeding fields with wildflower seed mixes, laying almost 0.9 miles (1.5km) of hedgerows in the traditional Devon 'steeping' style, and creating a new pond – which has been used already by emperor, broad-bodied chaser and common and ruddy darter dragonflies, as well as damselflies. As a working farm, this is a good place to spot farmland birds such as the yellowhammer and its relative, the cirl bunting, which occurs only in Devon and Cornwall in the UK. In spring and summer, you can listen out for song thrushes and may hear the iconic call of a cuckoo.

The reserve's hills provide brilliant

views to admire Exeter city from, and in summer, the fields are full of buttercups, ox-eye daisies, bird's-foot trefoil and knapweeds. These provide caterpillar foodplants and nectaring flowers for adult butterflies and moths. Looking out for meadow brown, common blue and marbled white butterflies, and day-flying moth species such as silver-Y and six-spot burnet.

Along the northwestern edge of the reserve, the Northbrook flows down to the River Exe. Although assessed as having poor water quality, species such as grey wagtail, kingfisher, dipper and, very rarely, otter can be seen.

CASTLE DROGO AND FINGLE WOODS

Drewsteignton, Exeter EX6 6PB • OS Explorer Map OL28 • Grid refs SX722900 (Castle Drogo), SX743899 (Fingle Bridge) • What3Words: triangles.driftwood.award (entrance to Castle Drogo), sits.surging.shuffles (Fingle Bridge)

How to get there: Take the 173 Stagecoach bus towards Chagford, and alight at the National Trust Castle Drogo stop (around a 45-minute journey). Walk along the driveway, which will take you to the reception building. You can turn off partway along the driveway to join the footpath which goes towards Fingle Bridge. Buses aren't very regular, so check the timetable online. • There are no recommended Sustrans routes to Castle Drogo or Fingle Bridge, but there are cycle racks at Castle Drogo.
Access and conditions: The majority of the paths between the reception, Castle Drogo and the gardens are flat and either tarmac or gravel, with ramped access into the castle. An electric mobility scooter (which must be booked at least three days in advance) and manual wheelchairs can be hired from reception, and there is also a shuttle service between the reception and the castle. However, the footpaths out into the estate are not suitable for wheelchair users. There are two designated Blue Badge parking spaces in the main car park. There are toilets, including an accessible toilet and baby-changing facilities, in the reception building. Assistance dogs are welcome in all parts of the property. • The walks are free to access. There is an admission fee to the castle and garden for non-members. The castle and garden are shut in January and early February.

•• A visit to the National Trust's Castle Drogo near Exeter provides the opportunity for a lovely wander around a castle and formal gardens, as well as a good walk out along the Teign Gorge and the River Teign. Springing up from the bogs of Dartmoor, the River Teign meanders up to the northern edge of the National Park, carving its way through the rocks, before eventually flowing south to Teignmouth.

There is a choice of two circular walks from the main car park, with leaflets available from the reception. The short walk is 1 mile (1.6km) in length and goes via Sharp Tor. The long walk is 4 miles (6.4km) in length, has a choice of two routes back along the river and visits both Sharp Tor and Hunter's Tor. Parts of both routes overlap with the Two Moors Way and the Dartmoor Way Walking Route.

Fingle Woods is a 334-hectare area made up of eight different wooded areas owned by the National Trust and the Woodland Trust. Look out for woodland birds, fabulous fungi including the iconic fly agaric, and butterflies – particularly fritillaries such as the pearl-bordered, small pearl-bordered and silver-washed. Summer brings out the glorious pinks and yellows of the heather and gorse on the hillside, and you can spot the large, busy nests of wood ants.

There are two species of deer to be seen – fallow and roe – though both can be elusive. Down by the river, look out for kingfishers and grey wagtails, and one of the most unusually behaved birds – the dipper. This bird will go swimming underwater in clean rivers and streams for its prey.

Autumn in Fingle Woods brings the chance to see one of the UK's most spectacular wildlife sights. Head down to the weirs along the River Teign, particularly after heavy rain when the river is in spate (high water). Keep an eye on the water, and if you're lucky, you may spot the fabulous jumps of Atlantic salmon and both sea and brown trout as they leap up the weirs. They are heading upstream in order to lay their eggs in gravel beds, returning to the spawning grounds from which they first hatched. The River Teign is also home to juvenile European eels, which will leave the river to spawn in the Sargasso Sea. These unusual fish have declined by 95 per cent since the 1980s and are hard to spot, so if you do, you're incredibly lucky.

The valley is steeped in history as well as wildlife. Fingle Bridge is a Grade II* listed building, with three Iron Age hill forts nearby: Prestonbury Castle, Cranbrook Castle and Wooston Castle.

Dipper.

RSPB AYLESBEARE COMMON

Joney's Cross car park, Devon EX10 OBL • OS Explorer Map 115 • Grid refs SY049906 (western entrance), SY056898 (southern entrance), SY074899 (eastern entrance) • What3Words: clipped.thrusters.flamenco (western), owes.hiring.noon (southern), ended.pocket.flattens (eastern)

How to get there: Take the 9/9A Stagecoach bus from Exeter bus station towards Honiton/Seaton or the 52 bus towards Seaton (around a 36-minute journey to the western entrance). You can alight at different stops according to where you want to access the reserve.
Western entrance: Alight at the Halfway House, then walk back towards the Hidden Oak equestrian shop. Turn right and walk up the road on the grass verge until you cross the road to access the public footpath.
Eastern entrance: Alight at the Burrow Lane bus stop in Newton Poppleford, and walk up Burrow (no pavement or verges) for about 480m. Where the road turns east, turn west instead and follow either of the public footpath signs.
• The local Buzzard Route cycling trail passes close to the reserve. There are no cycle racks.
Access and conditions: There are limited hard surface paths on the reserve, with a tarmac surface on the private road that runs down to Woolcombes Farm. The other paths can become wet and muddy in poor weather. • There are no toilet facilities. • The Joney's Cross car park off the Exeter Road does not have designated bays for Blue Badge holders.
• Assistance dogs are welcome on the reserve.

•• The lowland heaths of RSPB Aylesbeare Common offer up a variety of wildlife throughout the year, but the reserve particularly comes alive in summer. Look out for stonechats and Dartford warblers (often seen together), and if you can stay until dusk, you may be lucky enough to see nightjars – or hear their distinctive churring. It is an excellent site for dragonflies, including emperor, and as such is also ideal for seeing hobbies displaying their impressive hunting skills in catching these fast insects. The rare southern damselfly can also be found here, in the wet channels known as 'runnels' of the black bog rush mires. Having spent two years as a larva, an adult southern damselfly is alive for just a couple of

Minotaur beetle.

Common toad.

weeks. The wet heathland areas of the reserve are home to plants including cotton-grass and heath spotted orchids, small mammals such as harvest mice, and snipe in winter.

More than 30 species of butterfly have been recorded on the reserve, with highlights of silver-studded blue, white admiral, silver-washed fritillary and grayling. Alongside the bumbling dor beetle, you may also come across the impressive minotaur beetle, with the iconic male bearing his three 'horns'. These trundling dung beetles will take dung back to their nests for the larvae to feed on.

There are two circular walks shared on the reserve's leaflets, starting and finishing at the southern entrance. The shorter route is a little less than 1.2 miles (2km) in length, and the longer is 2.5 miles (4km) with a greater variety of habitats along the route. Both routes take in the famous Lone Pine and the Bronze Age barrows.

The Pebblebed Heaths NNR, including Aylesbeare Common, makes up the western edge of the East Devon National Landscape, which stretches from the NNR to Lyme Regis.

DAWLISH WARREN

East of Dawlish, Devon, EX7 0NF • OS Explorer Map OL44 • Grid refs SX983789 (visitor centre), SX980787 (entrance at car park) • What3Words: strike.submerged.snares (visitor centre), powder.decisions.rags (entrance)

How to get there: Catch a Great Western Railway train from Exeter St David's towards Paignton and alight at Dawlish Warren. Not all trains stop here, so check before boarding. The path off the station will take you down to the edge of the car park. Head northeast to access the reserve. • Alternatively, cycle down the National Cycle Network Route 34 and through Riverside Valley Park to where it joins Route 2, then continue south. The route passes close to Dawlish Warren; there are cycle racks in the Dawlish Warren Landward car park. From the Quay area of the city, the route is around 10.5 miles (17km).

Access and conditions: There is a path suitable for wheelchairs down to the visitor centre, but the paths beyond are unsuitable. There are no facilities at the visitor centre, but there are accessible toilets and baby-changing facilities off the Dawlish Warren Landward car park. There are designated bays for Blue Badge holders in the Dawlish Warren car park.

•• Dawlish is well known as a UK seaside resort, with a lovely sandy beach along a 1-mile (1.6km) sand dune spit that extends across the mouth of the Exe Estuary. The beach has consistently been awarded Blue Flag status and the Seaside Award by the Keep Britain Tidy charity for its water quality, facilities and environmental management. Behind the seaward-facing sandy beach, sheltered by the sand dunes, lies an important wildlife area, home to a variety of rare species.

Much of the Inner Warren is used for a private golf club, with very restricted access to the general public. The club works with Devon Wildlife Trust and Natural England to manage the course with wildlife in mind.

Winter at the warren brings large flocks of wading birds and geese on the sheltered side of the spit, including oystercatchers, dunlins and bar-tailed godwits. This area is designated as a Wildlife Refuge with only a few people granted access, in order to prevent disturbance to the wildlife here. On the seaward side of the spit, look out for a variety of wintering divers, grebes and ducks. Spring brings the passage of migrant birds, such as wheatears, terns and warblers.

Sadly the bird hide looking over the mudflats is currently unavailable to use as erosion on the dunes has meant that the footpath along to the hide is not safe. Hopefully a new footpath, or a relocated hide, will be made available in due course.

One of the ornithological highlights of Dawlish Warren has to be the cirl bunting, a pretty farmland bird that is related to the widespread yellowhammer. On the UK Red List, the cirl bunting was until recently only found in Devon in the UK, with its fortunes recently boosted by a reintroduction project in Cornwall. The species can be seen here year round.

Beyond the shorelines of the mudflats, at the mouth of the Exe Estuary lies a mysterious underwater world, home to one of the world's few flowering marine plants – eelgrass. As well as being

important for sediment deposition and stabilisation, the beds of eelgrass are nursery grounds for juvenile fish, and an important habitat for the UK's two species of seahorse, the short-snouted and the long-snouted (the latter also known as spiny).

There are more than 600 flowering plants at Dawlish Warren, and additional non-flowering plants such as the rare adder's-tongue and small adder's-tongue ferns. Orchid species include the bee orchid, autumn lady's tresses, marsh helleborine, and southern marsh orchid. Amongst the botanic delights of Dawlish Warren is the sand crocus, also known as the warren crocus. It is a small pale purple flower with curling leaves, which blooms in early spring and only opens its petals when the sun is shining. Although found elsewhere in parts of Asia, Africa and Europe, the sand crocus's range is very limited in the UK. In fact, until recently it was only known from Dawlish Warren, though it has now also been found in Lantic Bay in Cornwall.

Another rare plant is the petalwort, less showy and smaller than the sand crocus, and a non-flowering plant. Found at only seven sites in England, it is a small species of liverwort that looks a bit like a tiny lettuce. In 2024, translocation of the species was undertaken within the reserve, to areas less likely to be submerged by seawater.

Bee orchid.

CHUDLEIGH KNIGHTON HEATH AND BOVEY HEATHFIELD

CKH: Bovey Tracey, TQ13 0EY, BH; Old Newton Road, TQ13 9DU • OS Explorer Map OL44 • Grid refs SX842773 (Chudleigh Knighton entrance), SX837772 (southern half), SX824766 (Bovey Heathfield) • What3Words: sector.disband.crockery (start of the Ant Trail), reseller.joys.squeaking (entrance to southern part of BH)

How to get there: Take the 39 Stagecoach bus from Exeter Central station towards Newton Abbot and alight at the Village Hall stop in Chudleigh Knighton (around a 40-minute journey). Walk west along Homelea, keeping right to stay on The Chapelry. From the car park by the playground, follow the public footpath and the ant waymarkers to begin the Ant Trail. After crossing the road, either continue following the Ant Trail, or head out onto the reserve to the opposite side of the field to find the footpath to reach the other reserves. • Alternatively, to go straight to Bovey Heathfield, continue on the bus until after Bovey Tracey, and alight at the Heathfield stop outside the King Charles Business Park. At the southern end of the grass verge, cross the road and enter into the southern half of the reserve. Alternatively, walk into the business park and continue straight to find the entrance into the northern half of the reserve. • National Cycle Network Route 28 and the multi-use trail Stovey Way between Newton Abbot and Bovey Tracey run along the top of Bovey Heathfield. There are no cycle stands.

Access and conditions: No surfaced paths, facilities or parking. Paths are unsuitable for wheelchairs. Dogs are welcome, but must be kept on a lead.

•• Heathland habitat once used to stretch across the Bovey Basin, but is now limited to fragmented areas. Chudleigh Knighton Heath nature reserve is one of these areas, with a mixture of grassland, gorse and heather across its 42 hectares. Whilst it boasts some of the typical wild inhabitants of a heathland, it is also home to an incredibly rare insect, the narrow-headed ant. One of the wood ant species, which are the largest ants in the UK, the narrow-headed ant is found at just one site in England – Chudleigh Knighton Heath – and at five sites in Scotland, although it is widespread globally. Unlike other wood ants, narrow-headed ants do not build their nests within the shade of the forest. Instead, their slightly smaller nests need

Chudleigh Knighton Ant Trail.

more sun and so they are found on woodland and scrub edges. Intense conservation work has been undertaken in recent years to learn more about the species' ecology and the potential of translocation to other sites.

The 2-mile (3.2km) circular route, starting from the western edge of Chudleigh Knighton, takes you through

Bovey Heathfield.

the top of the southern part of the reserve, across the road and then around the northern part. This route is called the Ant Trail and is guided by ant waymarkers on the fence posts.

If you visit at dusk in summer, you may hear the churring of a male nightjar. The unusual call fills the air and can be accompanied by the bird clapping its wings in flight. Whilst you are there, keep a look out for the little lights of a female glow-worm trying to attract a male.

From Chudleigh Knighton Heath, you could also take in some or all of the Bovey Basin walk. This complete walk is roughly 4.5 miles (7.2km) in length, and takes in three of the local nature reserves. The online guide starts at Bovey Heathfield and ends at Chudleigh Knighton Heath, via Little Bradley Ponds, but you can visit them how you prefer. A visit to Little Bradley Ponds in summer is a treat for insect enthusiasts, as more than 20 species of Odonata have been spotted, including scarcer species such as hairy dragonfly and downy emerald dragonfly, and small red damselflies.

Little Bradley Ponds.

Bovey Heathfield is another wonderful heathland to explore. Here, look out for nightjars, solitary bees, grass snakes and adders. It is also home to the heath potter wasp, a master crafter. Over the course of 2–3 hours, the female wasp creates tiny clay 'pots' on branches of gorse or heather, in which she will lay a single egg, and then add in a number of paralysed small caterpillars as a food store for her young.

NORTHERN ENGLAND

CARLISLE

Beyond the ancient Roman landmark of Hadrian's Wall, Carlisle's rich and turbulent borderland history has left behind a wealth of natural wonders waiting to be discovered. Situated at the confluence of the Eden, Caldew and Petteril rivers, Carlisle offers access to tranquil inner-city parks and walks. Just 1 mile (1.6km) from Carlisle station, the River Eden can be explored through Rickerby Park (page 68), where urban respite can be found alongside spectacular opportunities for wildlife watching.

The city provides a particularly excellent base for carbon-free exploration of varied habitats – from ancient Atlantic oak woodland in the Lake District National Park (page 76) to reedbeds on the coast at Siddick Ponds Nature Reserve (page 73). Along with public transport, the Hadrian's Wall Path offers an adventurous, multi-day route to explore the particularly otherworldly landscape of Drumburgh Moss (page 72).

The changing seasons at Talkin Tarn Country Park (page 70) offer a wealth of natural wonders to enjoy. In autumn, the beech trees transform from emerald green to vibrant gold and umber, creating the perfect backdrop for fungi foraging and birdwatching expeditions. At the National Trust's Aira Force and Gowbarrow Park (page 76), red squirrels hide in woodland surrounding cascading waterfalls, and a lush tapestry of lichens and ferns adorn the landscape.

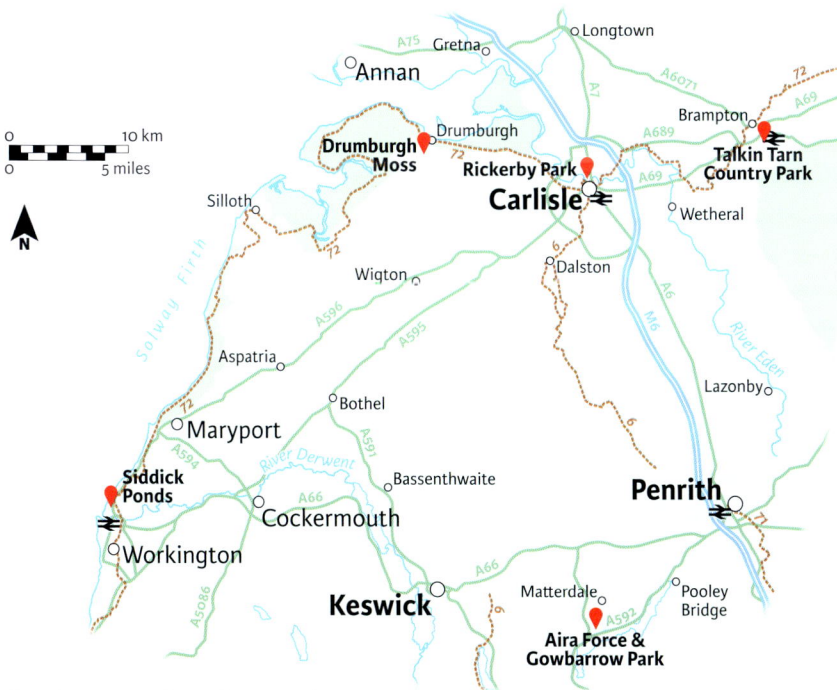

Opposite: Lower Ouseburn Valley, Newcastle.

RICKERBY PARK

There are numerous access points into Rickerby Park. Addresses for two mentioned in the directions are:
Memorial Bridge, 40 St Aidan's Road, Carlisle, CA1 1LS • OS Explorer Map 315 • Grid ref NY410564 • What3Words waddled.wins.reef
Carlisle Chinese/Italian Gardens, 10 Eden Bridge, Carlisle CA3 9AN • OS Explorer Map 315 • Grid ref NY400566 • What3Words: windy.pounds.cube

How to get there: Rickerby Park is situated on the northern edge of Carlisle city centre and can be visited with ease. The nearest train station is Carlisle, situated 1 mile (1.6km) to the southwest of Rickerby Park (Memorial Bridge entrance). From the station, walk northeast through the city centre until you reach the Memorial Bridge. Here you can cross onto the north side of the River Eden, or take a route west along the south shore.
• National Cycle Network Route 72 Hadrian's Cycleway, a 170-mile (274km) route from Ravenglass in Cumbria to South Shields in Tyne & Wear, passes through a section of Rickerby Park. Many routes within the park are accessible by bike. • A convenient bus stop for Rickerby Park is Carlisle Cricket Club, where the park can be entered via the Chinese/Italian Gardens to the east alongside Eden Bridge. Local services that visit this stop include 62, 79 and 382. The Richard Rose Central Academy bus stop also enables access from the south of the River Eden over the Memorial Bridge, and is a suitable bus stop if travelling from towns along the A69 using service 685.
Access and conditions: Most routes are suitable for wheelchairs and pushchairs. Lower sections along the northern edge of the River Eden can become flooded and saturated, but rough, surfaced paths run parallel along a higher path. Benches can be found along footpaths looking onto the River Eden. Toilets are available in neighbouring Bitts Park (subject to opening hours). • Along with an abundance of terrestrial and river wildlife, this public park often has unfenced, grazing livestock (cattle). Dogs should therefore remain under control.

•• An oasis in the city, Rickerby Park is popular with locals and visitors alike throughout the year. The park is an excellent place to search for wildlife along the meandering River Eden and its surrounding meadow and grassland habitats, dotted by beautiful mature trees.

The park is part of a green corridor which runs through Carlisle and borders the sinuous river to the north. Along the river, look for sand martins which nest in its banks in summer and can be watched zipping about feeding overhead. Goosanders can also be spotted moving through the river's course. Throughout the year, grey herons fish in the river and hunt along the banks, along with the UK's only aquatic songbird, the dipper. Look carefully at vegetation overhanging the river, or sit on a bench for a while, and you will likely spot the electric blue of a kingfisher.

The River Eden in Carlisle is perhaps one of the most wonderful locations for

watching otters. By keeping a respectful distance from the river and watching from the public footpaths, and with patience, you may well encounter these endearing mammals from Rickerby Park. Look out for their distinctive 'bubble trails' as they swim underwater and listen for their squeaky contact calls.

On the south side of the river, directly opposite Rickerby Park, The Swifts Nature Reserve can also be found. Continue west along 'Paul's Path' on the south, and you will reach The Swifts, and Bitts Park further on. It is certainly worth exploring the whole urban section of the River Eden and its surrounding habitats.

The Swifts is a 72-hectare site owned by Carlisle City Council and managed with Cumbria Wildlife Trust. In 2022, work was completed to make this former golf course into the first urban bee and butterfly oasis in the northwest through the Get Cumbria Buzzing project. It now features a stunning display of wildflower meadows, species-rich grassland and seasonal scrapes. Visit in summer to explore the transformation that has been made and to witness an abundance of butterflies, ladybirds, bumblebees and beetles now attracted to the site.

TALKIN TARN COUNTRY PARK

Talkin Tarn Country Park, Tarn Road, Brampton CA8 1H • OS Explorer Map 315 • Grid ref NY545591 • What3Words: woods.establish.ticket

How to get there: Talkin Tarn Country Park lies 9 miles (14.5km) east of Carlisle. It can be visited by train from Carlisle to Brampton (a 15-minute journey); after departing at Brampton station, walk along a country lane for around 10 minutes. Take care as cars can also use this lane. You will reach a field with a pedestrian gate leading south, which you can take to arrive at the main Talkin Tarn visitor area through fields and woodland. Please note that Brampton station is only partly accessible by wheelchair; level access is possible onto the platform to Newcastle, but the platform to Carlisle can only be accessed via a 3-mile (4.8km) journey by road. • The closest bus stop is Shoulder of Mutton in Brampton to the north of Talkin Tarn, which is serviced by Stagecoach bus 685. Talkin Tarn can be reached from this bus stop by walking south along the B6413 for 1.8 miles (2.9km). • Talkin Tarn can be cycled to from Carlisle by following Cycle Route 72 east along the River Eden through the village of Little Corby. When leaving the village, take a left at Langley Gardens and follow a country lane until reaching the B6413 directly to the south of Talkin Tarn.

Access and conditions: Toilet facilities are available by the site entrance between 09:00 and 17:00. A wheelchair-accessible toilet, also including a wheelchair-accessible shower and changing bench, is available near the car park, and there is a café for which the opening hours can be found on the Carlisle County Council website. A surfaced, mostly flat circular trail around the tarn makes the site accessible for wheelchairs, pushchairs and bikes. An all-terrain mobility vehicle (Tramper) is available to hire for Outdoor Mobility members. • Dogs are permitted under control; take note of the 'Dogs on Lead Zone' upon entering.

•• Close to the historic market town of Brampton lies picturesque Talkin Tarn Country Park, encompassing 49 hectares of mature woodland and meadow surrounding the glacial, kettle-hole lake (locally referred to as a 'tarn' from the Norse 'tjorn'). The main trail, which follows the edge of the tarn, is 1.3 miles (2.1km) in length, with branching routes available to explore the beautiful habitats further.

The northern side is hugged by woodland, with spectacular beech trees lining the tarn. In autumn, look amongst their fiery leaves for brambling in chaffinch flocks, as well as a stunning array of fungi such as brittlegills, fly agaric, stinkhorn, sulphur tuft and the death cap. In summer, search the ground from footpaths for orchids including common spotted and northern marsh. Jays, treecreepers and nuthatches are frequent in this area, and starlings can occasionally be spotted nesting in old great spotted woodpecker holes.

If visiting in summer, look for damselflies and dragonflies resting on waterside plants like willow and watermint. House martins, swallows,

swifts and hundreds of sand martins hawk over the tarn, taking advantage of the abundant insect life during the day. As the sun sets in summer, an incredible number of bats emerge from roosts including common and soprano pipistrelles, noctule and Daubenton's, to begin the 'night shift' of insect predation.

On winter afternoons, look to the sky for starlings which can form dramatic murmurations before settling into the small reedbed on the east side of the tarn. The site is home to a large rookery in mixed woodland neighbouring the reedbed; the rooks' captivating communication is best enjoyed from January into spring. Winter is also a wonderful time to wrap up warm and enjoy stargazing after sunset, particularly from the Stargazing Pavilion, a rural Dark Sky Discovery Site located on the southeast of the tarn. If visiting during the day, pop into the Pavilion to admire its structure, which was inspired by birds' nests. A small stone building can also be found nearby on the south of the tarn, housing a bird observatory where visitors can learn more about some of the local species.

As a large, inland body of fresh water, Talkin Tarn attracts an abundance of wetland birdlife such as mute swans, mallards and tufted ducks, as well as occasional rarities like scaup, red-necked grebes and black-throated divers. Reed buntings can be found in the reedbed in summer, while spotted flycatchers flicker amongst the trees.

DRUMBURGH MOSS NATIONAL NATURE RESERVE

Drumburgh Moss National Nature Reserve, Drumburgh, Cumbria CA7 5DR
• OS Explorer Map 314 • Grid ref NY255586 • What3Words: reserved.beard.flocking

How to get there: Drumburgh Moss is situated 12 miles (19km) to the west of Carlisle, around 1 mile (1.6km) to the southwest of Drumburgh village, and is best accessed by bike or bus. If travelling by bike, follow National Cycle Network Route 72 Hadrian's Cycleway west from Carlisle to Drumburgh. A small, brown tourism sign for Drumburgh Moss will direct you down a country lane, along which you can cycle south to reach the nature reserve. Please note there are no places to park or store bikes. • To travel by bus, take service 93 from Carlisle bus station to the Drumburgh Post Office bus stop (a 1-hour journey). After alighting, walk back a short distance along the road until reaching the brown Drumburgh Moss sign and continue walking along the lane for about 1 mile (1.6km).
Access and conditions: The reserve features a network of unsurfaced trails and narrow boardwalks, enabling visitors to enjoy various parts of the site while protecting its delicate habitats. Routes are not suitable for wheelchairs or pushchairs. Viewing platforms and a small bird hide can be visited following a circular trail along boardwalks. • There are no toilet or café facilities on site. Dogs must be kept on a lead to protect ground-nesting birds and other wildlife, as well as livestock.

•• For a complete change of scenery from the urban Carlisle landscape, venture out to the otherworldly scenery of Cumbria Wildlife Trust's Drumburgh Moss, a National Nature Reserve in the stunning Solway Coast National Landscape. This 121-hectare site of international importance supports a breathtaking expanse of lowland raised mire, a threatened habitat throughout western Europe. Part of the South Solway Mosses Special Area of Conservation (SAC), the reserve is one of only four remaining raised bogs on the southern Solway. Grazing by hardy Exmoor ponies and Longhorn cattle is contributing to restoration of the reserve by preventing scrub from dominating and keeping vegetation open. This complements extensive work by Cumbria Wildlife Trust to block drainage ditches and re-profile peat to help raise the water level.

Specialist bog-loving plants thrive at Drumburgh Moss including sphagnum moss, of which 13 species have been found here. All three UK species of the carnivorous sundew are recorded on the reserve too: round-leaved, oblong-leaved and the scarce great sundew. In spring, the bloom of bog rosemary, cranberry and heather is particularly stunning. Visiting in spring also offers the opportunity to enjoy the soundscape of displaying curlews, reed buntings and skylarks, as well as grasshopper warblers, snipe and redshanks. Between March and May, look for the impressive male emperor moth, adorned with regal feathery antennae, which can be spotted in flight during the day while females hide in vegetation.

As summer arrives, common lizards and adders can be spotted basking, and the

Common lizard.

White-faced darter.

boardwalk offers a good chance to see them – so step lightly and look ahead. Dragonflies are also a highlight, including the black darter (June to October), and the endangered white-faced darter, which is thriving thanks to an introduction project led by Cumbria Wildlife Trust in collaboration with the British Dragonfly Society. Peak flight period for the white-faced darter is May to August, with April and September also offering possible sightings. The nationally rare large heath butterfly also makes its home in the wet bog habitat; look for adults between late June and early August. Autumn brings short-eared owls quartering over the moss, along with hobbies, which can be seen hunting dragonflies on warmer days. Although Drumburgh Moss is best visited from late spring to early autumn, winter can offer sightings of small numbers of migratory wildfowl and waders among the thousands of annual overwintering birds on the Solway.

SIDDICK PONDS NATURE RESERVE

Siddick Ponds, behind Dunmail Park, Maryport Road, Workington CA14 1NQ
• OS Explorer Map 303 • Grid ref NY001300 • What3Words: late.hoping.lakes (reserve entrance) and exact.stays.pencil (Holmen Iggesund Gatehouse)

How to get there: Siddick Ponds Nature Reserve is situated on the coast of west Cumbria near Workington, 34 miles (54.7km) to the southwest of Carlisle city centre. It can be visited by taking a bus from Carlisle bus station and departing at the Dunmail Park bus stop in Siddick (just over 1-hour journey). Services include Stagecoach Cumbria service 300. From the bus stop, walk for 0.5 miles (0.8km) toward the J Edgar & Son car showroom; the entrance to the reserve can be found behind this. • Alternatively, catch a train from Carlisle to Workington station (50-minute journey), and walk 1.2 miles (1.9km) north on footpaths along the A597 to reach the reserve. • For an extended adventure, travel by bike along National Cycle Network Route 72 Hadrian's Cycleway, which can be followed for the entire journey from Carlisle city centre to Siddick Ponds, taking in the stunning Solway Coast National Landscape and west coast of Cumbria en route.

Access and conditions: A straight, flat cycle path passes along the length of Siddick Ponds, which is accessible for wheelchairs and pushchairs. Accessible entry onto the reserve can be found behind the J Edgar & Son car showroom. • The reserve does not have toilets or café facilities available; however, it directly neighbours the shopping centre, which does. • A bird hide can be found at the northern end of the pond, and you can request the key for this at the Holmen Iggesund Gatehouse. To reach the gatehouse, follow the cycle path north and cross the A596 to continue on the footpath on the west of the road. You will shortly arrive at another crossing point to return to the east of the A596, where you can enter the Holmen Iggesund estate. The gatehouse can be found by turning right when entering. The hide has a ramp to enter, and features windows at different levels facing onto the pond, along with interpretation panels. • Dogs on leads are permitted on the cycle path only.

•• Hosting a spectacular, extensive reedbed on the west coast, Siddick Ponds Nature Reserve is a Site of Special Scientific Interest (SSSI), recognised as a regionally and nationally important site for wintering and breeding birds. Two large ponds are distinctive features of the reserve, supporting both fresh water (east) and brackish water (west), boosting the diversity of species that use the reserve throughout the year. Nestled between farmland, scrub, retail and industry, Siddick Ponds is a hidden gem on the edge of the Irish Sea, set within the stunning West Cumbria Coastal Plain.

More than 170 species of birds have been recorded across the reserve's mosaic of habitats, including breeding reed warblers and an incredible number of swallows and sand martins feeding over the pools in summer. In winter, look for goosanders, goldeneyes, tufted ducks, pochards, shovelers, teals, little grebes, wigeons, whooper swans and reed buntings on the edges. A disused railway embankment bordering the west of the reserve has established with gorse and scrub, making it a valuable refuge for migrant birds in autumn.

Small blue.

One of the rarest butterflies in Cumbria, the small blue is confined to coastal grassland and open mosaic habitats between Maryport and Workington. Siddick Ponds is one such site that supports the species, thanks to the planting of kidney vetch on the reserve – the sole foodplant of its caterpillars. Look for adults on the wing between May and August from the footpath.

Siddick Ponds is the best location to

see wintering bitterns in Cumbria. The hide on the northern edge of the reserve is a great place to look for them; take extra care at dusk to look for these masters of camouflage settling in to roost amongst the reeds. You might also be fortunate enough to spot an otter hunting or to visit during a winter starling murmuration; tens of thousands of the birds have roosted in the reeds in previous years.

The reserve is managed by the Workington Nature Partnership, a joint venture between Workington Town Council and Allerdale Borough Council, with the management and care for the reserve also contributed to by the Friends of Siddick Ponds. Both groups welcome enquiries from those keen to volunteer, which can be explored through the Workington Nature Partnership website.

AIRA FORCE AND GOWBARROW PARK

Aira Force and Gowbarrow Park, Matterdale, Penrith CA11 0JS • OS Explorer Map OL05 • Grid ref NY400200 • What3Words: reward.green.indulgent

How to get there: Visiting this rural spot in the Lake District National Park, situated 30 miles (48km) to the south of central Carlisle, is possible via a surprisingly simple 1.5-hour journey using public transport. To begin your journey, catch an early train south from Carlisle to Penrith station (15-minute journey); from Penrith station, you can then take the Stagecoach Cumbria bus service 508 to Matterdale. Get off at the Aira Force bus stop after a 45-minute journey that takes a beautiful route along Ullswater. The bus stop is 150m from the site; when departing the bus, cross directly over the A592 and follow the brown signs for Aira Force Waterfalls along the footpath. Be sure to note the time of the last return bus, as the service is infrequent. • As an alternative, multi-day adventure, National Cycle Network Route 6 passes through central Carlisle, south along countryside toward Becksess, east of Troutbeck. From here, you can continue cycling south along Route 71 between Great Mell Fell and Little Mell Fell before reaching Aira Force through Dockray. Bike hire can be arranged in advance from Carlisle through Border City Cycle Hire, and electric hybrid bikes can be arranged through family-owned Arragons Cycling Centre for routes beginning from Penrith station.

Access and conditions: Much of this site includes trails that can only be accessed by foot and are not suitable for wheelchairs, including the route to the Aira Force waterfalls. There are waymarked trails throughout; paths cover grass, gravel and mud surfaces, with steep gradients and steps in some areas. There are benches throughout the route. • There is a welcome building with a tearoom on site. Toilets, including baby-changing facilities and an accessible toilet, are available near the welcome building. • Dogs are permitted on leads. • Weather in the Lake District can be changeable, so be prepared by wearing walking boots and packing suitable clothing along with seasonal items such as suncream. You might also like to print or download an electronic trail map from the National Trust Aira Force website before travelling.

•• The National Trust's Aira Force and Gowbarrow Park offer a wealth of natural wonders for visitors to explore. Lush Atlantic oakwood, cascading waterfalls, tranquil glades and spectacular scenery await. Five waymarked trails of varying distances and elevation gains cater to hikers of all skill levels, from easy 0.5-mile (0.8km) strolls to more challenging 4.5-mile (7.2km) treks up Gowbarrow Fell (480m summit). While the Lake District is a popular summer destination, those seeking a quieter experience can opt for the longer trail routes to avoid pinch-points.

Entering the woodland, you'll discover a steep ravine carved by the rushing waters of Aira Beck, its banks teeming with vibrant plant life including rare ferns, mosses and bryophytes, and also lichens. In fact, hundreds of lichen species have been identified in the area, with data now available online through the Cumbria Lichen and Bryophyte Group. Continuing north, the trail leads to the impressive Aira Falls, best viewed from the aptly named Falls View Bridge. Keen-eyed visitors may even spot the elusive red squirrel, as this area of the Lake District is one of the few remaining strongholds for these enchanting mammals in England. This is in part due to considerable effort by the Penrith and District Red Squirrel Group, and habitat connectivity projects in the Lake District landscape. Check treetops for their dreys (nests), look on the ground for feeding signs, and keep your eyes peeled for their distinctive flash of red. Upon reaching an opening by High Cascades Bridge, Gowbarrow Fell can be seen to the northeast; this trail offers breathtaking vistas across Ullswater. In summer, listen out for cuckoos, pied flycatchers and redstarts, and scan the skies for ravens, buzzards and peregrine falcons throughout the year. Autumn brings a vibrant display of fungi including fly agaric, giant polypore, blusher, waxcaps and boletes.

Red squirrel.

HULL

Sitting above the largest tidal estuary on the east coast of Britain, the Humber, the port city of Hull offers an ideal hub to explore rewilded urban oases, ever-changing peninsulas and breathtaking clifftop wildlife encounters. Within the city, a grassroots urban, passive rewilding project can be explored at Noddle Hill Nature Reserve (page 81), a 50-hectare site where 400 species have been recorded.

The Humber is best enjoyed during autumn migration peaks, when the estuary provides a crucial stop-over and wintering ground for tens of thousands of wading birds and pink-footed geese. A great way to encounter this spectacle is to pay a visit to the Far Ings National Nature Reserve (page 79). Where the Rivers Ouse and Trent meet, 35 miles (56.3km) west of Hull, the second largest expanse of tidal reedbed in England can be found at RSPB Blacktoft Sands (page 83). The presence of nesting and wintering marsh harriers is a real conservation success story for the site, and a series of hides enables excellent viewing opportunities.

With irregular buses from Hull to Spurn National Nature Reserve (page 85), the journey to this awe-inspiring landscape requires a lot of forward planning – but it is certainly worth it. Enjoy a day trip or consider making a break of it, particularly during Spurn Migration Festival (Migfest). For a real sensory break from the city, an early morning journey to Flamborough Cliffs (page 87) will bring views of striking white chalk cliffs and exceptional coastal wildlife within a couple of hours.

FAR INGS NATIONAL NATURE RESERVE

Far Ings National Nature Reserve, Far Ings Road, Barton-upon-Humber, North Lincolnshire DN18 5RG • OS Explorer Map 281 • Grid ref TA017233 • What3Words: invest.giving.sparrows

How to get there: Directions are to the visitor centre, situated 8 miles (12.9km) to the southwest of central Hull. However, different routes can be taken to enter the reserve from the south side. • Enjoy spectacular views of the Humber across the Humber Bridge Cycling/Walking Route, before joining a level, surfaced trail on the southern edge of the Humber to the visitor centre. Details of joining this route via different cycle lanes from central Hull can be found on Hull City Council's 'Travel Hull' website. Cycling is not permitted within the nature reserve, but cycle racks can be found in the visitor centre and Ness End car park. • Regular Stagecoach East Midlands bus services run from central Hull to Barton-upon-Humber Rail Station, which is the closest stop. • The nearest train station is Barton-upon-Humber, located 1.3 miles (2.1km) to the southeast of the visitor centre.

Access and conditions: Many paths are surfaced and suitable for wheelchairs and pushchairs, including access into two hides. However, gates when livestock are on site may impact this. Toilets, including an accessible toilet and baby-changing facilities, are available in the visitor centre, which is also fully accessible. • Dogs are permitted along the Viking Way trail and on leads in the visitor centre, but are not permitted on the reserve. • The visitor centre is open Tuesdays to Sundays 10:00–16:00, with seasonal variations.

•• Situated on the south bank of the impressive Humber Estuary, the 59-hectare Far Ings National Nature Reserve supports an abundance of wildlife. The mix of reedbed, meadow, scrub, freshwater and saline habitats are cared for and managed by Lincolnshire Wildlife Trust, and you can explore them all via circular, waymarked trails.

It is worth popping into the visitor centre, if open, to look at recent sightings and upcoming events, and to ask for tips on the best routes to take for encountering any seasonal highlights from the informative volunteers.

Leaving the visitor centre with the breathtaking backdrop of the Humber Bridge to the east, you will walk west along the Bittern Trail (which follows the Viking Way) to reach the interior of the nature reserve. The walk along the Humber itself is worth taking the time to enjoy, particularly at low tide when the banks are bustling with wading birds busily feeding in the mudflats.

A series of trails wind through a mosaic of flooded clay pits in the reserve, which were created in 1986 to restore some of the wetland lost in Lincolnshire through drainage. These freshwater habitat niches have helped to restore diverse microscopic life, which provides a rich food-base for fish, in turn attracting kingfishers, grey herons and grebes, including Slavonian grebes on occasion.

The situation of this reserve on the Humber Estuary, its diversity of habitats and its successful reclamation for nature by Lincolnshire Wildlife Trust make it a wonderful place to watch wildlife at any time of the year, though there are seasonal highlights to take note of.

Far Ings and the Humber Estuary offer a truly wild spectacle during spring and autumn passage, forming a major east–west flyway for migrating birds, with passage waders including curlew sandpipers and whimbrels. As you walk between Ness Pit and Hotel Pit, look through the screen to check for resident bearded tits, which can also be spotted from Ness Hide.

Marsh harriers can be observed displaying here in spring, as well as above the Scrapes, and otters are frequently sighted. In recent years, the rare Norfolk hawker dragonfly has been sighted in summer, a real highlight for entomologists, along with more than 250 species of moth recorded on the reserve and 19 species of butterfly. In winter, tens of thousands of starlings form shapeshifting murmurations above the reserve and estuary as dusk falls, before settling into the reedbeds.

The jewel in the crown for Far Ings is its value as a vital UK stronghold for breeding, as well as wintering, bittern; a species which returned to Far Ings in 2000 after a 21-year absence. With comparatively high chances of seeing bitterns at Far Ings, as well as hearing their booming calls in March, the Ness End Farm hide is a recommended viewing platform. This 'double-decker' hide offers a higher chance of seeing bitterns over the high reeds; particularly due to the channels, well managed by Lincolnshire Wildlife Trust, which offer opportunities for bitterns to fish from the visible edges.

Bittern.

NODDLE HILL NATURE RESERVE

Noddle Hill Nature Reserve, Noddle Hill Way, Hull HU7 4YP • OS Explorer Map 293 • Grid ref TA110348 • What3Words: owls.zeal.laying

How to get there: Numerous Stagecoach East Midlands bus services visit the estate, which neighbours Noddle Hill. The closest bus stop is Enstone Garth. Enter the reserve by taking a 5-minute walk along Bransholme Road. • The nearest train station is Hull Central, located 5 miles (8km) to the south of the reserve.

Access and conditions: Trails through the reserve are undulating, rough and narrow; this site is therefore unsuitable for cycling or wheelchairs. • There are no toilet facilities on site. • Dogs are permitted on leads.

•• This is a real hidden gem for those who love urban scrubland, and an excellent example of the opportunities for wildlife and communities that passive rewilding can bring to a city.

Situated in the heart of one of Hull's most densely populated housing estates, Noddle Hill Nature Reserve has been recognised as a hotspot for biodiversity by the UK Centre for Ecology and Hydrology, with songbirds in particular benefitting from this habitat. The site became Hull's first officially recognised nature reserve in 2012 and now, following decades of passive rewilding, encompasses a wildlife wonderland of around 50 hectares with more than 400 species recorded to date.

There are a couple of different routes to take which can be walked within an hour. However, as these follow very narrow channels through the scrub at times, it is worth settling in on one of the central viewpoints to wait for wildlife to 'come to you'. If arriving from the Bransholme Road entrance, you can enter the main body of the scrubland by following the footpath to the southeast of the fishing lake, before entering to the north.

In recent years the reserve has become dominated by extensive scrub thickets with bramble, hawthorn, hazel, dog rose and willow highlighted by a mix of vetch, umbellifer, thistle and nettle species, alongside cuckooflower, comfrey, teasel and other plants. People living local to Noddle Hill take advantage of the excellent foraging opportunities there, such as blackberry, rose hip, wild spearmint, cinquefoil and fern-leaved yarrow. A series of freshwater pools are dotted within, which can be spotted by looking for reed-swamp in the hollows.

To date, the pools and ditches throughout Noddle Hill have been found to support at least 16 species of dragonfly and damselfly, including willow emerald and blue-tailed damselflies, migrant hawker, black-tailed skimmer, ruddy darter and emperor.

The acoustic landscape of Noddle Hill is a real spectacle, from the rhythmic, almost mechanical hum of invertebrates, such as Roesel's bush-crickets, lesser marsh grasshoppers and long-winged coneheads, to a breathtaking dawn chorus. Best enjoyed from mid-April to June, the dawn chorus features familiar songsters such as robins, goldfinches, song thrushes and blackbirds, along with habitat specialists such as common and lesser whitethroats, yellowhammers, greenfinches, reed buntings, and reed, grasshopper, Cetti's, sedge and willow warblers.

Look out for kestrels, buzzards and sparrowhawks overhead throughout the day, and barn owls and tawny owls hunting alongside common pipistrelle and noctule bats during early mornings and at sunset. Roe deer, fox, hedgehog and weasel are some of the other mammals frequently spotted at Noddle Hill, with a population of harvest mice another success story for the reserve.

Noddle Hill is expected to continue developing through passive rewilding,

with support from the local community, so with every passing season throughout the years to come, new wildlife sightings can be enjoyed as the habitat continues its transition from an industrial past into a diverse haven for wildlife.

RSPB BLACKTOFT SANDS

> RSPB Blacktoft Sands, Goole, East Riding of Yorkshire DN14 8HR • OS Explorer Map 291 • Grid ref SE842230 • What3Words: marsh.moss.likely
>
> **How to get there:** RSPB Blacktoft Sands is approximately 35 miles (56.3km) to the west of Hull, on the southern bank of the River Ouse. However, public transport to the site is very simple. First, take a train from Hull to Goole (30-minute journey), then hop on either Stagecoach East Midlands bus service 360 or 361 to Blacktoft Sands (30-minute journey), which will drop you off at the entrance to the reserve. Be sure to check your return journey back to catch the last bus.
>
> **Access and conditions:** The linear trails are level and composed of loose gravel. Several hides are accessible. The site is wheelchair accessible and a push-style wheelchair is also available to hire. Toilets, including a unisex accessible toilet and baby-changing facilities, are available. Binocular hire is available. • Dogs are not permitted on the reserve, with the exception of assistance dogs. • The reserve and toilets are open 09:00–18:00. The visitor centre is open during daylight hours, with seasonal variations.

•• Where the River Ouse and River Trent meet at the inner Humber Estuary, RSPB Blacktoft Sands is perfectly situated on the south bank of the Ouse. Boasting the largest expanse of tidal reedbed in England, and the second largest in the UK, the reserve supports brackish lagoons, managed pools, willow scrub and grazing marsh alongside the reedbed.

Following the entrance trail to the north, you will first arrive at the 'Reception Hide' where you can pop in to speak with an RSPB volunteer and find out about recent sightings. Altogether there are seven hides at Blacktoft Sands, which overlook the lagoons and reedbed.

The site has highlights throughout the year and is a vital reserve for waders during spring and autumn passage. For this reason, be sure to look out for scarce birds, with little stint and curlew sandpipers spotted in recent years.

The reserve follows a linear path, with the hides dotted throughout looking northwards onto different aspects of the site. To the west the Marshland Hide is particularly worth a visit, along with the Xerox Hide, where you can enjoy close views of some 40 breeding pairs of avocets in summer.

To the east, First and Reedling are 'double-decker' hides where great views across the reedbed can be enjoyed. Look out for marsh harriers here as they have been known to nest close to the hides, offering spectacular views of behaviours such as courtship displays, food-passes and chicks taking first flights. Marsh harrier is a speciality of Blacktoft Sands, with the first birds nesting in 1994 (after the species' recovery from extinction across Britain in the nineteenth century). Now, at least eight pairs nest on site, and around 15 individuals overwinter.

The reserve is a great place to see black-tailed godwits in their spectacular breeding plumage, along with greenshanks, spotted redshanks and ruffs.

Good views of snipe and water rails are also possible on the watery edges of the reeds, and spotting a bittern is increasingly likely thanks to the ongoing efforts of the RSPB. In the reedbeds you will likely hear bearded tits, joined in summer by the reserve's large reed warbler population – more than 300 breeding pairs.

Barn owls are also frequently viewed hunting over the reserve, particularly in summer, along with peregrine falcons, sparrowhawks and kestrels.

Across the reserve in autumn, from Ousefleet Hide in particular, tens of thousands of ducks can be viewed feeding, including large numbers of pintails, wigeons and teals.

If you can pull your eyes away from the spectacular birdlife, look out for other wetland species including otter and water vole (the latter is known to be hunted by grey herons on the reserve), along with brown hare in the surrounding arable fields.

SPURN NATIONAL NATURE RESERVE

> Spurn National Nature Reserve, (south of) Spurn Road, Kilnsea HU12 0UH
> • OS Explorer Map 292 • Grid ref TA416155 • What3Words: owls.howler.transmits
>
> **How to get there:** Between March and November, on Saturdays only, the East Yorkshire 71 Spurn Explorer service runs from Hull Interchange to the Spurn Discovery Centre bus stop. Services are irregular, so set off early and take note of the last return bus, or book accommodation in advance to extend your adventure. The journey will travel around 25 miles (40km; 1 hour 45 minutes) to the southwest. A Spurn Discovery Centre Bus Service timetable can be viewed online via the Yorkshire Wildlife Trust.
>
> **Access and conditions:** Ground coverage is susceptible to inclement weather and tides, meaning soft sand and changeable conditions make wheelchair access difficult across much of the reserve. Detailed accessibility information is available online. An accessible toilet is available in the YWT Discovery Centre during open hours. • Dogs are not permitted on Spurn Point, but they are permitted on short leads around other parts of the site. • Spurn Bird Observatory and YWT Discovery Centre and toilets are subject to seasonal opening hours.

•• One of the most iconic and spectacular bird migration sites in Britain, Spurn National Nature Reserve has enchanted generations of visitors with its evocative landscape, dedicated birding community and as a mecca for birdlife.

There are a few walks that can be enjoyed, depending on the time you have available, and any key wildlife encounters you're hoping for. Spurn Point itself is a striking feature on the east coastline, a narrow spit of sand curving out from the Holderness Coast between the North Sea and Humber Estuary offering a true sense of wildness for visitors to this ever-changing landscape. The Spurn Point peninsula is over 3 miles (4.8km) long but very narrow, as little as 50m wide. Access to and from the point is subject to the tides.

Following a dynamic history of natural processes and human use through the ages, from longshore drift to military defences, Spurn has been a Yorkshire Wildlife Trust reserve since 1960 and now features a mosaic of habitats including mudflats, saltmarsh, saline lagoons, grassland, dunes covered in marram grass, and sea buckthorn scrub. The saltmarsh supports a wonderful array of coastal plants, with a seagrass protection area reinstating some of this drastically threatened habitat to the coast, situated to the west of the point before the Chalk Bank Hide.

The Yorkshire Wildlife Trust's 35-hectare Kilnsea Wetlands Nature Reserve, situated to the north of Kilnsea village, is worth visiting at high tide. This site was created in 2012 to offer refuge for roosting waders, which relocate from the Humber to spend a few hours on the wetlands. It is also a good spot to look out for birds of prey including short-eared owls. The reserve can be reached by walking a circular 4-mile (6.4km) route from the Spurn Discovery Centre, which encompasses the Canal Scrape Hide, and passes tight along the coast to the west.

Testament to the long-standing birding community here is the Spurn Bird Observatory Trust (SBOT). Located in Kilnsea, the observatory is a 'must-visit', both online to prepare for a visit by viewing recent sightings and in person. Look out for their expert-led seasonal events, as well as their work parties throughout the year, which offer the popular opportunity to contribute to essential habitat work and stay in on-site accommodation.

Opportunities for wildlife watching at Spurn are vast and variable throughout the seasons. Peak activity for 'visible migration' is between March and May in spring, and August and November in autumn. The site is well known for the Spurn Migration Festival, known as Migfest, run by SBOT and the British Trust for Ornithology (BTO) each year in early September – an event worth adding to your calendar.

One of the greatest wildlife encounters at Spurn is the spectacular passage of thousands of swifts in early to mid-summer. If timed right, the birds push down toward land around the peninsula, offering the incredible chance to be surrounded by screaming parties as they arrive back from wintering in Africa. 20th June to 10th July is considered to be the best time to visit, with tens of thousands of swifts recorded flying through daily.

FLAMBOROUGH CLIFFS

Flamborough Cliffs, North Marine Road, Bridlington, East Riding of Yorkshire YO15 1BJ • OS Explorer Map 301 • Grid ref TA239719 • What3Words: quick.plankton.wiping (for North Landing)

How to get there: Take an early train from Hull to Bridlington, then the East Yorkshire 14 bus service from Bridlington bus station to the North Landing bus stop. Overall the journey will take around 2 hours. Plan your journey back before setting off as signal may be limited at the site.

Access and conditions: The clifftop terrain is hilly with steep slopes to beaches. Paths away from the car park are rough and can become muddy in wet weather. Sections of trails include steps and raised boardwalks. • There are no toilet facilities on site, but cafés with facilities for customers can be found in the car park and there are public toilets 1 mile (1.6km) away in Flamborough. • Dogs are permitted on the footpath on a lead.

•• Spectacular seawatching and seabird colonies await at Flamborough Head. A clifftop walking route from Yorkshire Wildlife Trust's Flamborough Cliffs to Flamborough Lighthouse can be enjoyed within a 45-minute walk (covering 1.5 miles /2.4km), but with colonies of seabirds and coastal wildlife to enjoy en route, this is a place best enjoyed by packing a picnic and taking your time.

This coastline is one of the most beautiful in the east, with striking geological features, including white chalk cliffs, sea stacks, rock arches and bays, offering mesmerising foregrounds onto the vast backdrop of the North Sea.

Flamborough Head's rich marine wildlife is largely due to aspects of the landscape that are not visible, but are certainly worth acknowledging when visiting. Europe's largest chalk reef extends 3.7 miles (6km) offshore into nutrient-rich waters, which, along with submerged sea caves, offers a diverse and complex underwater environment for an array of marine life carpeting the seafloor, from sponges and anemones to lobsters, crabs and dense seaweed forests.

In summer, the cliffs on the north side of the headland come alive with the cacophony of hundreds of thousands of nesting seabirds, making Flamborough Head one of the most important and captivating seabird colonies in Europe, and the largest seabird colony in Britain. The best time to immerse yourself in this 'seabird city' is between April and July when, from mid-May, puffins nesting in cliff-face burrows can be viewed from the clifftops, along with cliff-nesting fulmars, kittiwakes, gannets, shags, herring gulls, razorbills and guillemots. If you're particularly keen to see and learn about puffins, perhaps check whether you can coincide your visit with the annual Yorkshire Puffin Festival, which takes place in late May or early June.

After the breeding season, some species can continue to be viewed year-round, including fulmar and shag, as well as gannets, which continue to amaze visitors with their dramatic dives between January and October. During peak passage (mid-September to mid-October), migrant passerine birds are unrivalled in abundance and in the number of extreme rarities which are spotted, along with the October spectacle of thousands of thrushes making landfall.

An online visit to the Flamborough Bird Observatory is worthwhile to check for recent sightings of rare visitors and find out about events such as Migweek in October and Seawatch Festival in August.

One of the most captivating wildlife encounters at this site is with the Flamborough Head Atlantic grey seal colony. These magnificent marine mammals have increased in number here over the past few years, with around 500 seals counted in recent years and hundreds regularly hauling out onto secluded bays. Although the seals are visible year-round, the breeding period between November and May is an excellent time to visit to hear their wonderful, vocal breeding displays on pebble beaches. In recent years, pups have been sighted hauled out with adults in summer. Seals are highly sensitive to disturbance, so give them space by only viewing them from the clifftops in order to enjoy wonderful views whilst respecting the needs of the colony.

Puffin.
Grey seals.

LEEDS

West Yorkshire's proud industrial heritage shines on today through a vibrant creative culture cultivated in the city of Leeds. Woven throughout the city's urban fabric and into the surrounding countryside, pockets of exceptional natural beauty can be found in areas protected, and reclaimed, from the industrial age. At RSPB St Aidan's (page 90), nestled in the River Aire catchment east of Leeds, kestrels and little owls welcome visitors from their perches on a mechanical memorial of the site's history as an open cast coal mine. Today, the enigmatic, wild seasonal soundscape of this reserve is one of its biggest draws, provided by booming bitterns, pinging bearded tits and more, alongside sightings of wildlife such as the rare black-necked grebe. Whilst there is much to discover on the city's outskirts, immersion in nature is possible without venturing far in central Leeds – such as the city's longest linear waterfront park, Whitehall Riverside Pocket Park (page 98), and Meanwood Valley (page 93), which cocoons a 7-mile (11.3km) trail through an incredible array of important habitats from the city centre to rural fringe. Nearby, Kirkstall Valley Nature Reserve (page 96) packs a punch with more than 130 plant and 65 bird species recorded in a 10-hectare site – a testament to nature's ability to recover, even on the site of a former power station. While some wildlife sites in northern England cities have been reclaimed from an industrial past, others have remained rooted for generations. To the south of central Leeds lies Middleton Woods (page 92), the largest remaining ancient woodland site in West Yorkshire.

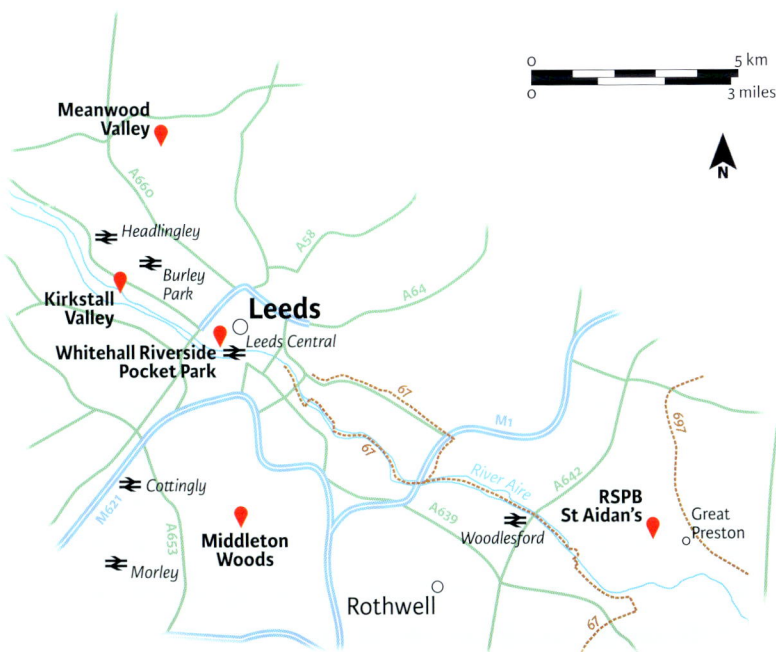

RSPB ST AIDAN'S

RSPB St Aidan's Nature Park, Astley Lane, West Yorkshire LS26 8AL • OS Explorer Map 289 • Grid ref SE398286 • What3Words: lakeside.pocket.plantings

How to get there: St Aidan's is situated around 10 miles (16km) to the southeast of central Leeds, and can be accessed via several cycle routes. The Linesway from Garforth connects directly into the reserve from the east, and the Trans Pennine Trail connects from three access points on the south side. The nearest National Cycle Network routes are National Route 67 – Trans Pennine Trail Central, Yorks and Derbyshire, and National Route 697, which run alongside the site. • The Northern 168 bus service can be used from Leeds centre. Get off at Bowers Row and walk west on Astley Lane until reaching the entrance. The visitor centre is 320m from the bus stop. • The nearest train station is Woodlesford, located 3 miles (4.8km) to the west of the visitor centre. It is possible to walk from the train station along the River Aire, before crossing over a bridge to enter the reserve by the Western Reedbed.

Access and conditions: The reserve has excellent, surfaced footpaths throughout the interior of the reserve. Due to the site forming part of a floodplain, it is recommended that local weather conditions are checked in advance of visiting. • Mobility scooters and binoculars are available to hire. Toilets, including an accessible toilet with baby-changing facilities, can be found by the car park. • Dogs are permitted on leads in the recreational area of St Aidan's (excluding the Little Owl Café); assistance dogs are welcome throughout. • The visitor centre, toilets and café are open seven days a week, with seasonal opening hours.

Kestrel perched on 'Oddball' excavator.

Black-necked grebe.

•• Demonstrating the huge benefits of reclaiming land for nature, St Aidan's is the jewel in the crown of the River Aire catchment. A former open cast coal mine, this post-industrial floodplain is now brimming with life in new reedbed, wetland, meadow and woodland habitats.

On arrival you will likely be greeted by some of the regulars: kestrels and little owls, who have adopted the historic Sunshine Miners Landmark Memorial to nest and roost in. Look closely at and around this huge dragline excavator (nicknamed 'Oddball') for the russet tones of kestrels perching or hovering, and in the surrounding scrub and grass for little owls resting and hunting.

A small RSPB welcome hut can be found here too, with information on the site's history, recent sightings, upcoming events and routes to take. Alongside this are the reserve's toilets, and the Little Owl Café, which has outstanding views across the Aire Valley.

Perhaps the most spectacular feature of St Aidan's is the enigmatic soundscape it offers in each season. Spring brings booming bitterns and an astounding dawn chorus, along with hundreds of chattering sand martins and black-headed gulls on pools. The summer soundtrack features screaming swifts, echoing cuckoos, an excellent common tern colony cacophony and the hum of invertebrate life – dragonflies in particular. The metallic pinging of bearded tits can be heard amongst the spectacular autumnal arrival of wintering birds, from the deep bugling of whooper swans to the high-pitched 'winking' of pink-footed geese.

There are visual spectacles at St Aidan's too. One speciality of the reserve is the rare black-necked grebe, which returns to St Aidan's each year to breed. The site now supports around 30 per cent of the UK population. In April, great crested grebes share their captivating courtship displays and lapwings call, swoop and dive. The wildflower-rich footpath verges are full of colour in late spring and summer, with flowers such as snake's-head fritillary and lady's smock beginning to establish as the site develops.

If you can pull your eyes away from the flora and invertebrate life in summer, look out for hobbies hunting dragonflies over the pools. In winter, you might be lucky enough to encounter a starling murmuration before the birds tuck up into the reedbeds at sunset.

MIDDLETON WOODS

> **Middleton Woods, Middleton Grove, Leeds LS10 3SH • OS Explorer Map 289 • Grid ref SE301287 • What3Words: honey.sticky.gates**
>
> **How to get there:** Middleton Woods is located 4 miles (6.4km) to the south of Leeds city centre, from which several bus routes can be taken to visit the site including LeedsCity service 2 to Beeston Park Ring Road, which stops just outside the west entrance of the woods. Additionally, the LeedsCity 47A/47 services from Leeds Corn Exchange to Newhall Road Newhall Chase, and services which end at the Middleton Park bus stop, allow entry from the south (main) entrance. • The nearest train stations are Cottingly, 2 miles (3.2km) northwest of the park, and Morley, located 2.6 miles (4.2km) to the southwest. • Surfaced paths throughout the park and woods make this site accessible for those arriving by bike.
>
> **Access and conditions:** Toilet facilities, including an accessible toilet, can be found at the visitor centre near Middleton Park Lake, available during opening hours. There are tarmacked paths around the woods and park. Mobility scooters are available to hire from the centre. • Dogs are permitted across most of the site. • Seasonal and daily opening hours apply for the visitor centre.

•• Nestled amidst the urban outskirts of south Leeds lies the largest remaining fragment of ancient woodland in West Yorkshire: Middleton Woods. Covering around 81 hectares, towering cathedrals of oak stand amongst beech, hazel, elder, birch and sweet chestnut. Soft, dappled light is a beautiful aspect of this woodland, with the array of tree species and heights bringing ever-changing views to explore. The tranquillity afforded by standing beneath the ancient, winding branches of these trees is an exceptional opportunity for grounding oneself in nature and peace in the urban landscape. It is this rare opportunity which makes Middleton Woods such a precious place, along with the habitat it provides to a wealth of wildlife.

In spring the woodland is adorned with vibrant bluebells, between carpets of bright white wood anemone, wood sorrel, delicate wood forget-me-not and sunshine-coloured lesser celandine. Amidst the carpets of wildflowers in spring and summer, and the windfall of leaves, seeds and berries in autumn, a richness of deadwood is dotted throughout.

This valuable habitat fulfils the life cycle of these ancient trees and provides different habitats to explore on a micro level. Look closely and you will discover an array of fungi and lichen, from distinctive jelly ear and candlesnuff fungus to chicken of the woods, wood oysterling and hairy curtain crust in autumn. On the 'snags' of

Jelly ear fungus.

standing deadwood, and in the nooks and crannies of the ancient bark, birds such as treecreepers search for insects. Jays, nuthatches and great spotted woodpeckers can be heard and seen throughout and are particularly notable in late summer and autumn as they take advantage of the bounty of acorns and hazelnuts.

The gnarled and decaying trunks provide roosting opportunities for bats, such as common pipistrelle, which can be observed flitting amongst high stands and woodland edges in summer at dusk. Whilst exploring the woodland, look out for the historical and archaeological features which help to share the story of this land's influence on Leeds' historical past, from medieval bell pits used for early coal mining to tracks and wagonways now enshrouded by trees.

MEANWOOD VALLEY

Meanwood Park, Green Road, Meanwood, Leeds LS6 4LT • OS Explorer Map 289 • Grid ref SE281373 • What3Words: horns.goat.rungs

How to get there: Meanwood Valley can be explored via the Meanwood Valley Trail (an inspiring landscape strategy for green space in Meanwood), with many routes and locations to enjoy in this area. The information included here is based on arriving at the main southern entrance of Meanwood Park, which can be cycled via paths and bridleways with some planning in advance. • Meanwood Park is 3.5 miles (5.5km) northwest of Leeds city centre, and several bus services can be taken to arrive at the park's southern entrance within 30 minutes, including numerous LeedsCity services from

Meanwood Valley

Leeds University to Weetwood Avenue. After leaving the bus, take a 10-minute walk along Hollin Lane to the entrance opposite Weetwood Avenue. Alternatively, LeedsCity service 38 from Headrow K to Green Road can be taken, which also passes by Meanwood Valley Urban Farm. • The nearest train station is Headingley, located 1.6 miles (2.6km) southwest of the southern entrance.

Access and conditions: Main paths throughout the park are wide and level; woodland paths are more uneven. Toilets are not available along the trail itself, but accessible toilets (including baby-changing facilities) are available to visitors of Meanwood Valley Farm during opening hours. • Dogs are permitted; they must be kept on a lead if visiting Meanwood Valley Farm.

•• Celebrated as a 'green artery' of Leeds, the waymarked Meanwood Valley Trail begins around 3 miles (4.8km) to the north of Leeds city centre. The 7-mile (11.3km) route encompasses a wonderful array of opportunities for discovering wildlife amidst a nature-minded community and features several circular walks to enjoy as well as the full stretch.

The full trail by which Meanwood Valley can be explored features an astounding array of important habitats which connect the city of Leeds to the wider rural fringe, including lowland heath, woodland, meadow and wetland. Stretching from the southern tip by Woodhouse Moor, the route follows through alongside Sugarwell Hill and

Woodhouse Ridge to Meanwood Local Nature Reserve in the centre, through to Adel Woods alongside Adel Moor and emerges in the north at Golden Acre Park near Breary Marsh.

One circular trail on the southern edge of the valley begins near Meanwood Valley Urban Farm, a vibrant hidden gem of a community farm well worth visiting for its environmental EpiCentre and natural setting. From here, Sugarwell Hill can be explored. This site, following a tree planting scheme in the 1980s, now has several wooded areas and neighbouring acid grassland supporting specialist wildflowers. If entering via the northern aspect, head along toward Breary Marsh (a Local Nature Reserve and Site of Special Scientific Interest), a well-managed area of wet valley alder wood and floodplain habitat featuring wet meadow, and fen, alder and willow carr.

The mosaic of habitats which Meanwood Valley supports makes it a spectacular inner-city home to an abundance of wildlife, including red kites, common lizards and the endangered white-clawed crayfish for which Meanwood Beck is one of the few remaining locations in Leeds. Look out for dippers and kingfishers on Meanwood Beck too.

Meanwood Valley Nature Reserve itself, situated in the centre of the trail, was designated in 1989 and has since been protected and advocated as a vital refuge for wildlife in the city. There are a number of groups situated throughout Meanwood Valley working to protect its natural and cultural heritage, including Friends of Meanwood Park, Friends of Breary Marsh, and Meanwood Valley Volunteer Rangers, who meet every month to improve and maintain habitats for wildlife.

KIRKSTALL VALLEY NATURE RESERVE

Kirkstall Valley Nature Reserve, Redcote Lane, Leeds LS4 2AW • OS Explorer Map 289 • Grid ref SE268344 • What3Words: throw.layers.mass

How to get there: The reserve is located 2.5 miles (4km) to the west of Leeds city centre and can be reached easily by bike from Leeds Central station. Head west along the Aire Valley Towpath until crossing the Aire Valley Marina onto Redcote Lane. The wooded trail to the reserve can also be cycled; however, parts of the reserve itself are unsuitable for cycling and bikes will need to be pushed. • Many bus routes pass within walking distance of the reserve entrance, such as LeedsCity services A1 Flyer, 60 Aireline and 34, and the most suitable stop to get off at is Kirkstall Road ASDA. From here, walk 0.5 miles (0.8km) west along Redcote Lane until reaching the entrance gate. • The nearest train station is Burley Park, 1 mile (1.6km) to the northeast.

Access and conditions: Access is via permissive footpaths, some of which are uneven and narrow. Wheelchair access is limited throughout. • There are no toilet facilities on site. • Dogs must be kept on a short lead.

Sedge warbler.

Tucked in between river, canal and railway, on the site of the former Kirkstall Power Station, the orchard, grassland and meadow of Kirkstall Valley is a peaceful oasis for urban wildlife and humans alike. Despite its small size, just 10 hectares, this Yorkshire Wildlife Trust site packs a punch with the spectacular diversity of plants, birds and mammals it supports. The location for Kirkstall Power Station until the 1980s, this site is a testament to nature's ability to recover.

When arriving at the reserve gates on Redcote Lane, venture along the linear path until you reach a small path and sign on your right. Here you will take a narrow path alongside a meadow, which bends to the left through more grassland and scrub before reaching the orchard. From here you can enjoy time in the tranquil setting, before continuing onto a wooded path along the River Aire and back through the reserve toward Redcote Lane. To extend this visit, a longer route can be taken by combining the Leeds and Liverpool canal.

The 0.5-mile (0.8 km) circular route of the reserve can be enjoyed within an hour.

However, with over 130 plant, 65 bird and 16 butterfly species recorded to date, along with an array of dragonflies and mammals, this tranquil spot is the perfect place to settle in – particularly on a warm summer day.

Each season shares its own distinctive beauty, particularly in the orchard where, in spring, the apple blossom provides a stunning display and an early source of nectar for an array of invertebrates such as comma and small copper butterflies. In autumn, the fruits of sloe, apple, pear, quince and medlar offer a heady, sugar-rich lure for invertebrates, mammals and birds alike.

It is not only wildlife tempted by the bounty of fruit in Kirkstall Valley. The area is renowned by the local community for its yearly abundance of bramble (blackberries). Each September an annual Blackberry Pickers event is hosted by Leeds LGBT+ Sport Fringe on the reserve – a great opportunity to meet with others to explore and connect with nature on the site. Viper's bugloss, field scabious, bush vetch, germander speedwell and wood avens are just some of the ground flora you can encounter in summer.

In spring, sedge warblers, willow warblers, blackcaps and chiffchaffs can be heard, whilst in autumn fieldfares and redwings join blackbirds to feast on fruit. Resident birds include grey wagtails, dippers, kingfishers and grey herons, which can be spotted along the River Aire, whilst sparrowhawks and kestrels are regularly spotted overhead. Keen eyes might also see an otter for which the area is known, an excellent indicator of the gradual restoration of the health of the River Aire following its degradation during the industrial revolution.

WHITEHALL RIVERSIDE POCKET PARK

Whitehall Riverside Pocket Park, Glove Road, Leeds LS11 5QG • OS Explorer Map 289 • Grid ref SE293330 • What3Words: empire.bubble.birds

How to get there: Leeds Central station is located 0.5 miles (0.8km) from the reserve; walk west from here along the Aire Valley Towpath. • There are many LeedsCity bus services which pass the site; the closest bus stop is Wellington North.

Access and conditions: The location of this site within Leeds city centre makes it very accessible. The paths are level and surfaced, with room for multiple users. There is seating along the length of the park. • There are no toilet facilities on site.

•• A new addition to the cityscape for 2023, the Whitehall Riverside Pocket Park fits between the River Aire and the Leeds and Liverpool Canal. Just 0.5 miles (0.8km) from Leeds Central station, a visit to the park can be made whilst commuting through the city or integrated at the start of a full-day urban wildlife adventure.

The waterside pocket park was a partnership project between the Canal & River Trust, Leeds City Council and Groundwork and has revitalised a once unloved section of canalised water into a haven for wildlife and people. This is the city's longest linear waterfront park, stretching 230m with planted wildflowers, trees, seasonal plants and grassland. It can be enjoyed slowly, with plenty of benches throughout to sit and immerse oneself in the returning wildlife.

The artificially re-naturalised bank is already proving to be beneficial for an array of wildlife, including the familiar sight of mute swans, which can be spotted cruising the river and canal with cygnets. Grey herons and the electric-blue flash of a

kingfisher are also occasionally sighted here.

Throughout summer look out for mesmerising banded demoiselles, along with red-eyed, blue-tailed and common blue damselflies. Territorial male demoiselles, catching the eye with their broad, dark-banded wings and iridescent blue bodies, can be found performing striking wing-flicking display flights along the watercourses. Females, iridescent green with green- or bronze-tinted wings, hunt nearby while observing the dancing males. Check the establishing vegetation for resting individuals. Butterflies including ringlet, orange-tip and small tortoiseshell can be spotted on the flowers too. The list of hoverfly, shield bug, mining bee, bumblebee, moth, ladybird, beetle and many other invertebrate species in the park is growing each year, offering the perfect opportunity to see which 'wildlife firsts' you can discover for the site.

LIVERPOOL

On the eastern edge of the Mersey Estuary in northwest England, the lively city of Liverpool embraces the coastline, its landscape shaped by generations of human activity. This sheltered estuary supports more than 100,000 non-breeding waterbirds, alongside other species such as the globally threated European eel. Tucked away in the industrial Port of Liverpool, a surprisingly wild spot can be explored at Seaforth Nature Reserve (page 103). This complex of saltmarsh, reedbed and grassland habitats on the mouth of the Mersey lures an outstanding number of waders and seabirds. Close by, the sweeping green corridor of Rimrose Valley Country Park (page 105) connects coast to country alongside the Leeds–Liverpool canal – an excellent place to cycle to explore the abundant birds, invertebrates and mammals seasonally. Also near the city centre is Sefton Park (page 107), a beautiful public park with excellent accessibility. In summer, bluebells blanket the roots of beech trees and bats hunt at dusk, while winter brings flocks of tits and thrushes.

With excellent cycling and public transport networks, Liverpool provides a great base for venturing further afield too. To the north, the Ribble Estuary provides the third most important wetland site in Britain, welcoming 250,000 migrant birds each winter. RSPB Marshside (page 101) can be visited from the neighbouring town of Southport, with nesting avocets a spring and summer highlight, and huge skeins of migrating pink-footed geese an unmissable autumn spectacle.

Another coastal highlight to rewild the senses is Hilbre Islands (page 109). This is one of the best sites in the country to see Leach's storm petrel during autumn migration, alongside hundreds of shelducks, and hundreds of grey seals in summer.

RSPB MARSHSIDE

Marine Drive, Southport PR9 9NT • OS Explorer Map 285 • Grid ref SD352205 • What3Words: slam.relate.host

How to get there: The National Cycle Network Route 62 (Trans Pennine Trail) encompasses a largely traffic-free 24-mile/40km (approximately 2.5 hour) route between Liverpool and RSPB Marshside, passing from the urban centre into wider countryside and finally to the coast. Please note that, although much of the reserve can be enjoyed along Marine Drive, some trails on the reserve may be unsuitable for cycling. • Alternatively, there are many public transport options. First travel to Southport via train or bus, such as Arriva North West service 47 to Bridge Wills Lane. Then hop on Arriva North West bus service 44 from Southport War Memorial Lord Street and get off at Elswick Junction. Continue walking north along Marshside Road for 200m to the reserve. • The nearest train station is Southport Chapel Street, located 2.6 miles (4.2km) to the southwest of RSPB Marshside. From here, catch a bus, hire a bike or enjoy a scenic stroll along on the wide, surfaced, level footpath of Marine Drive.

Access and conditions: Hide/screen trails on the reserve are level and surfaced and at least 2m wide with passing places, making many wonderful parts of the reserve accessible for wheelchair users and those with mobility aids as well as pushchairs. An accessible portable toilet is located outside the visitor centre. • Dogs must be kept on leads; assistance dogs only are permitted in hides. • Toilets and hides open throughout daylight hours.

•• On the northern edge of Merseyside, the Ribble Coast and Wetlands Regional Park encompasses internationally significant wetland habitats, with the Ribble Estuary National Nature Reserve at its heart supporting an astounding 250,000 ducks, geese, swans and wading birds annually.

A short distance from Southport, RSPB Marshside provides an ideal location for those looking to immerse themselves in the wild, windswept landscape of the northwest coast. Featuring some of the best lowland wet grassland in the region, along with dynamic swamp, saltmarsh and scrub habitats, RSPB Marshside offers a base to enjoy a diversity of wildlife throughout the year.

A small visitor centre (Sandgrounder's Hide) offers panoramic views across marsh, pools and lagoons of the coastal grassland, and is a recommended stop-off point to view the site map, trails, recent sightings and seasonal highlights. Across the reserve there are a couple of other viewpoints and Nel's Hide, which offer views onto the dynamic grassland habitats. During spring and summer, the footpath verges are vibrant with wildflowers and insects.

The spectacle of the autumn migration and winter bird flocks make the reserve a particularly excellent place to visit during colder months. In early autumn, the sky-filling skeins of pink-footed geese, gently 'winking' (calling) as they approach land, is breathtaking. Marshside is also a favourite wintering site for impressive flocks of lapwings and golden plovers, as well as pintails, shelducks, wigeons, pochards, teals and black-tailed and bar-tailed godwits.

Look and listen out for huge flocks rising and wheeling in defensive displays, as aerial predators such as peregrine falcons, kestrels, marsh harriers and hen harriers hunt the 'winter larder', and for short-eared owls quartering over unsuspecting small birds and mammals.

The first nesting birds begin to arrive from mid-February, with avocets a particular highlight. These distinctive, graceful waders can be observed foraging in shallow waters and hosting dramatic nest defence displays, often within good viewing distance of the path and hide. In the fields, brown hares can be seen boxing from March, whilst meadow pipits and linnets can once again be seen flitting through the grassland, and skylarks serenade in the skies.

Marshside has welcomed a few unusual visitors over the years too, prospecting the Ribble's prime real estate, including American wigeon, buff-breasted sandpiper and Wilson's phalarope, to name a few. Some scarce visitors are increasing in number, including spoonbills and little and great white egrets, with little stints and curlew sandpipers often seen on passage.

Make the most of your time at RSPB Marshside by ending your day enjoying the beautiful sunset over the lake and estuary, with a front-row seat from the sand dunes.

Little egret.

SEAFORTH NATURE RESERVE

Seaforth Nature Reserve, Royal Seaforth Docks, Liverpool, Lancashire L21 1JD • OS Explorer Map 275 • Grid ref SJ323971 • What3Words: royal.tulip.beam (for registration building)

How to get there: A day pass is required to enter the reserve, which must be obtained online from Lancashire Wildlife Trust in advance of your visit. Once approved, day passes can then be collected from the Port of Liverpool Police, on site, on the day of your visit. Lancashire Wildlife Trust Members can apply for an annual port pass. • A cycle lane runs for 5 miles (8km) along the edge of Liverpool docks on Regent Street, and the reserve itself can be reached on bike through the port. Cycling is not suitable around the reserve; however, bikes can be pushed alongside on short paths to reach hides. • Many bus routes are available from the city centre to the Port of Liverpool stop, including Arriva North West service 47. After departing the bus, walk along footpaths for 5 minutes to the Port of Liverpool Police to collect your pre-arranged day pass, and continue walking for 10 minutes to reach the nature reserve. • The nearest train station is Seaforth & Litherland, located 1.2 miles (1.9km) to the east of Seaforth Nature Reserve.

Access and conditions: Low-gradient paths throughout the reserve with surfaced, gravel substrate. • There are no toilets on site. Seats around site, including benches within hides. • Dogs are not permitted. • Once Lancashire Wildlife Trust have accepted your day pass request, you will be forwarded more useful information about visiting the nature reserve, including a site map of the docks.

•• Cocooned within the Port of Liverpool, one of the world's leading ports with a deep-rooted history, lies an innovative and unexpected sanctuary for birds. Covering an area of 33 hectares on the mouth of the Mersey, the surprisingly tranquil Seaforth Nature Reserve hosts a major roosting site for an incredible diversity of birds. Managed by the Wildlife Trust for Lancashire, Manchester and North Merseyside, the site features a complex of saltmarsh, grasslands and reedbed, with two lagoons – one salt water and one fresh water – and is home to hundreds of thousands of waders and seabirds.

The first of a few interpretation boards greets you upon arrival, along with a map sharing the locations of hides. Walk slowly along the paths and listen for birds, which may be singing along species-rich grass banks or resting in the sheltered borders of bramble, hazel, willow, hawthorn and alder, particularly during spring and autumn migration. Listen out for Cetti's and grasshopper warblers, chiffchaffs, blackcaps, wheatears, whinchats and redstarts.

On warmer days, take note of invertebrates along the path edges; small copper, comma, red admiral, common blue and speckled wood are just some of the butterfly species spotted, along with rarer sightings of hummingbird hawkmoths. In summer, look closely at the diverse array of bees, hoverflies, wasps and sawflies. You might also spot a bee orchid hiding amongst the rich ground flora.

Arriving to wetland viewpoints, the unique spectacle of Seaforth is unmistakable with the calls and constant activity of birds drawn to this industrial haven. To make the most of your trip, try to visit when wading birds come together to roost on the reserve. They gather 2–3 hours before high tide. For information on recent sightings and counts, along with scarce and rare visitors, visit the southern hide, which is frequented by local birders.

If gulls are your particular interest, Seaforth is a must for your list, with at least 15 gull species recorded on the reserve. The reserve also holds one of the largest breeding colonies of common tern in northern England, with 150–180 pairs.

Around 2,000 roosting terns makes for a spectacular wild cacophony in summer! During the spring migration, hundreds of little gulls stop by the reserve on passage to breeding grounds in Finland.

From March, the numbers of summer arrivals begin to increase, including shelducks, teals, goldeneye, godwits, redshank, lapwings, oystercatchers, little ringed and ringed plovers and, increasingly, avocets. In autumn, knots arrive to spend the winter at Seaforth in their thousands, along with congregations of bar-tailed and black-tailed godwits. Throughout the year, look out for the passing flights of ravens, which have adopted dock towers as nesting sites.

RIMROSE VALLEY COUNTRY PARK

The 2.5-mile (4km) long site encompasses a large green corridor on the northern edge of Liverpool, and there are at least 25 entrances from different aspects of the country park. As a general location: Litherland, Sefton, Liverpool L21 0EP • OS Explorer Map 275 • Grid ref SJ333989 • What3Words: plant.stroke.shunts

How to get there: The country park offers excellent cycle paths throughout and due to the size of this green corridor, taking a bike would be an excellent way to explore the whole country park with ease. The park encompasses part of the Sefton Circular cycle route, which can also be used to arrive to the site. It is worth noting that a couple of areas cannot be easily accessed by bike, including the southern entrance. • Multiple bus routes are available; for example, if arriving to the west of the country park, travel to Bramhall Road or Sycamore Road via the Arriva North West 47 service. • The nearest train station is Seaforth & Litherland, located a 5-minute walk from the southern entrance of the country park via the Seaforth Nature Trail. Alternatively, Waterloo station is situated 0.5 miles (0.8km) to the west, and access can be made into the southwest edge of the country park after a 15-minute walk.

Access and conditions: Wide, surfaced and levelled paths run throughout, excluding the southern entrance which is accessible on foot via a narrow, rugged path. There are no toilets on site.

•• Tucked in between the Leeds–Liverpool canal and the Liverpool–Southport rail line, the peaceful, green lung of Rimrose Valley Country Park offers an oasis within the dense urban environment. Rimrose Valley provides a beautiful natural corridor for wildlife and people to move through on the northern edge of Liverpool. Within the park are two Special Local Biological Interest Sites: Brookvale Local Nature Reserve to the south and Fulwood Way to the north.

As soon as you enter the park, the leafy canopy encasing this green corridor muffles the urban sounds of traffic and industry, offering calm against the rush of the city.

From the southern (Princess Way) entrance, Brookvale Local Nature Reserve (LNR) can be passed through en route to the wider country park. The narrow path passes through dense scrub of guelder rose, blackthorn, hawthorn and bramble, with interspersed self-seeded trees of alder, apple and sycamore, the more mature adorned with ivy. After a short while, the path opens into rough grassland and scrub, edged by semi-mature trees. This route passes reedbed swamp, damp meadow and willow carr, which supports diverse plant life such as marigold and greater spearwort, along with southern marsh and spotted orchids in the drier grassland.

The mosaic of habitats supports an abundance of birdlife too, including snipe, water rails and woodcocks, along with good numbers of greenfinches, blackcaps, reed buntings, and grasshopper, garden and reed warblers. This section offers real immersion in the habitat, where birds resting in the scrub can be quietly observed, and an abundance of invertebrates are attracted by the heady aromas of sun-kissed bramble in late summer, such as gatekeeper, red admiral and speckled wood butterflies. Look out for elephant hawkmoth caterpillars feasting on rosebay willowherb here during the summer too.

Continuing north through the country park, the landscape opens largely into rough grassland and woodland. The main body of the park is worth visiting during the quieter, crepuscular hours of dusk and dawn. At this time, roe deer, foxes and barn owls are regular sightings along scrub and grassland edges, and pipistrelle bats can be seen flitting along tree lines. Look to the skies for hunting kestrels and sparrowhawks throughout the day.

On the northern edge of the country park, Fulwood Marsh is home to reed and sedge warblers in summer, with elder scrub offering breeding habitat for blackcaps, common and lesser whitethroats, chiffchaffs and other scrub specialists and migratory warblers. Dragonflies including broad-bodied chaser and southern hawker can be spotted in summer. Take an exit on the east of the country park to join the Leeds–Liverpool canal path, a regular haunt of kingfishers and water voles.

SEFTON PARK

Sefton Park, Aigburth, Liverpool L17 1AP • OS Explorer Map 275 • Grid ref SJ377876 • What3Words: skip.boot.enjoyable

How to get there: An ideal, comfortable place to cycle to and through, Sefton Park features wide, level, surfaced paths throughout which can be accessed via numerous entrances around the circumference of the park. • There are many regular bus routes from Liverpool city centre which pass by Sefton Park, such as Arriva North West services 75, 80 and 80A which travel from Lime Street to the Ullet Road stop, enabling entry into the park from the north side. • The nearest train stations are St Michaels, located 1 mile (1.6km) to the southwest of the park, and Mossley Hill, situated 1 mile (1.6km) to the east of the park; it is approximately a 20-minute walk from each station.

Access and conditions: Sefton Park has well-maintained, surfaced paths throughout and plenty of benches and seating areas. Male, female, accessible and Changing Places toilets can be found in the centre of the park by the café, as well as baby-changing facilities. The Palm House has been renovated as an accessible, single-level building.

•• Public parks can be excellent places for wildlife watching. Many have been established as green spaces for communities to enjoy for decades – some for centuries – allowing habitats to mature, with the bonus of being accessible to allow 'bites' of nature exploration to fit into the everyday.

Sefton Park is an urban gem. A Grade 1 listed park covering over 80 hectares, its curved routes venture through fields, lakes, woodland and ponds along tree-lined paths. In spring, bluebells carpet the woodland beneath impressive stands of beech.

On the ponds and lake, little grebes, great crested grebes, grey herons, cormorants, moorhens and coots are regular sightings, whilst in summer house martins can be seen hunting insects over the water. Kingfisher are frequently seen along the water courses; listen out for their distinctive high-pitched call accompanied by a flash of vibrant blue.

Take extra care to look along the banks of streams, as water voles may be seen commuting through – though these can at times be mistaken for brown rats, which also live in the park! Alongside the telltale 'plop' as a water vole enters water, these rodents have shorter and blunter snouts, and smaller eyes and ears, than brown rats. Their tails are also short and furry, compared to the long bare tails of rats, and their fur a rich dark, reddish brown. On warm evenings, bats such as common pipistrelle and Daubenton's take flight to hunt insect prey over the habitat edges and water.

Heading into the larger wooded section at the east of the park, look out for nuthatches, treecreepers, jays and great spotted woodpeckers, as well as tribes of long-tailed tits and goldcrests gleaning insects from the canopies. As with many urban parks in recent years, ring-necked parakeets can be seen and, most evidently, heard in stands of trees through Sefton

Park, and may form considerable winter flocks. In winter, thrush flocks made up of redwings, fieldfares, mistle thrushes and blackbirds feed on the park's fields.

If you find yourself in need of warming up on a winter visit or are keen to make the most of your exploration, it is certainly worth stopping by the beautiful, refurbished Palm House in the centre of Sefton Park. The Palm House features plants that are endangered, threatened with extinction or already extinct within their native habitats. The local RSPB Liverpool Group host occasional events from here too, including the annual Big Garden Birdwatch.

The beauty of such well-visited, urban wildlife watching sites is that they provide wonderful opportunities to join a community of like-minded individuals. The Sefton Park iNaturalist account is worth browsing to understand species in the area, and using to share your discoveries with others.

HILBRE ISLANDS

Hilbre Island, Wirral CH47 1HZ • OS Explorer Map 266 • Grid ref SJ184880
• What3Words: fishnet.safe.leader

How to get there: The only way to access the Hilibre Islands is by walking from the starting point of West Kirby marine lake and across the beach at low tide. Good public transport options are available from central Liverpool, to travel the 13-mile (20km) journey west. Some bus routes can be taken in a single journey from central Liverpool to West Kirby bus station, including North West services 407 and 437 (approximately a 1-hour journey). When leaving the bus, continue west along Dee Lane until you reach West Kirby marine lake. • The nearest train station is West Kirby; when departing walk along Dee Lane until you reach the marine lake.

Access and conditions: Access to the islands is on foot only. The walk from West Kirby to Hilbre Island is 2 miles (3.2km) each way, and takes around an hour to complete. Visits can only be made in accordance with tide times: walking from West Kirby 3 hours after high tide and returning at least 3 hours before the next high tide. The route passes across sand, puddles and rocks. • Along with online guidance, an information board with tide times and wildlife of Hilbre can be found on the promenade north of the water sports centre, just before you reach the beach. • There are composting toilets on Hilbre Island. • Dogs must be kept on a short lead at all times.

Hilbre Islands.

If you're looking for an adventure to rewild your senses, a day-long pilgrimage across the Hilbre Islands is spectacular. The unoccupied archipelago encompasses three islands – Little Eye, Middle Eye and Hilbre – just 2 miles (3.2km) from the shore of West Kirby, and offers panoramic views across the River Dee Estuary and North Wales coastline.

There is one recommended and safe walking route to follow, which thousands of people use each year to visit the island. Set off from the Dee Lane Slipway and head west toward the smallest island, Little Eye. Keeping the island on your right, continue north toward Middle Eye, keeping this island on your left. Finally, pass over a rough track and rocks to approach Hilbre Island, before joining a footpath on the southern tip of the island.

Throughout most of the year, hundreds of waders can be seen feeding around the islands, taking advantage of the inaccessible exposed rocks to roost at high tide. Good numbers are present from August to April, with October to February being the busiest time.

Some Hilbre specialities include the purple sandpiper, which forages around seaweed-covered rocks from November to April, and Hilbre offers one of the best sites in the country to view Leach's storm petrels during the autumn migration, whilst shelducks can be seen in their hundreds.

Seawatching from the island can produce gannets, Manx shearwaters, skuas, common scoters and other sea ducks, and red-throated divers, along with common, Sandwich and little terns in August. The Hilbre Island Bird Observatory was established in 1957, and has since continued to survey and count birds, seals and invertebrates on and around the islands. Their seasonal records can be found online.

Another incredible summer encounter is the Hilbre grey seal colony. En route to Hilbre Island, scan the rippled sands from Little Eye to search for their mottled grey forms. Numbers peak in July with around 400 grey seals often spotted on the West Hoyle sandbank.

If you are waiting for the tides, take a stroll 1.3 miles (2.1km) north along West Kirby beach to explore the mesmerising Red Rocks Marsh Nature Reserve, managed by Cheshire Wildlife Trust. It features a diverse range of sands dunes, and a highly specialised plant system with more than 50 floral species, including local and national rarities such as sticky stork's bill. Brackish pools support the only breeding population of natterjack toads on the Wirral Peninsula, which can be heard croaking throughout evenings between April and July.

Red Rocks Marsh.

NEWCASTLE

The rich industrial heritage of the Newcastle–Gateshead Quayside, forged through coal transport and shipbuilding, has fostered a unique wildlife haven along the River Tyne. In summer the world's most inland colony of black-legged kittiwakes can be visited. A short walk from Newcastle on the Gateshead Quayside at Dunston Staiths, a remnant of the Tyne's vast tidal estuary can be discovered (page 116). Here, hundreds of waders including redshanks and curlews gather to spend the winter feeding on the mudflats, and shelduck nurseries gather in summer. Dunston Staiths is just one hotspot for wildlife along the Tyne Derwent Way, a 9-mile (14.5km) route which can be enjoyed on foot or bike, with a local bus service nearby. This route takes in an impressive array of habitats, from industrial wildflower meadows to reclaimed rail lines along the River Derwent leading toward the stunning semi-natural oak and birch woodlands of Thornley Wood (page 120).

The Lower Ouseburn Valley offers a captivating urban rewilding experience (page 112). The tidal burn brings opportunities to see otters and sand martins alongside pubs, kingfishers outside bakeries, and more. Upstream along the route of the newly-developed Ouse Burn Way, Gosforth Nature Reserve – a wetland jewel in Newcastle's nature crown – can be found (page 114).

The North Tyneside and Northumberland coast is stunning – with castles, islands and wildlife a bus ride away. One of the most accessible coastal locations for wildlife watching is St Mary's Island (page 118), where basking grey seals and shorebirds await.

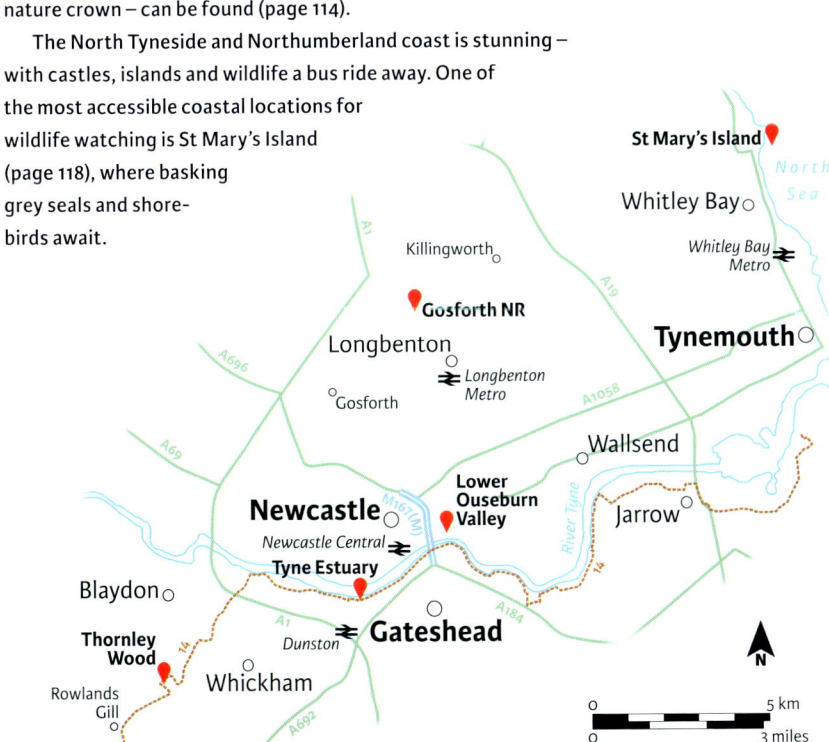

LOWER OUSEBURN VALLEY

Gleann Ouseburn, Newcastle-upon-Tyne NE6 1BU • OS Explorer Map 316 • Grid ref NZ264641 • What3Words: game.waddle.daisy

How to get there: The closest train station is Newcastle Central (1.3 miles/2.1km west); however, there are also Metro stations 0.5 miles (0.8km) to the east (Byker) and west (Manors) of Ouseburn. From Newcastle Central station, walk or cycle east along the Newcastle Quayside to enjoy views of the River Tyne before reaching Ouseburn, where the mouth of the Ouseburn meets the River Tyne. • Stagecoach North East bus services including 1/12/22/39/40/62/63 travel from Central Station Clayton Street West to Newbridge Street – Blackfriars. From here, walk east down Stepney Bank to reach the Ouseburn Valley. In summer, hop on the Toon Tour bus (blue route) from Central station, which encompasses Ouseburn in its sightseeing service.

Access and conditions: Ouseburn can be explored via paved/surfaced public footpaths, although the sections into the woodland feature steep gradients. • There are no public toilets, but there are many pubs and visitor attractions with facilities for customers. • Dogs are permitted.

•• From its industrial past, the Lower Ouseburn Valley has transitioned into a vibrant landscape of arts, independent businesses, music, and food and drink. In recent years, this hidden gem in Newcastle has also gained recognition for the diversity of wildlife it supports.

The Ouseburn itself runs from the rural northern edge of Newcastle until joining the River Tyne. As the River Tyne is tidal, so too is this lower section of the Ouseburn, bringing unique opportunities to experience wildlife with every ebb and flow.

If visiting in spring and summer, check for sand martins around the mouth of the burn, which turned up in 2023 to nest in a retaining wall along this urbanised stretch of the River Tyne. Following two successful breeding seasons, a community crowdfunding campaign launched by the Wild Ouseburn project enabled installation of an artificial sand martin

Sand martins.

bank in 2025, which can be viewed at the mouth of the burn.

From here, follow the burn upstream. Throughout the year, grey wagtails, moorhens and mallards are everyday sightings. In recent years, grey wagtails have nested in industrial remnants with excellent views of chicks possible during late spring and summer. Ouseburn is also locally 'famous' for mute swans, which can be seen throughout the year and often opt to nest close to the public footpath.

Grey wagtail feeding chick.

In winter, check overhanging vegetation along the burn for visiting kingfishers. In recent winters, redshanks and curlews have also entered the burn during low tide to feed from mudbanks, while mallards congregate in large flocks and attract other waterfowl including teal. On a high tide, look for cormorants which enter the burn to feast on flatfish and salmon, particularly during autumn and winter. Otters are also sighted on the burn in the evenings, receiving a great deal of admiration from the local community.

The Lower Ouseburn Valley is a fascinating site to visit as it forms a vital part of the urban 'Ouseburn Wildlife Enhancement Corridor'. There are therefore wildlife spectacles to enjoy other than on the burn itself. Once you reach the end of the burn (where it flows underground beyond Crawford's Bridge), look north toward the Ouseburn Viaduct where kestrels have attempted to breed in recent years. Check the metal girders for them resting in between hunting forays.

Ouseburn Woods and the neighbouring City Stadium is frequented by roe deer, which pass through from Heaton Park to the north. The abundance of scrub in this section of the valley makes it an excellent spot to enjoy the dawn chorus between April and May. An early morning visit is also the best time to spot roe deer. The woods annually support a diversity of nesting birds including wrens, goldfinches, long-tailed tits, greenfinches, bullfinches, song thrushes and mistle thrushes, as well as wintering redwings and siskins.

Walking through the woods on a summer evening, you may encounter foraging common pipistrelles, which have benefitted from recent wildlife-friendly grassland management in the valley. There are many places worth visiting in the valley such as Ouseburn Farm and the Ouseburn Trust. For an extended urban wildlife adventure, follow the course of the Ouseburn north into Heaton Park and Jesmond Dene. Before visiting the Lower Ouseburn Valley, check the Wild Ouseburn website for information on recent wildlife sightings, as well as opportunities to take part in seasonal wildlife surveys, events and celebrations.

GOSFORTH NATURE RESERVE

Gosforth Nature Reserve, Lake Lodge, Salters Lane, Gosforth NE3 5EP • OS Explorer Map 316 • Grid ref NZ260698 • What3Words: freed.foal.saves

How to get there: There are several bus services that run from Newcastle Haymarket bus station to Gosforth Nature Reserve. The nearest bus stops to and from the reserve are both called BT Call Centre, located around 0.5 miles (0.8km) from the reserve entrance. Bus services include X8, X7 and X63. • A cycle path runs along the length of the A189 Salters Lane from central Newcastle, 4.5 miles (7.25km) north to the entrance of Gosforth Nature Reserve. From the city centre you can largely travel through greenery to the reserve by cycling along the Ouse Burn Way through Jesmond Dene to Killingworth Road, or alternatively passing through the open vista of the Town Moor. A cycle rack is available inside the reserve. • The nearest Metro station is Longbenton, situated 1.3 miles (2.1km) to the south of Gosforth Nature Reserve. The Metro can be taken straight to Longbenton from Newcastle Central station.

Access and conditions: Much of the reserve can be explored along unsurfaced trails. Toilets, including an accessible toilet and baby-changing facilities, can be found in the Field Station building by the entrance, along with an eco-loo within the reserve itself. • Dogs are not permitted on the reserve, with the exception of guide dogs. • Public entry times are 09:00–16:00 (last entry 15:00) daily, year-round. Natural History Society of Northumbria (NHSN) members can enjoy extended opening hours. Entry is free for NHSN members, otherwise a Visitor Pass must be purchased online or at the entrance gate at £5 per adult, £2 per student and £1 per child. If you would like to join NHSN as a member after visiting, the cost of Visitor Passes can be reimbursed.

•• On the northern horizon of Newcastle lies the wildlife oasis of Gosforth Nature Reserve. Since 1924 the reserve has been under the management of the Natural History Society of Northumbria (NHSN), whose volunteers care for its 61 hectares of mixed woodland, open water, reedbed and meadow. This Site of Special Scientific Interest (SSSI) provides a vital stronghold for local wildlife with over 1,600 species recorded to date.

When entering the reserve, you will be greeted at the Welcome Hut by an NHSN volunteer – an excellent opportunity to hear about recent wildlife sightings. Secluded circular paths including the Reedbed Trail (1.4 mile, 2.2km), Meadow Trail (1.4 mile, 2.4km) and Woodland Trail (1.6 mile, 2.5km) enable exploration of the reserve.

The Lawrence Hide by the entrance is a good first stop. Scan the feeding station for woodland birds such as great spotted woodpeckers, marsh tits, nuthatches, treecreepers and jays. Sparrowhawks are often spotted here.

Taking the circular Meadow Trail you will have the opportunity to visit three hides and a viewing screen situated along different aspects of Gosforth Lake. Follow this route to the left (south path) to first reach Ridley Hide, accessible along a boardwalk through the reedbed.

In summer Ridley Hide offers brilliant views of common tern and black-headed gull colonies, which return to nest yearly on rafts. Look out for reed buntings, sedge warblers and reed warblers darting amongst the reeds. Return along the boardwalk and take the path to the right to find Beck Hide, the Meadow Screen and Pearce Hide.

Wildfowl on the lake include gadwall, goldeneye, pochard, mallard, teal, tufted duck, shoveler and wigeon. Great crested and little grebes are also present in spring and summer, along with a wonderful heronry around the edge of the lake. Water rails are resident; listen out for their piglet-like squeal from the hides.

Otters are a star species of the reserve, with many encounters enjoyed by visitors throughout the year from the hides. Roe deer can be spotted resting amongst trees or feeding in the field on the southern edge of the Meadow Trail. In summer, the botanical richness of the reserve is stunning, with beds of melancholy thistle, rare orchids, and scarce aquatic species being just some of the highlights. Some winters see thousands of starlings enlivening the sky with murmurations before settling into the reedbed.

Gosforth Nature Reserve's urban setting makes it an enchanting site, where even chance encounters with badgers are possible, so take your time to enjoy this special place quietly.

TYNE ESTUARY

Dunston Staiths, Gateshead NE8 2GS • OS Explorer Map 316 • Grid ref NZ234627 • What3Words: animal.call.almost

How to get there: Cycling and walking directions are from Newcastle Central station to Dunston Staiths on the Gateshead Quayside, where the Tyne Estuary and the tidal basin can be best viewed. These routes also encompass views of the summer Tyne kittiwake colony. The Tyne Estuary can also be viewed on the Newcastle Quayside, on the north side of the River Tyne, directly opposite Dunston Staiths. • To cycle, head west along Neville Street before heading south along Marlborough Close. From here you can join the B1600 leading onto the Newcastle Quayside. Follow the Newcastle Quayside east before crossing over onto the Gateshead Quayside via the red Swing Bridge. From here, cycle west to reach the Dunston Staiths. • To walk, head east along Neville Street and Westgate Road toward Newcastle Castle. From here you can walk along the northern edge of the castle down a side street, leading eventually to Newcastle Quayside and the Tyne Bridge. Walk along the red Swing Bridge to reach the Gateshead Quayside and then head west until reaching Dunston Staiths; around 2 miles (3.2km). • The closest train station is Dunston, situated under 1 mile (1.6km) to the south of Dunston Staiths. Newcastle Central station is situated around 2 miles (3.2km) to the north. • Go North East bus routes run close to Dunston Staiths, including 10/10A/10B Tyne Valley services, and the 47 Red Kite Ranger. The closest bus stop is called Gas Works Bridge Road – Riverside Inn, situated 500m from Dunston Staiths.

Access and conditions: The Tyne Estuary is situated between the cities of Newcastle and Gateshead; both of which have paved quaysides. No public toilets are available on the route, but there are some establishments en route with facilities that customers can use. Dogs are permitted.

•• The Newcastle–Gateshead Quayside is perhaps best known as a tourist destination for arts and culture, as well as its night-life. Opportunities for nature exploration in both locations are excellent, however, and a little-known natural wonder can be found connecting the two: the Tyne Estuary.

The River Tyne's connection to the North Sea makes it subject to the daily rhythms of the tide. This natural phenomenon enabled the region to excel in shipbuilding during the industrial revolution, and remnants of this rich heritage are now contributing in a surprising way to a vital natural resource.

One of the best examples of the North East's industrial past influencing its wild future can be found at the Dunston Staiths, a wooden structure opened in 1893 to transport coal onto ships. In the years since its closure in 1977, this structure has trapped silt and mud from the Rivers Tyne and Team. This now forms vital intertidal zones on this inland section of the Tyne Estuary. Mudflats provide an ideal habitat for saline invertebrates to live within, attracting in turn an array of birdlife seasonally. This site is therefore best visited during a changing tide.

In summer, the tidal basin located on the southern edge of the Staiths supports an annual nursery for shelducks and their chicks. This also becomes a welcome feeding ground for waders, which can be viewed from the footpath, particularly on a changing tide. In winter, listen for the piping calls of hundreds of redshanks mingling with the calls of curlews.

The Staiths themselves offer a welcome roost for cormorants, grey herons and, for a brief period during their autumn migration, hundreds of lapwings, which congregate to roost on on inaccessible parts of the structure. Kestrels have also roosted on the structure in recent years, and peregrine falcons can occasionally be seen perching and hunting in this area. Buzzards are occasionally sighted above the Dunston Staiths, flying between Gateshead and Newcastle.

If visiting in summer, a visit to the famous Tyne kittiwake colony is a must. Renowned as the most inland breeding colony of black-legged kittiwakes in the world, the Tyne kittiwakes are a fascinating example of urban human–

Kittiwake with chick.

wildlife co-existence. You will likely hear these city seabirds before you see them, as individuals call their own name, *kitti-wake*. Most of the colony favours nesting on the Tyne Bridge and the surrounding buildings and lamp posts, as well as the Baltic Centre for Contemporary Art and Saltmeadows Tower. Look out for Tyne Kittiwake Week and other seasonal experiences to learn more about these pelagic gulls.

The Tyne Estuary is a highlight of the Tyne Derwent Way, which is a waymarked route that can be walked or cycled from St Mary's Heritage Centre on the Gateshead Quayside to National Trust Gibside. The Tyne Derwent Way website is a great place to discover more about the area's nature, heritage and culture, as well as seasonal events and volunteering opportunities.

Peregrine falcon.

ST MARY'S ISLAND

St Mary's Island Causeway, Whitley Bay NE26 4RS • OS Explorer Map 316 • Grid ref NZ351752 • What3Words: played.with.fishery

How to get there: St Mary's Island is around 12 miles (19.3km) northeast of Newcastle. The 309 Cobalt & Coast Blyth via Whitley Bay bus service offers a direct route from Newcastle Haymarket station to Hartley Square (1-hour journey). From here, walk southeast toward the Old Hartley car park, from which you can follow a surfaced track for 1 mile (1.6km) south along the cliffs toward St Mary's Island Nature Reserve.
• An alternative route can be taken from Newcastle Central station. Take the yellow Metro route St James via Whitley Bay, and get off at the Whitley Bay station (35-minute journey). From here, walk to the Park Avenue – York Road station and catch the Cobalt & Coast 308/309 (Blyth) bus service to The Links – Cemetery station. From here, walk 0.5 miles (0.8km) northeast along footpaths adjacent to The Links to reach St Mary's Nature Reserve and St Mary's Island.

Access and conditions: Access to St Mary's Island is dependent upon low tides to enable access across the causeway. Step-free, surfaced paths run along the coastline and causeway. Some potholes and damp sections may occur. • Public toilets are available in the St Mary's Island (North) car park; opening hours are variable. An accessible toilet with baby-changing facilities is available in the visitor centre on the island. A small hide is present on St Mary's Island, and viewing screens are situated around the terrestrial wetland. • Dogs are permitted on a short lead, and should remain off the rockpool areas. • It is free to visit the nature reserve, but an admission charge applies to visit the St Mary's Lighthouse and visitor centre on the island.

•• St Mary's Island Local Nature Reserve is a scenic go-to spot for local wildlife enthusiasts hoping to quench their ornithological, marine and geological interests throughout the year. Intertidal features such as rockpools, mud and sand support a diversity of marine life, making this landscape a spectacular part of the Coquet to St Mary's Marine Conservation Zone. As well as the island, which is managed by North Tyneside Council, and its intertidal habitats, a wetland managed by the St Mary's Island Wetland Conservation Group brings a wealth of birdlife to this part of the coast. The wetland, situated between the North and South car parks, is managed through regular volunteer effort, as well as conservation grazing by Exmoor ponies in winter.

The island is accessible via a causeway at low tide, and has become a popular spot for enjoying views of grey seals on land at a respectful distance. The voluntary work of a second community group, the St Mary's Island Wildlife Conservation Society, has been instrumental in protecting this grey seal haul out through the implementation of a wildlife refuge area. When visiting, you will likely encounter one of the helpful volunteers who can direct you to an excellent viewing point by the lighthouse, away from the rocks where the seals rest. The shoreline attracts overwintering shorebirds, including dunlins, ringed plovers, redshanks, sanderlings, turnstones, oystercatchers, lapwings, bar-tailed godwits, curlews, and large flocks of golden plovers. Along the cliff bases, look for rock pipits and the occasional wintering water pipits.

Another top draw of this site is its prime position during the spring and autumn migration. In autumn, walk slowly around the wetland and clifftop footpath to Old Hartley and you may spot freshly landed birds which, if timed fortunately with the weather, can be spectacular in their abundance. From goldcrests to short-eared owls, and scarce species such as the yellow-browed warbler, the autumn migration brings many birds to this North East coastline, attracted by the St Mary's wetland and its surrounding habitats. It's important to allow the birds to rest after their lengthy journey by viewing them only from the public footpath. In summer, the wetland supports snipes, coots, grey herons, gadwalls, shovelers, tufted ducks and other wetland specialists. The surrounding vegetation attracts chiffchaffs, common whitethroats, willow warblers, sedge and grasshopper warblers, blackcaps and stonechats. Adjacent farmland is good for skylarks, lapwings and brown hares, whilst kestrels are frequently observed hovering above.

The clifftops are a good spot for seawatching throughout the year. Depending on the time of year, you can search offshore for eiders, divers, skuas, terns, auks, gannets and fulmars, and there's the chance of passing bottlenose and white-beaked dolphins, and harbour porpoises. If you are keen to extend your visit, another great wildlife site nearby is Holywell Dene, which runs along Seaton Burn to the southwest of Old Hartley.

Eider.

THORNLEY WOOD

Thornley Wood, Rowlands Gill, Gateshead NE39 1AR • OS Explorer Map 316 • Grid ref NZ178604 • What3Words: wooden.puddles.oiled

How to get there: Directions are to Thornley Wood, situated 6 miles (9.7km) southwest of Newcastle, from which various aspects of the wider Derwent Walk Country Park can be enjoyed. Hop on the 47 Red Kite Ranger or X45 X-lines bus service from Newcastle Central station or Newcastle Haymarket bus station and travel 30 minutes directly to the Lockhaugh Road – Glamis Crescent bus stop, alighting directly outside the entrance to Thornley Wood. • Derwent Walk follows an old rail line which now forms part of the waymarked Coast to Coast Cycle Path (C2C) National Cycle Network Route 14, so cycling is another great option to explore this beautiful area. Some trails around Thornley Wood are unsuitable for bikes. Derwent Walk can be joined from central Newcastle by crossing the Swing Bridge or High Level Bridge to Gateshead, and following the waymarked Tyne Derwent Way route on foot or bike. To visit Thornley Wood, cross over the Nine Arches Viaduct to join the waymarked sculpture trail to the south.

Access and conditions: The Derwent Walk cycle and footpath is surfaced. Some trails in Thornley Woodlands Centre and other sites along the route include gradients and steps. • Trail information can be requested from Thornley Woodlands Centre, which also houses a café, toilets and information on local wildlife (subject to opening hours). • Thornley Wood is open 24 hours a day, year-round. • Dogs are permitted on leads. • Hides can be visited along the route; however, a key must be purchased from Thornley Woodlands Centre.

•• To the west of Gateshead town centre, picturesque opportunities for nature immersion can be found in the Derwent Valley. The Derwent Walk Country Park follows a reimagined railway track, now providing a 12-mile (19.3km) route to walk or cycle between Consett and Swalwell, encountering river, woodland, meadow and ponds along the way.

There are many sites worth visiting along the route, with Thornley Wood a particularly special place to spend a day exploring. Recognised as one of the few remaining areas of semi-natural woodland in the Lower Derwent Valley, Thornley Wood is designated a Site of Special Scientific Interest (SSSI). Birch and oak fills much of the canopy, though variable soil conditions throughout this site make the ground full of ferns, flora and fungi, including the evergreen hart's-tongue fern, fragrant meadowsweet and appropriately named common stinkhorn.

When arriving, you will see the Thornley Woodlands Centre nestled amongst the ancient woodland. If visiting during opening hours, the centre is a good place to begin your journey to find out about local conservation initiatives and to purchase a hide key. You might also like to pick up a trail guide for the wildlife sculpture trail, created from fallen trees.

The key will enable you to enjoy access to six wildlife hides: two in Derwent Walk

Country Park, one at Shibdon Pond, one at Lamesley Pastures and two at Clara Vale Local Nature Reserve. The Thornley Hide can be accessed a short walk across the road (A694) from the centre. Frequent sightings from this feeding station hide include tits, nuthatches, jays, treecreepers, great spotted woodpeckers, bullfinches, sparrowhawks and roe deer.

There are several waymarked trails which can be taken from the centre, such as the 0.5-mile (0.8km) sculpture trail or the 2-mile (3.1km) Thornley Woods and Clockburn Lake circular. By taking the path to the west you can enjoy a 2.5-mile (4km) walk through Paddock Hill Wood and down to the River Derwent, a great place to look out for dippers, before passing riverside meadows and impressive views of the historic Nine Arches Viaduct.

Derwent Valley is home to one of the North East's most high-profile wildlife initiatives, the Northern Red Kites Project, which released around 100 red kites in the valley between 2004 and 2006. Thornley Woods is included in a 12-mile (19.3km) circular Red Kite Trail, the free guide for which can be downloaded via the Friends of Red Kites website. Thornley Wood is a highlight of the Tyne Derwent Way; see the Tyne Derwent Way website to learn more about the area.

Grey heron.

WALES

ST DAVIDS

Pembrokeshire, located on the southwestern coast of Wales, is one of the most spectacular regions in the UK for wildlife watching. The region boasts a fabulous diversity of life, all found along a beautifully rugged coastline with extensive woodlands and beautiful beaches ready to explore. Pembrokeshire has plenty to offer, whether you are interested in birds, cetaceans, flowers or butterflies – there is something for everyone. From seabirds on dramatic cliffs to seals basking on sandy shores, the area is home to an abundance of species, making it a must-visit destination for wildlife-lovers. The beautiful miniature city of St Davids and its larger neighbour, Haverfordwest, are well connected by public transport, making it easy to explore some of the best wildlife spots in the region, including the Pembrokeshire islands of Skomer, Skokholm and Grassholm (page 127), as well as Bosherston Lily Ponds and St Govan's (page 132).

Local train and bus services, including routes from Haverfordwest, Pembroke Dock and Swansea, make it easy to access the region's most stunning natural areas, with shuttle buses travelling around the area during the summer months. You may want to plan a day of communing with the puffins on Skomer, or try seawatching at the dramatic headland of St Govan's. For a gentler option, enjoy a stroll around Tenby (page 130) or go rockpooling at Marloes (page 125).

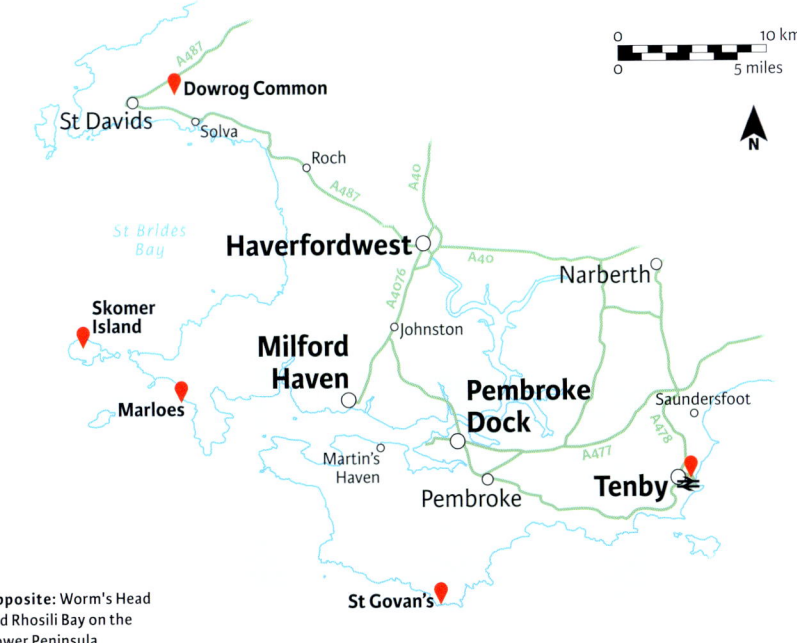

Opposite: Worm's Head and Rhosili Bay on the Gower Peninsula.

DOWROG COMMON

Dowrog Common, A487, St Davids, Haverfordwest SA62 6BX • OS Explorer Map OL35 • Grid ref SM7726 • What3Words: musician.triathlon.active

How to get there: This beautiful heath is accessible by bus from St Davids via the Puffin Shuttle or Celtic Coaster, departing from the Pembrokeshire Coast National Park Visitor Centre. The road itself goes through this reserve and you can hop out and explore. • Alternatively, it is possible to walk the 1.6 miles (2.5km) from St Davids, taking in the breathtaking sites of the heathlands as you trek north.

Access and conditions: Aptly named Dowrog, meaning 'wet' or 'watery', this site can be boggy underfoot and difficult for walking. Wellies or waterproof walking boots are a must. You may enter the reserve on either side of the road by climbing over stiles and following cut pathways, avoiding electrical fences laid out for the grazing cattle. • Should you wish to explore in a more leisurely way or with the use of a wheelchair, it is possible to see orchids and birds from the roads that surround the wet heath. • There are no toilets at this site. You can visit other amenities at Dr Beynon's Bug Farm, which is directly opposite the reserve and well worth a visit if time allows.

•• Adjacent to Britain's smallest city, St Davids, this wet heathland is a mixture of gorse, heather and other wet-heath specialists, with cotton-grass along the roadsides, billowing in the wind. The site, managed by the Wildlife Trust of South & West Wales, has been a designated SSSI since 1954, and is part of the North West Pembrokeshire Commons SAC. Whilst some of the 101 hectares are suitable for exploring, the remainder of the area is dedicated to conservation and not accessible, with work being carried out to protect the plants and invertebrates. However, that is not to say that the available exploring areas will not provide the wildlife you seek. Of particular interest during the late spring months is the range of orchids on display. Southern marsh orchid, common spotted orchid and fragrant orchid are all common, and perhaps the main target for many is the lesser butterfly orchid, which flowers on

Lesser butterfly orchid.

Blue-tailed damselfly.

the roadside verges. There are also plenty of interesting and uncommon insects here, including marsh fritillary, scarlet tiger moth, small red damselfly, hairy dragonfly and the scarce blue-tailed damselfly.

There are few amenities nearby, but a picnic amongst the flowers is a great way to spend your day with dragonflies and damselflies flying overhead, the unmistakable calling of cuckoos, and the air fragrant with coconut-scented gorse and sweet-smelling heathers as you peer among the dog-violets and bog pimpernel. The best time to visit for orchids and invertebrates is between April and July, but the birds are spectacular from October to February, with short-eared owls, hen harriers and merlins all roosting on site. The site is teeming with life and a slow pace is definitely recommended to fully take in the different species on offer.

MARLOES

Marloes Sands and Mere, Pembrokeshire SA62 • OS Explorer Map OL36 • Grid ref SM794083 • What3Words: drain.tinted.airstrip

How to get there: It is very simple to get to Marloes for Marloes Sands, Mere and the Deer Park by public transport. The Pembrokeshire Coastal Cruiser bus and Puffin Shuttle are available every day throughout the summer months and run two days a week in the winter months. The Puffin Shuttle (400 service) departs from St Davids New Street and St Davids Visitor Centre and the journey will take 90 minutes as it takes you on the scenic route of the Pembrokeshire coast. • If you want to explore further and fancy a bit of an adventure, you can join the Pembrokeshire Coastal Path, part of the Welsh Coastal Path route. This route can be hiked from any point in Pembrokeshire, with train access to Pembroke Dock and easy bus access to the main towns of the region.

Access and conditions: Access to the beach is not possible for wheelchair users or those with mobility issues due to the steeply descending steps and uneven terrain. It is possible to explore Marloes Mere by wheelchair, especially with off-road attachments, or mobility scooter. • There are no public toilets at Marloes, but there are facilities for customers in the nearby cafés should you wish to stop for a drink or a bite to eat.

•• With one of the most beautiful beaches in Pembrokeshire, the region of Marloes is known primarily for its unique scenery that combines the sea, the rugged rocks and the evergreen countryside that surrounds the town. It is definitely a wildlife enthusiast's dream, with a different range of species to see at different points of the year and opportunities to experience wildlife in different ways, be it sitting in a hide, walking the clifftops or even taking a dip in the sea. The beach at Marloes Sands is a golden stretch of sand below the towering cliffs. The southern edge of the beach consists of sedimentary sandstone and on a low tide the rockpools are a great place to spend the day looking for marine life among the seaweeds such as velvet swimming crabs, starfish and rock gobies. Or put on your snorkel and head out for a swim, looking for scarce species such as the sea fan sea slug, pink sea fan, sponge crab, and many more that live around the various wrecks offshore. Between April and June, it's possible to see an unforgettable underwater spectacle when spider crabs gather in their thousands in the shallow bays to shed their exoskeletons. There are so many of these crabs that the seafloor looks to be moving.

If you're not the beach-loving type and would prefer a land-based excursion, then the cliffs of the Deer Park are a great location to start. You can reach the Deer Park from Marloes village by walking west along the only track towards Martin's Haven for 2 miles (3.2km). Walking through the remains of the Iron Age fort dating back 2,000 years, the scenery is utterly breathtaking. The fort was once the largest promontory fort in South Wales, and is a great piece of history to explore as you make your way into the clifftop Deer Park. Named after a failed attempt to establish a deer park at Marloes in the late eighteenth century, the Deer Park is a fantastic viewpoint to seawatch offshore with Manx shearwaters, gannets, harbour porpoises and a breeding colony of grey seals all possible to see from the clifftop. Through the Deer Park, you may also see choughs, peregrine falcons and Dartford warblers. As you head back to the bus stop, it is worth popping to Marloes Mere, a small wetland that punches above its weight wildlife-wise. It is a 1.5-mile (2.4km) walk from the Deer Park to Marloes Mere. There is a dirt track where you can walk among the willows and a hide that overlooks the pool. The mere hosts breeding birds such as reed warblers and sedge warblers, but is also a stopping-off point for migrant and wintering species, with teals, swans such as whooper and mute, reed buntings and the occasional rarity such as blackpoll warbler, American

black duck, golden oriole, isabelline shrike and spotted sandpiper turning up among the vegetation.

Taking a short 1.2-mile (2km) trek to the nearby Dale Airfield is a great way to end your day. Dale Airfield originally opened in 1942 as a satellite runway for RAF Talbenny, but was closed in 1948, allowing the wildlife to move in. It is a great location for wintering and autumnal birds with chough being regular, alongside occasional visits from more unusual species – the list includes short-toed lark, dotterel and many more.

SKOMER ISLAND

Martin's Haven, North Lane, Marloes and St Brides SA62 3BJ • OS Explorer Map OL36 • Grid ref SM7726 • What3Words: waistcoat.gadgets.denim

How to get there: To embark on an exciting journey to Skomer Island, you'll need to first reach the picturesque Martin's Haven, from where you can get a boat over to Skomer. Boats depart five times a day in the morning (excluding Mondays) with the return boat allocated according to departure time. The journey to the island takes around 15 minutes.
• Travelling from St Davids, the main option is to take the 400 Puffin Shuttle from St Davids to Martin's Haven, which runs three times a day between May and September and takes 90 minutes. Trips book up quickly, so pre-booking online is recommended. • Skokholm is also reached from Martin's Haven, but there are no day visits to this island – instead book your stay in advance via the Wildlife Trust of South and West Wales. This is also where the boats for Grassholm Island, an RSPB reserve famous for its gannet colony, depart from; tickets can be purchased online or in St Davids.
Access and conditions: The island is open to visitors during the spring and summer months. There is a steep climb up a set of steps from the boat landing spot to the top of the island. There are areas to stop on the climb. The journey is unfortunately not possible for wheelchair users as there is no alternative path to reach the top of the island from the boat landing. • An interpretation centre, toilet facilities and other amenities can be found on the top of the island at the Farm. • Skokholm is similar in terms of access.

•• Spring and summer on Skomer offer one of the most remarkable experiences you could have. Not only is every inch of the island fragrant with the sweet smell of chamomile, but you will see birds and marine wildlife aplenty. As you reach the top of the steps, head towards the Farm where the toilets and accommodation are located. From here there are several paths you can take depending on your interests and whether you are looking for a gentle amble around the island or looking to find a spot to relax and watch the dazzling display of breeding birds. A short but rewarding option is the route down to South Pond (0.7 miles/1km) where breeding oystercatchers, wheatears and stonechats can be heard from the blooming campions, as butterflies and damselflies flit across the boggy ground either side of the pathways. The South Plateau is a great location if you are looking to extend your walk; as well as seeing visible remnants of an Iron Age roundhouse that once stood here, you may also catch glimpses of curlews and more wheatears and stonechats.

No visit to Skomer is complete without a visit to The Wick. This point of the island is a dramatic spectacle with a sheer drop of 61m on one side – and every inch of the steep cliff-face is filled with birdlife. There are around 41,605 puffins breeding on Skomer with the majority concentrated around The Wick. Spend some time here to watch these adorable sea-parrots as they fly in from the sea to run around your feet, bringing bill-loads of fishy delights to their partners down in the nesting burrows.

The Wick is also home to thousands of kittiwakes, hundreds of fulmars, 6,000 pairs of razorbills and 15,000 pairs of guillemots, which you can see on the rocks from the viewpoint. Although fulmars breed elsewhere on the volcanic rocks of the island, the population's stronghold is here. And if that is not enough, Skomer is also home to breeding gulls, choughs, peregrine falcons and Manx shearwaters, with 350,000 pairs of these breeding in burrows beneath the soil.

Alongside the vast array of seabirds, Skomer and its surrounding waters are also home to mammals, including the Skomer vole, a large subspecies of the bank vole found only on Skomer. It is not easy to see but you may catch a glimpse of this plump, blunt-nosed rodent running between the bracken paths. Offshore you may spot fins emerging from the sea as common dolphins and harbour porpoises chase shoals of fish around the island, along with grey seals. Taking the longer route around the island (4 miles/6.5km) will allow you to take in the vast host of wildlife Skomer has to offer.

For a longer adventure, you can visit Skomer's sister island, Skokholm, for stays

Razorbills.

of two or more nights in basic but comfortable off-grid accommodation, bookable through the Wildlife Trust of South and West Wales. The summer nights offer a particularly otherwordly experience, as Manx shearwaters return from the sea under cover of darkness, creating a cacophony of haunting calls as they make contact with their mates down in the nesting burrows.

Puffin.

TENBY

Tenby Harbour Office, Main Quay Wall, Tenby, Pembrokeshire SA70 8BY
• OS Explorer Map OL36 • Grid ref SM72485 • What3Words: farms.swarm.limes

How to get there: As one of the biggest towns in Pembrokeshire, Tenby is well served by public transport. There are buses that run between St Davids and Tenby, although there is not a direct service – you will need to take the T11 service (51-minute journey) from St Davids to Haverfordwest before then taking either the 349, X49 or 381 services to Tenby (60 minutes) or the Transport for Wales train south towards Tenby (50 minutes). The train station is a 0.5-mile (0.8km) walk from the harbour itself where you will be able to get a boat to the nearby Caldey Island. The island is open to day-tripping visitors from Easter to October, Monday to Saturday. Boat tickets can be purchased from the Caldey Island Kiosk located in the harbour. The boat departs every 20 to 30 minutes with the first boat at 10:00 and the journey lasting 20 minutes.

Access and conditions: The town itself is mostly accessible although some streets are cobbled and have hills. There are public toilets stationed around the town. • If you wish to travel to the islands offshore, this is currently not possible in wheelchairs or motorised scooters due to access on the boats.

•• Tenby is an iconic part of the Pembrokeshire coast, and visits are a staple part of many a Welsh person's childhood. A beautiful coastal town, offering some of the most unique dining experiences in South Wales as well as fantastic scenery and wildlife, it is an ideal location for a short trip away.

One of the best options for watching wildlife is Caldey Island, located just off the Tenby Harbour entrance. The island is managed by Cistercian monks who have graced the island with their prayer and quiet living for thousands of years, making for a tranquil and peaceful trip. Successful efforts to preserve and enhance the island's diversity, including the eradication of a population of rats, have resulted in a 400 per cent increase of the general wildlife population. From a quiet island with little wildlife, it is now a thriving landmark in the land and sea. One of the beneficiaries of this has been the hedgehog, which is becoming more abundant on the island. Across the surrounding cliffs, there are shelves adorned with razorbills, guillemots and fulmars and the skies have kestrels and peregrine falcons hunting those below. In the sea, it's possible to see the thriving population of grey seals and occasionally harbour porpoises. One of the island's biggest claims to fame is the walrus that visited between March and May 2021, affectionately named Wally and now a famous symbol around the town.

There also is now also a thriving population of red squirrels after the introduction of a founder population of three individuals in 2016. Now more than 60 red squirrels live on Caldey, to the delight of the visiting wildlife-lovers hoping to catch a glimpse of these bundles of red fur. The squirrels are currently given supplementary food during June, July and August, but a variety of newly planted trees will in due course provide them with abundant natural sources of food. It is easy to spot them as they visit feeding stations around the island.

Only a small hop, skip and jump away from Caldey Island is the adjoining island of St Margaret. Whilst it is not possible to land on St Margaret's Island itself, you are able to take a boat journey around both this island and Caldey Island to take in all the wildlife. The island is home to a medieval chapter of the same name, which was later converted to house the men who quarried the island's limestone during Victorian times. Cliff-nesting guillemots and razorbills can be seen adorning the shelves of the island and you may also pick out the colourful bills of puffins, which breed on the slopes facing Tenby. There have been gannets and cormorants nesting regularly and the hope is that the island will develop into another South Wales gannetry.

Gannet.

Caldey Island.

ST GOVAN'S

St Govan's Head, Bosherston, Pembrokeshire SA71 5DR • OS Explorer Map 153 • Grid ref SM968931 • What3Words: downward.ballooned.firms

How to get there: St Govan's is somewhat difficult to reach via public transport due to its remote location. However, you can get there by either the Puffin Shuttle from Tenby or Haverfordwest (see page 130 for details on getting to these towns from St Davids), or the Coastal Cruiser, which operates on a winter and summer timetable from all major towns in Pembrokeshire. If you are looking to extend your walk, then the nearby options for pick-ups and drop-offs are Stackpole Head or Bosherston Ponds.

Access and conditions: Open all year round. Toilets can be found at the nearby Stackpole Café and Bosherston Ponds. There can be restrictions to access to Castlemartin on entry to St Govan's Head as the Castlemartin Range is an active MOD zone. • Access is somewhat challenging in some areas of the site with the steps down to the St Govan's Chapel being very steep and particularly difficult to navigate on windy days. The nearby headland around St Govan's and Stackpole Head is more accessible, particularly if you are looking to go for a stroll or have the use of a mobility scooter. The ponds at Bosherston are generally accessible as the slope down to the ponds is tarmacked (although the walk back up is strenuous) and the loop around the lily ponds themselves is made up of gravel paths and wooden bridges.

•• St Govan's Head is a place of beauty and legend. There is plenty of wildlife to see around the headland, with an abundance of sea thrift and rock sea-lavender bursting out of the rocks like pink jewels on the surrounding slate-grey landscape. The cliffs of the headland itself are bursting with life, with herring gulls and lesser black-backed gulls adorning the pillars offshore, their calls filling the sea air. During the summer months, migratory birds arrive to delight visitors with song and dazzling flight. One of the most common species that you will see on the headland is the wheatear. There are also plenty of stonechats, which are often seen around the gorse bushes.

One of the best things to do here is to sit down with a pair of binoculars or spotting scope and enjoy some seawatching. Looking offshore, you can see species such as storm petrels and

Rock sea-lavender.

Chough.

Manx shearwaters dancing above the waves as they begin their foraging journeys to and from the nearby islands of Skomer and Skokholm (see page 127), where both have globally important breeding populations. The most iconic species, and one that everyone loves to try to spot when they visit, is the chough, which is often seen in pairs or small groups, perched on the rocks or calling in the sky above.

The prime visitor attraction at St Govan's is the chapel itself, a small stone building carved into the limestone cliff. Govan himself was believed to be an Irish abbott who was on his way to Wales when he was attacked by Irish pirates offshore. He was forced to flee to the cliff, where the rocks allegedly morphed into a secret cave for him to hide in. After this, he set up a monastic hermitage in the cove and lived off the surrounding land. If you make the journey down to the chapel, count the steps on your journey as legend says that the count on the way down is never the same as the count back up!

You can extend your trip to St Govan's with a visit to Stackpole Head and Bosherston Lily Ponds. The lily ponds are truly a beautiful place to visit, offering a very different wildlife-spotting experience to the rest of Pembrokeshire, comprising parkland and peaceful waters, alive with insects and plants. The ponds were created by the Cawdors, a noble family from Pembrokeshire, who drained several acres of 'wet wasteland', damming the valley of two rivers to form ornamental lakes with a mansion on a hill nearby. Stone bridges were built across one lake where the footpath takes you down to Broad Haven South beach. The best vantage point is the wooden bridge, which gives you a close-up of the lily pads themselves. Whilst walking around, keep your eyes open for the vast array of dragonflies and damselflies around the pads, but keep your ears primed and ready too, as at any moment you could hear a splash as an otter fishes around the lily pads.

St Govan's Chapel.

SWANSEA

This vibrant city on the south coast of Wales offers a unique blend of urban life and stunning natural beauty. Surrounded by diverse landscapes, from sandy beaches to lush woodlands and rugged cliffs, Swansea is an excellent base for wildlife watching trips, with plenty of accommodation options and camping areas. With its accessible public transport network, you can easily explore the city's natural wonders and nearby wildlife hotspots, including the Gower Peninsula and nearby Mumbles Bay (page 139). Llanelli is another fantastic base to consider, located just a short train ride from Swansea. This town is home to the WWT Llanelli Wetland Centre (page 142), an incredible reserve that attracts a variety of wading birds including spoonbills and great white egrets, as well as wildfowl such as pintail and teal.

Rhosili Bay (page 135), at the southwestern tip of the Gower, offers panoramic views and is a prime location for spotting migrating birds. The nearby cliffs are also home to seal colonies, and if you're lucky, you may even spot dolphins or porpoises swimming off the coast. Public transport options from Swansea to the Gower include buses that run regularly from the city centre to popular sites like Rhosili, Oxwich Bay and Port Eynon, making it easy for visitors to explore the peninsula's rich wildlife.

Not only does Swansea have an extensive network of buses and trains connecting the city to nearby nature reserves, beaches and coastal paths, but the range of cycle paths also offers good access to the different wildlife hotspots.

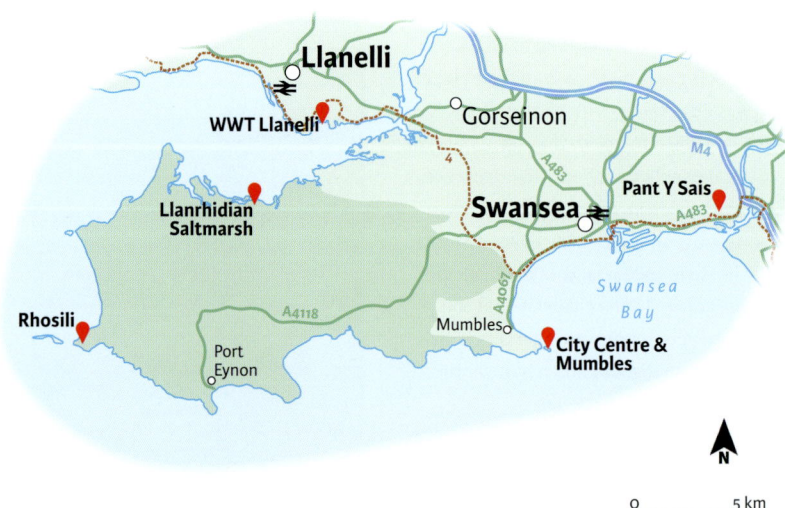

RHOSILI

Rhosili, Swansea SA3 1PR • OS Explorer Map 159 • Grid ref SS414880 • What3Words: adjusting.empty.funny

How to get there: The easiest and most reliable way to reach Rhosili is to take the 118 bus from Swansea City Centre bus station, located at the Quadrant. Alight at the bus stop next to the National Trust car park after around 75 minutes. • It is also possible to cycle from Swansea City Centre down to Rhosili by taking the A4118 (19.5 miles/29km) or the National Cycle Network Route 4 (24 miles/39km), passing through various villages on the way. • For those looking for a bigger adventure, you can take in all the beautiful landscapes the Gower has to offer by walking the 18-mile (29km) Gower Coastal Path from Mumbles Head in Swansea around the coast to Rhosili.

Access and conditions: Worm's Head is only accessible 2 hours either side of high tide. Be sure to check the tide times on the coastguard boards before setting out. • There are no designated paths at Rhosili; the coastal path is mostly grass so motorised wheelchairs are the preferred method of travel for wheelchair users. Accessing Worm's Head and the beach is not possible for those requiring wheelchair use or having limited mobility, due to the rocky nature of the causeway and the naturalised pathways leading down from the car park either side of the beach below. • There are toilets in the main car park, where accessible and baby-changing facilities are also available.

•• Rhosili is the crowning gem at the tip of the Gower Peninsula. With its rich history, naturalised farming practices and diversity of species, it's a fantastic site to look for most of the wildlife on offer in the surrounding peninsula. The Gower is a real treasure within this stretch of coastline – it was the first place in Britain to be named a National Landscape (formerly Area of Outstanding Natural Beauty). The core strength of this rugged coastline is the diversity of the landscape, with towering trees, golden beaches and beautiful downs. A weekend trip here is definitely needed to fully immerse yourself in the true beauty of South Wales.

Perhaps one of the most iconic sites of the Gower is Worm's Head. This is a rocky promontory shaped like a snake, which sits proudly off Rhosili. The name 'worm' comes from the Viking name for 'sea serpent', which would be much more fitting than 'worm'!

The adventure out to Worm's Head is a fantastic trip. Walking out from the end of Rhosili headland, you will cross a rocky terrain before reaching the serpent-like headland of Worm's Head. Be sure to take your time as this causeway is dotted with rockpools full of wrasse, starfish and plenty of crabs, a wealth of intertidal life that is more than worthy of a stop to appreciate. Worm's Head itself is home to breeding fulmars, guillemots, razorbills and kittiwakes, with the calls of choughs filling the sky above. Be sure to scan the waters too, as common dolphins and grey seals are frequently seen off the rugged ridges.

If adventuring across rocks is not your thing, then a trip to the golden beach of

Rhosili should definitely be on the cards. The 3 miles (4.8km) of blissful golden sand is regularly featured on 'world's best beaches' lists, and it is clear to see why, with very little disturbance and a plentiful supply of space and wildlife. Harbour porpoises and grey seals are a regular sight throughout the year in the glossy blue waters surrounding Rhosili, whereas the winter months will see thousands of scoters forming rafting flocks offshore – be sure to scan through these as they occasionally host unusual visitors to the area such as long-tailed ducks and surf scoters. You may also see red-throated and great northern divers surfing the waves offshore, as their human equivalents also like to do here.

If you're still looking for more, a walk down to the Vile is a must whilst visiting. The National Trust has gone back to the roots of Rhosili and transformed the area using traditional farming techniques to enhance the soil and the general area, to the benefit of wildlife. Traditional arable crops and wildflower meadows are a

Worm's Head.

beautiful sight to see during the summer months. One addition that has been particularly welcome is the developed hay meadows, which have seen numbers of pollinators, mammals and birds thrive. The crop fields have wide margins, allowing wildflowers to grow, and the crops are undersown with red clover, which is both a treat for bees and butterflies and also protects the soils after the harvest, allowing the wildlife and plants to develop year on year. Highlights of the flower-filled fields range from badgers, weasels and stoats, to skylarks, meadow pipits, choughs and kestrels. The hay meadows, sunflower fields and ample amounts of gorse provide food for the pollinators and insects to thrive. Some highlights to look out for are common carder bee, red-tailed bumblebee, tawny mining bee and commoner species such as buff-tailed and white-tailed bumblebees, along with common blue, small tortoiseshell and meadow brown butterflies and six-spot burnet moths. You may also see hummingbird hawkmoths migrating during the late summer.

Rockpools at Rhosili.

LLANRHIDIAN SALTMARSH

Mill Lane, Llanrhidian SA3 1ER • OS Explorer Map 159 • Grid ref SM72485
• What3Words: openly.waddled.sending (cattle grid)

How to get there: Bus is the primary way of travelling around the Gower and the journey from Swansea to Llanrhidian is no different. From Swansea City Centre bus station, board the 116 service to Landimore, alighting at Llanrhidian after around 40 minutes. To reach Llanrhidian Marsh, walk down Mill Lane before joining Marsh Road and walking to the cattle grid for the best views of the full saltmarsh (around 0.9 miles/1.5km). • It is also possible to cycle from Swansea City Centre to Llanrhidian by joining the National Cycle Network Route 4 (15 miles/24km).

Access and conditions: Access is fully supported at this site, with tarmac paths and also several benches if you need to sit down along the way. If walking is slightly challenging for you, then you might opt to sit in the pub gardens and use a spotting scope to view the saltmarsh below. • There are no public toilets available.

•• Located on the North Gower coast, Llanrhidian's greenery and marshy habitats offer a very different landscape to the golden sands of the southern parts of the Gower. Llanrhidian is where some of the best wildlife spectacles in South Wales can be found, due to the extensive saltmarsh systems running alongside the Burry Inlet estuary. This estuary has played host to many exciting species including Pacific golden plovers and long-tailed ducks and is a Ramsar site and SSSI, recognised for wildfowl such as pintail, wigeon, shelduck and shoveler, and waders including knot, oystercatcher and redshank. You can admire the wintering spectacles of wildfowl and waders from just about anywhere from Llanrhidian to Crofty, but Dalton's Point in Penclawdd (opposite the pharmacy) is a prime location for a good view of the feeding waterfowl using the sandbanks to find crunchy cockle delights.

Should you be looking to make a day of your trip to Llanrhidian, then a trip to the Dolphin Inn pub is recommended. After you have eaten some of the best food Wales has to offer, including the must-have cawl, you can walk to the saltmarsh down the winding Marsh Road where the extensive saltmarshes are in full view. There is a prime location to observe wildlife on Llanrhidian Marsh throughout the year: walking northeast towards Wernffrwd from Llanrhidian, you will come across a track between Marsh Road and New Road where Nant Y Wrach Farm is located. There is a cattle grid here; position yourself on the road connecting to the cattle grid and look out towards the coast. This is a popular spot where birders and wildlife watchers arrive to watch the winter spectacles of roosting birds. Take up position an hour or so before sunset to see waders such as golden plover and lapwing coming in to roost on the saltmarsh crevices, calling out as they do so. The eerie calls of curlews can also be heard as they hunker down for the evening. Looking west, you will notice a

white house among the trees – this is where you should focus your attention as birds on their way to roost will begin to appear from that direction. Thousands of herons, including grey herons, little egrets and great egrets all come drifting above you, while hen harriers do their last night-time scans before dusk.

Keen observers will notice the silent wings of short-eared owls and barn owls as they glide above the reeds and marshlands, looking for voles and mice using the reeds as cover. Occasionally you can be treated to the spectacle of flocks of jackdaws or starlings swirling in the sky before departing to their roost.

CITY CENTRE AND MUMBLES

The Old Lifeboat Cottage, Mumbles, Swansea SA3 4EN • OS Map ref OL165 • Grid ref SS6188 • What3Words: daring.height.observer (Mumbles Pier)

How to get there: A very popular way of navigating around Swansea and the nearby towns is to use the ample buses available. There are several discounts and passes available to purchase from the Quadrant bus station located in the city centre, allowing you to take full advantage of the routes around Swansea city and nearby Mumbles. Many a journey has been enjoyed travelling from the city centre to Mumbles, hopping off at various points to enjoy the beach and to fill up on delicious ice cream – a staple of any visit to Mumbles.

Access and conditions: Access around Swansea is very good. The city centre and Mumbles have smooth tarmac pathways, pavements and crossings. The only difficulty is the steep incline ramp between Mumbles Pier and the Bracelet Bay car park where the regular bus visits; the alternative is to exit the bus at Verdi's café and make your way to the pier from there. • There are toilets available at the pier and nearby public ones available near Verdi's café.

•• For a city, Swansea is absolutely beautiful and filled with wildlife. There are various points where you can enjoy a bit of respite from the hustle and bustle of city life and take a wander around the parks, of which one of the most popular is Singleton Park. Often enjoyed by university students and local workers, this park is located on the edge of the city centre. With 101 hectares of green grass and mature towering trees, this former country estate has been open to the public for more than 100 years and houses a botanic garden. Depending on the time of year, you may see jays collecting their autumnal surplus of nuts, tawny owls calling in the twilight, or common pipistrelle, soprano pipistrelle and noctule bats aplenty hunting for prey as dusk approaches, particularly from the Old Swiss House.

Just outside of Swansea city centre, you have the Mumbles. Well connected to the city centre, Mumbles is very easy to visit and should be on any visiting wildlife-lover's list as an ideal location for a short break. If you are not immediately sold by the picturesque town and moored boats in the bay, then a trip along the promenade will soon win you over. You can embark on the 5-mile (8km) walk between Singleton Park and Mumbles Pier along the promenade, taking in the sights of Swansea Bay where it's possible to see turnstones, oystercatchers and sanderlings running and feeding on the sand below. There is also a cycle lane, making this route great for cycling (or rollerblading!) too. Also check the water for grey seals looking for fish using the tidal bay. On reaching Mumbles Pier, a

short walk along it provides many delights, particularly if you are fond of gulls, as black-headed gulls, herring gulls and lesser black-backed gulls are a common sight and Mediterranean gulls are also regular visitors during the summer and winter months. There is also a very noisy colony of kittiwakes that breed underneath the pier in late summer. They have been here for generations and allow for close views of their silver, black-tipped wings as they come soaring from the waves to their nesting ledges on the old lifeboat station.

The tip of Mumbles allows access to Bracelet Bay, where you will find a small rocky bay adorned with pebbles and worm casts. This is a very popular area with tourists due to its location and safety – with coastguards being an active presence throughout the summer – as well as the range of wildlife that can be found in the relatively easy to access rockpools, such as hermit crabs, various starfish species, common prawns, whitebait, blennies and

Common dolphins.

anemones. The rocks are also great hunting grounds for fossils; there have been several important discoveries, but more common finds are ammonites and corals. It is a beautiful and peaceful beach to enjoy, and if you scan beyond the rocks towards the sea you may spot more marine life, with grey seals and common dolphins a regular sight throughout the year, but most common during the spring, summer and autumn.

WWT LLANELLI WETLAND CENTRE

WWT Llanelli, Llwynhendy, Llanelli, Carmarthenshire SA14 9SH • OS Explorer Map OL186 • Grid ref SS5398 • What3Words: grows.ruffling.elated

How to get there: It is possible to cycle to WWT Llanelli from Swansea City Centre by taking the National Cycle Network Route 4 from the Swansea seafront down to Bynea cycle track (13 miles/21km). • A train service between Swansea and Llanelli takes 15 minutes and runs several times a day; from here you will need to take the 11 service bus to WWT Llanelli, again taking around 15 minutes. • By bus from the city centre, take the 111 service to Llanelli, disembarking in Bynea after 20 minutes; from here, walk the cycle track to WWT Llanelli (2 miles/3.2km).

Access and conditions: The reserve is open from 09:30 to 17:00 in the winter months and to 18:00 in the summer months. The site is fully accessible with tailored hides and observation areas suitable for wheelchair users. Paths are mostly tarmac on the zoological collection side, with some gravel paths on the reserve. Motorised wheelchairs can be rented from the reception; it is recommended to call up and book prior to visiting. There are toilets dotted around the site, with accessible toilets in the main visitor centre, along with baby-changing facilities, and in the Heron's Wing Hide.

•• One of the most popular nature reserves in South Wales, WWT Llanelli lies on the Burry Inlet estuary, sitting like a crown jewel amongst the emerald saltmarshes. The site comprises 182 hectares of glistening lakes, reedbeds, towering woods and lagoons and, as if that is not enough, there is also extensive saltmarsh visible from the numerous hides dotted around the grounds and reserve. The site is divided into two zones: one focused on captive species and saltmarsh, and the other more wildlife-focused with created lagoons and lakes adorned with trees and hedges, making it a paradise worthy of any wildlife-lover's visit.

As you explore the site, there are some distinct areas that you'll find particularly worth a visit. During the winter months, head down towards the estuary and pop into the British Steel Hide or Michael Powell Hide to see wintering waders in their masses. Feeding flocks of black-tailed godwits, greenshanks, redshanks and oystercatchers can be seen probing the mud for tasty treats, and you may also be able to see flocks of shovelers feeding on the scrapes and tufted ducks flying in for the winter. Elsewhere on the reserve, otters are a common sight during the autumn and winter months. It's possible to see them fishing among the reeds from the Heron's Wing Hide or the Peter Scott Hide, where you may spot them on the Deep Water Lake. Great white egrets and bitterns are also great spots during these seasons from either of the hides.

Summer is a great time to explore the vast reedbeds and green edges of the reserve. Willow warblers, chiffchaffs and blackcaps flit around the willows, while breeding gulls add their loud voices to the soundscape. There are several large colonies of black-headed gulls on the site

Mediterranean gull.

Lapwing.

and a quick scan through these flocks can produce a few Mediterranean gulls, which also breed on the islands. There may also be snipe, lapwings and other local breeding birds.

The spring and summer months are also a fantastic time to see numerous dragonflies and damselflies whizzing around the various streams and pools. You can find them throughout the site but looking around the Deep Water Lake is a great spot for emperor dragonflies patrolling the walkways, common darters on the benches and common blue, emerald and blue-tailed damselflies dotted around the various lakes. Botanists will not miss out either, as the reserve is filled with wildflower meadows providing swathes of flowers and plenty of pollinators. Keep an eye out for the standout bee orchids.

PANT Y SAIS NATIONAL NATURE RESERVE

Pant y Sais NNR, Skewen, Neath SA10 6JR • OS Explorer Map 165 • Grid ref ST696945 • What3Words: rang.could.powering

How to get there: The easiest way to arrive at Pant y Sais is to take the 45 service bus from Swansea City Centre bus station to Jersey Marine where you can disembark and walk 0.8 miles (1.3km) to the car park along Ashleigh Terrace. Other buses that can take you there are the T6 TrawsCymru, numbers X1 and 31, all of which leave from the Swansea bus station. • Should you wish to take in the beautiful coastal scenery, you can walk or cycle along the beach front for 4.6 miles (7.4km).

Access and conditions: There is a circular boardwalk with passing places and ample seating and benches. • There are no toilets available at this site, but customers of the nearby Towers Hotel & Spa can use the facilities in their restaurant.

- Whilst it is possible to visit Pant y Sais during any season, a trip during the summer months offers the best experience. Enjoy a gentle stroll on the boardwalks surrounded by tall towering reedbeds and you will be serenaded by reed warblers and sedge warblers singing from their reedbed perches, punctuated with bursts of loud song from Cetti's warblers and set against the gentle buzzing of grasshopper warblers. You may glimpse water rails as they dash out from the reeds, and marsh harriers, buzzards and red kites are often seen overhead.

The site is a SSSI and has developed naturally on a former course of the Neath River. Its complexity and habitats are made up of diverse wetland with several plant communities thriving in this formed bogland. Species include wetland staples such as fen-sedge, bogbean, bulrush, creeping jenny and purple moor-grass, as well as other moist-ground species such as devil's-bit scabious and southern marsh, pyramidal and early purple orchids, which provide a pop of purple amongst the moss. Not only is it a bustling site for birds and plants, but it is also a hub for a range of invertebrates. One of the standout species is the fen raft spider, which is adapted to a semi-aquatic lifestyle and is found at only a handful of sites in the UK, with this population first recorded in 2003. The boardwalks are a great site to try to spot these arachnids and they particularly gravitate towards stiff-leaved tussocks where they can weave their nursery-web systems.

Should you wish to extend your visit, then pop across to Crymlyn Bog, the largest lowland fen in Wales. As at Pant y Sais, there is an extensive boardwalk system in place to ensure your feet stay dry as you wander through the various reedbeds and fens. Butterflies, including brimstones and silver-washed fritillaries, and dragonflies are numerous around both of the reserves. Listen for the gentle rustle of adders hiding among the tree edges and keep your eyes peeled on the boardwalks at both sites as common lizards are often spotted scuttling between the wooden cracks.

Whilst the summering birds are a delight to behold during the warmer months, winter is also a great time to visit with barn owls, marsh harriers, bitterns and a slim possibility of bearded tits.

Water rail.

Fen raft spider.

LLANDUDNO

Llandudno is a well-loved seaside location on the North Wales coast, providing a great base from which to explore the well-connected wildlife sites. Located just a short distance from Llandudno, the Great Orme (page 148) offers a wealth of wildlife watching opportunities with public transport options making it an easily accessible day trip. The area is home to a wide variety of species, including the famous wild goats that roam freely across the headland and often even come to nearby Llandudno town. The Great Orme is also a great site for spotting marine life, including dolphins and porpoises, which are often seen swimming just offshore. Whilst exploring the clifftops you'll come across a variety of insect and plant life, making the area an exciting place in Wales where birds are perhaps not always the central point of interest.

Gronant Dunes (page 151), located along the North Wales coast near Prestatyn, is another excellent wildlife destination that is easily accessible from Llandudno. The area is particularly famous for its nesting colonies of sand martins and little terns, which return to the dunes each summer. The site also provides an important refuge for wading birds such as oystercatchers, curlews and lapwings. Gronant Dunes is easily reachable by train from Llandudno to Prestatyn, followed by a short bus ride to the dunes – an easy journey for a fantastic wildlife-filled day out.

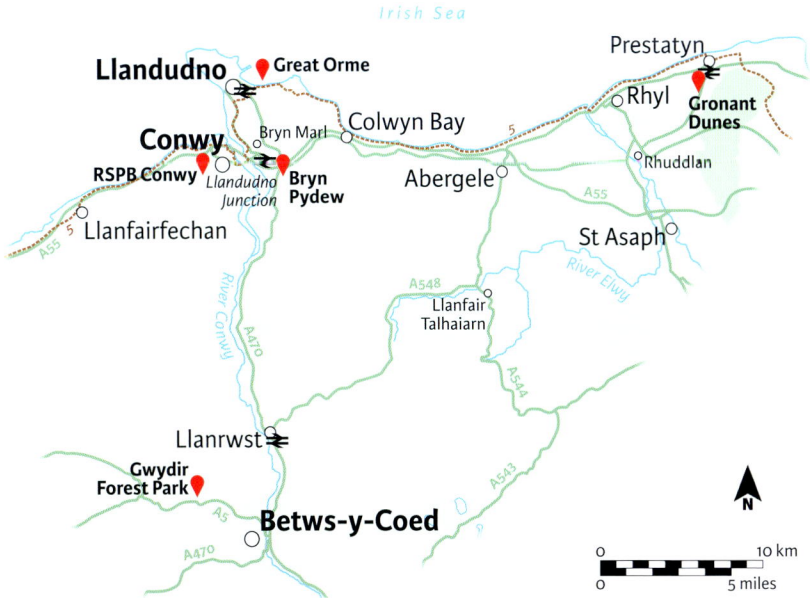

RSPB CONWY

RSPB Conwy Nature Reserve, Llandudno Junction, Conwy LL31 9XZ
• OS Explorer Map OL265 • Grid ref SH79467737 • What3Words: lives.lurching.graced

How to get there: There are several ways to travel between RSPB Conwy and the nearby Llandudno, given the short distance – it is the perfect place to combine with a short trip to the area. To travel by bus, the 25 (Eglwysbach) and 27 (Tan-lan) services will take you from Llandudno Junction station to Tesco Superstore (a 5-minute journey) where you can then walk the 0.7 miles (1km) to the RSPB reserve entrance. • You can also cycle or walk from Llandudno town centre to the reserve along the National Cycle Network Route 5 (4.5 miles/7.25km). • Those travelling by train from further afield can claim a free hot drink from the RSPB café on site by showing a valid rail ticket.

Access and conditions: The nature reserve is accessible for wheelchair users and mobility scooter users, although there are some grassy areas that are less suitable. The viewing screens and hides have slots at varied heights, and there are wheelchair-friendly picnic tables available. • There are toilets, including accessible toilets and baby-changing facilities, and a shop on site.

•• A true testament that nature can thrive anywhere, this site was originally formed between 1986 and 1991, when the A55 North Wales bypass was built. At that time, it was a barren wasteland, before conservation work transformed it into the wildlife haven that it is today. The site terrain is varied, with several routes available. Taking a summertime stroll through the reedbeds on the purpose-built boardwalk, you will see

plenty of dragonflies and damselflies, with many common species flying down to lay eggs at the water's surface. At this time of year, it is also a prime location to listen out for and spot reed warblers, sedge warblers, Cetti's warblers and reed buntings. In the winter months, you may be lucky enough to spot a water rail darting from the reeds into the lagoons. As you finish your trail through the boardwalks, you will enter the mature scrubland where roaming flocks of long-tailed tits and goldcrests may be observed; there are occasionally feeders placed around the scrub, which provide great views of resident bird species.

There is an ample supply of orchids to be found at RSPB Conwy, including common spotted, early purple, southern marsh and early marsh. As you enjoy the walking loop through the various habitats, keep your eyes peeled for the uncommon coccinea form of early marsh orchid, and for the ever-popular bee orchids.

The lagoons are the prime feature of this estuary-side nature reserve, with multiple hides located around them. The water levels in these lagoons are adjusted at different times of the year to allow wildlife to flourish. In the summer months they are filled with water to protect the islands from mammals attempting to steal eggs from nesting birds. You may see avocets and black-headed gulls breeding on the islands during this time. Water levels are lowered during autumn, winter and spring, and this is when the array of waders on view can be spectacular. Curlews, redshanks and greenshanks are in abundance, with moving flocks of black-tailed godwits putting on a show and ducks such as teal and wigeon enjoying respite on the lagoons. Recent vagrants have included green-winged teal, Bonaparte's gull and Lapland bunting. Walking the circular loop of the reserve takes you straight past the estuary with breathtaking views of Conwy Castle. This is a joyous way to end a winter visit, with mergansers, goosanders, goldeneyes and waders often seen feeding on the tidal banks.

GREAT ORME

Great Orme, Llandudno, Conwy LL30 2XF • OS Explorer Map OL264 • Grid ref SH780827 • What3Words: divide.funky.geology

How to get there: There are several ways to reach the Great Orme summit; one of the most popular, and a thorough joy, is to take the Great Orme tramway departing from Victoria station in Llandudno. Opened in 1902, this is Britain's only funicular tramway that travels on public roads. • There are also buses that travel from Llandudno up towards the summit, namely the Arriva 26 and Alpine Great Orme Explorer which runs from Llandudno Pier. Note that the No.26 does not run on Sundays or bank holidays and the Explorer only runs between 10:00 and 17:00. • Should you want a challenge, it is possible to cycle or walk up to the summit (1.5 miles/2.5km) along the pathway.

Access and conditions: Great Orme is open all year round, although public transport options limit the times possible to reach the summit. There is a visitor centre with toilets, including accessible toilets and baby-changing facilities, available on the top, overlooking the sparkling blue sea of Llandudno. • For wheelchair users, it is possible to use the gravel path to travel halfway to the headland but the remainder of the terrain is on grass. The best way to experience the bay for wheelchair users is to stay on the base level and use the pathways to travel the whole loop of the headland. There are also plenty of seating spots and viewpoints to take a break and admire the wildlife.

•• An absolute gem adorning the North Wales coast, the Great Orme is a mixture of sea cliffs, heathland and limestone grassland with the odd bit of garden and shrub vegetation around the lower parts of the headland. With such a variety of habitats, the ease of transportation and the clear views across the bay, it is one of the best places to go birding in Wales.

The botany of this headland is one of the most exciting parts of a visit. Due to the shallow limestone-covered soil, many botanical rarities thrive here, particularly the Great Orme berry, a cotoneaster endemic to the Great Orme and found growing in the more isolated areas of the headland. Other plants of note during the spring and summer months are bloody cranesbill, sea campion and pyramidal orchid. Dark-red helleborines can be seen on the cliffs near the summit car park, often surrounded with cages to protect them from grazing animals, including the famous Llandudno mountain goats.

Another interesting plant to be found here is the white horehound, found growing on the western slopes. The history of this plant's residence on the island is somewhat unknown but one of the local legends tells that this tiny white beauty was cultivated by fourteenth-century monks who lived in the Bishop's Palace, which is now in ruins. Not only is this plant a delight to see, but also the very rare horehound plume moth lays its eggs on the leaves, with the caterpillars relying solely on the horehound as a foodplant. The horehound plume moth is not the only unusual Lepidoptera you can attempt to spot during your visit; two species of butterflies have endemic subspecies on the Great Orme. The local forms of silver-studded blue (ssp. *caernesis*) and grayling (ssp. *thyone*) have adapted to life on the limestone edge; they appear earlier in the year and are somewhat smaller than their mainland relatives.

Birdlife is a major draw for wildlife-loving visitors to the Great Orme, with many coming here to see one of Wales' iconic birds, the chough, which can be seen dancing overhead. The cliffs also provide homes for guillemots, razorbills and fulmars, which arrive at their nesting sites in spring ready for the breeding season. Due to the Great Orme's prominent location on the coastline, autumn provides opportunities to see unusual species such as dotterels and ring ouzels, which are occasional visitors, as well as other rarities. Don't forget to look down into the bay below here too, as harbour porpoises, common dolphins, minke whales and grey seals are often seen. Birdlife in the bay is also interesting with black guillemots a regular sight, as well as grebes and scoters in winter.

BRYN PYDEW NATURE RESERVE

Bryn Pydew, Penrhyn Bay, Conwy LL31 9JT • OS Explorer Map OL17 • Grid ref SH818798 • What3Words: grapes.certified.rugs

How to get there: The reserve is located in the village of Bryn Pydew, which is served by a bus from Llandudno Junction on Tuesday, Wednesday and Thursday with the stop operating on request online. Alternatively, you can reach the site on foot with a 1.5-mile (2.4km) walk from Llandudno Junction station. • Should you be travelling from Llandudno centre, it is possible to take the 25 service from Llandudno bus station to Conwy, which runs throughout the day and takes 20 minutes. From here you can walk the 3-mile route (4.8km) across the glorious Conwy Road Bridge past the castle and up the hill to Bryn Pydew. It is also possible to disembark the bus at Bryn Marl which will cut your walking distance down to 1.5 miles (2.4km). • Alternatively, you can cycle from Llandudno centre to Bryn Pydew for 4.5 miles (7.2km) along Gilfach Road.

Access and conditions: The terrain is very challenging to navigate with the site being mostly made up of limestone outcrops. It is not possible for wheelchairs or motorised scooters to travel around this site. It may be possible for individuals with limited mobility to explore parts of the site, but walking poles or other aids would be strongly recommended. Care should be taken when walking around the clints of limestone on this site as these can be very slippery when wet.

•• Nestled above one of the quietest towns in North Wales, the special habitats of Bryn Pydew are an under-explored refuge for many species of wildlife. Similar to the Great Orme (see page 148), the limestone and unimproved grasslands provide an absolute treat for any botanist looking to spot a range of species within one site. One can easily fill a day exploring the green grasslands and the tall standing flowers that provide pops of colour. As you first head into the reserve, you'll be able to spot carline thistle, cowslip and common rock-rose, but the standout species are the various orchids adorning the green carpets. Some highlights to spot when wandering around are early purple, green-winged and pyramidal orchids, and scarcer species such as dark-red helleborine and autumn lady's tresses.

Dark-red helleborine.

Due to the abundance of plants throughout the nature reserve, there are records of an impressive 22 butterfly species and nearly 600 types of moths on the reserve, with highlights of the latter including reddish light arches, heath rustic, cistus forester and chalk carpet moth, which can be seen at various times of the year. As well as butterflies and moths, there is also a small population of glow-worms at Bryn Pydew, which can be seen between June and July.

There are opportunities to see birds at Bryn Pydew NNR, in particular migratory species. The prime time to see them is between April and September, when the likes of blackcap, garden warbler and willow warbler visit the site. Raptors such as kestrels and buzzards can also be seen gliding overhead.

Glow-worm.

GRONANT DUNES

Gronant Dunes, Gronant, Prestatyn LL19 9TT • OS Explorer Map OL265 • Grid ref SJ091833 • What3Words: repelled.lively.outlawing

How to get there: Train is the fastest way to reach Gronant Dunes from Llandudno. Take the train from Llandudno Junction to Prestatyn, which takes 30 minutes. The trains run several times a day and are fully accessible. • Should you wish to take a bus instead, take the 18 service from Llandudno to Rhyl, then the 11C, 11F, 11M or 11X services from Rhyl to Gronant Village. From Gronant village, there is a 1.6-mile (2.6km) walk down Gronant Hill and Mostyn Road towards the Natural Resources Wales Ranger Hut where the dunes open out and allow you to begin your wildlife watching.

Access and conditions: Gronant Dunes is one of the most accessible sand dunes and beaches you can visit in the UK. With an innovative approach, Natural Resources Wales have installed a Mobi-Mat made from recycled plastic that runs to the beach. This mat allows the dunes to move and change, whilst enabling more people to enjoy the beach. You can also rent beach wheelchairs by contacting Natural Resources Wales and booking in advance. • Public toilets, including disabled stalls, can be found at the car park near the start of the hiking trail to Gronant Dunes.

Gronant Dunes

•• Gronant Dunes NNR is a beautiful sandy stretch between Prestatyn and Talacre. On your walk down the pathway from Gronant village, you will pass the first of the varied habitats that Gronant has to offer. Whilst not the core focus of a visit to the dunes, the bushy scrub provides great respite for many migratory species of birds including reed warblers, blackcaps and chiffchaffs, and you may even hear a Cetti's warbler. Pyramidal and marsh orchids can also be seen standing tall among the grasses. The change in wildlife is apparent as you walk down onto the dune systems, most noticeably in the range of plants you'll see – gone are the scrub and bushes, and in their place is sea holly. Here you may see or hear serenading skylarks and meadow pipits. Look out for dunlins, ringed plovers and gulls on the sea and beach. The white rumps of wheatears can also often be seen as these dapper birds flit along the coastline.

The primary focus of a visit to Gronant is to see Wales's only little tern colony. During the breeding season, between May and August, there is a visitor centre with wardens on site to answer any of your questions and tell you more about the breeding population of terns. These charismatic seabirds are monitored each year and protected by an electric fence, which was installed to keep away predators such as foxes. To keep human disturbance to a minimum, the team have also installed a perimeter rope, giving the

terns a wide boundary to keep the colony protected. Not only are there little terns, but you can also spot ringed plovers scuttling down the rocky beach and oystercatchers are known to breed – listen for their loud peeps carried with the wind.

Offshore it is possible to see common, Arctic and Sandwich terns fishing, cormorants flying by and gannets diving into the waves. Every inch of the dunes and coast is bursting with life.

A worthwhile addition to your visit is a trip to the nearby Talacre site, home to the only population of natterjack toads in Wales. The site was once a hotspot for the species, but the toads disappeared from Wales in the 1950s after habitat loss from urban development. A reintroduction project was undertaken in 1995 in which spawn was translocated to the site. The project was a success and there is now a thriving colony here. The project has been so successful that it is now a donor site for other reintroductions of the species.

Natterjack toad.

GWYDIR FOREST PARK

Gwydir Forest Park, Holyhead Road, Betws-y-Coed, Conwy LL24 0AA • OS Explorer Map OL17 • Grid ref SH778542 • What3Words: intrigues.convert.gardens

How to get there: The nearest train station is in the town of Llanrwst which is about a 1.5-mile (2.4km) walk from the Gwydir Forest Park Visitor Centre. Llanrwst station is located on the Conwy Valley Line which links Llandudno to Blaenau Ffestiniog. • You may also get the bus down to Gwydir Forest; there are various buses to Betws-y-Coed where you can exit at the entrance to the Forest Park.

Access and conditions: Visitor centre opening hours vary throughout the year; check the Natural Resources Wales website for information. • As this is an extensive forest and forms part of Wales' National Forest, there are many different routes to suit various needs. The Forest Park itself mostly consists of hiking and biking routes through the taller parts of the forest where accessibility is limited. There is a gentle route (0.5 miles/0.8km) from the visitor centre round the most central part of the site. The boardwalks and smooth pathways allow for wheelchair users and those less mobile to enjoy some scenic viewpoints and there are also some wheelchair-suitable picnic tables. • Accessible toilets and baby-changing facilities can be found at the visitor centre.

•• Formerly a zinc and lead mining area, this impressive forest has been transformed for the better and is now one of the best forest systems in Wales for wildlife. While exploring the various trails, you may encounter remnants of the site's mining past such as old engine houses, waste tips and reservoirs. Some of the mine remains have been made safe to explore and you can enter the openings and experience the wildlife and history within. Cyffty Mine and Hafna are two with the most history on show.

The capped mines are popular with bat species using the area for maternity roosts and hibernation. One of the most notable records is that of a lesser horseshoe bat, which was found hibernating in one of the capped mines in 2001. This is the furthest north the species has been found in the UK and this particular individual was ringed in the Forest of Dean in 1999. Taking a walk in the evening, you're likely to see common and soprano pipistrelles and noctules whizzing around the paths, hunting for insects.

The birds of Gwydir Forest are worth the trek around the different routes. Notably, the forest is a hive of activity for raptors, with buzzards, peregrine falcons and merlins all present here, but the big draw for many is the numerous goshawks that are seen hunting over the pines. Other species to listen out for include tawny owls and nightjars, which can be heard churring away from dusk in the summer months. There are babbling creeks that often host species such as dippers and grey wagtails, and the fields surrounding the forest can be good for redstarts. Whilst you're enjoying the forest itself, commoner species such as goldcrests can often be heard with their high-pitched calls echoing amongst the Douglas firs and Norway spruces.

BANGOR

Surrounded by a mix of coastal, woodland and mountainous habitats, Bangor offers easy access to some of the best wildlife watching locations in Wales. With its efficient public transport network, visitors who base themselves here can easily explore nearby natural attractions such as Anglesey, the Menai Strait and the Eryri National Park.

The Isle of Anglesey is a paradise for wildlife enthusiasts, especially those interested in birdwatching, seal spotting or discovering coastal plants. South Stack (page 164), located on the west coast, is home to a large seabird colony with one of the UK's most accessible puffin colonies. The cliffs provide a nesting site for puffins, razorbills and guillemots, making it a top spot for birdwatching during the summer months. There is plenty of other wildlife to see around Bangor and nearby Anglesey. A spectacle to witness during the winter months is at RSPB Cors Ddyga (page 162) where starling murmurations grace the skies above the reedbeds and hen harriers, short-eared owls and barn owls hunt the wintering waders around the pools. Visit Plas Newydd (page 158) to look for the resident red squirrels hopping between the towering trees in the summer.

Travel around Anglesey can be somewhat complex but there are a range of places connected by public transport, including direct trains from Bangor to Holyhead, the island's largest town, and a bus network connecting the major towns and reserves.

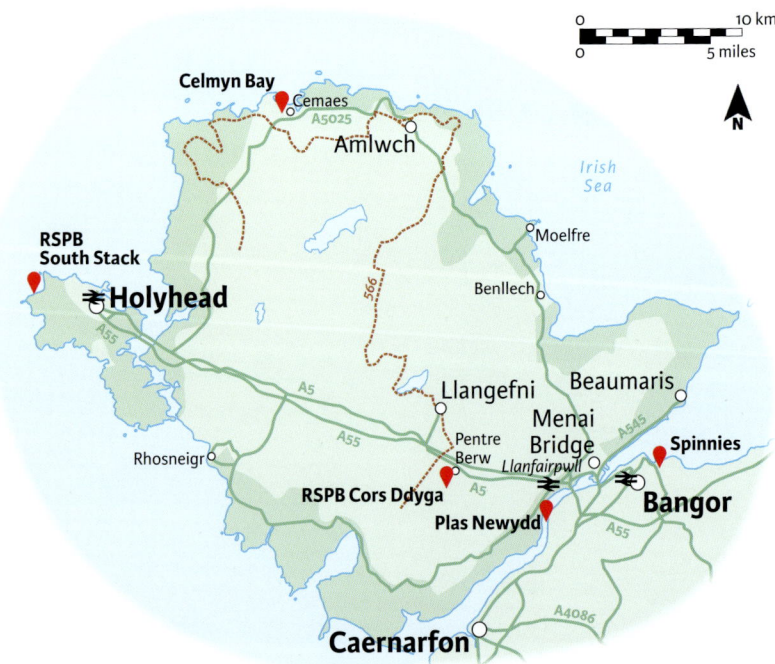

SPINNIES ABEROGWEN NATURE RESERVE

Spinnies Aberogwen Nature Reserve, Bangor LL57 3YH • OS Explorer Map OL17
• Grid ref SH613720 • What3Words: radiated.really.companies

How to get there: To reach the reserve from Bangor, take the number 5 bus from Bangor bus station towards Llandudno and disembark at Eglwys St Cross. From there, it is a 0.8-mile (1.3km) walk along Ponc-y-Lon towards Spinnies on the coast. • It is also possible to walk or cycle from Bangor to Spinnies (approx 4 miles/6.5km) with various routes available, depending on which part of Bangor you're in.

Access and conditions: The reserve is open during daylight hours; times vary in different seasons. For up-to-date information, visit the North Wales Wildlife Trust website.
• There are various routes to explore around the reserve with plenty of accessible paths. The paths are well marked; note that the path towards the shoreline is not accessible due to the sand and shingle ridges. Two of the three bird hides are accessible. The Cuddfan Bird Hide has a level pathway suitable for wheelchairs and three low windows designated for wheelchair users. • There are no toilets at this site, although the nearby towns of Tal-y-bont and Llandygai (both around 1.5 miles/2.4km away) provide amenities such as toilets, cafés and parking.

- Located in Aberogwen on the River Ogwen, Spinnies is a series of lagoons and a beautiful and tranquil location to observe wildfowl, waders and passerines. The history of the lagoons is not well known, but it is thought that they were once 'borrow pits', from which sand and gravel material was extracted for use in construction. They now provide a stopping point for birds during the spring and winter months with waterfowl being most numerous during this period. It is possible to see the tidal flats of Traeth Lafan, which, in the winter, provide great views of oystercatchers, dunlins, lapwings, bar-tailed godwits and curlews. The river itself provides ample food for grey herons and little egrets and there is also the possibility of seeing great crested grebes and red-breasted mergansers, particularly during the summer months.

The reedbeds that hug the edges of the lagoons are also teeming with life. The Kingfisher Hide allows users to sit and eagerly await the passing by of kingfishers, which hunt sticklebacks and minnows in the waters below. During the winter months the squeals of water rails can be heard from the reedbeds and the well-camouflaged common snipe may also be spotted.

A walk through the woodlands offers some fantastic plants. Dog's mercury and hart's-tongue fern are two common plants here, but the standout species is the broad-leaved helleborine, which can be found in the more shaded areas and adorning the paths. These woodlands are also filled with birdsong, with species such as chiffchaffs, bullfinches, firecrests and blackcaps providing pops of colour between the emerald leaves.

PLAS NEWYDD

Plas Newydd House and Garden, Llanfairpwllgwyngyllgogerychwyrndrobwllllantysiliogogogoch, Anglesey LL61 6DQ • OS Explorer Map OL30 • Grid ref SH521696 • What3Words: skis.idealist.indulgent

How to get there: An easy route to Plas Newydd is to take the 42 bus from Bangor to Llangefni, alighting at Brynsiencyn Road after around 25 minutes, which is next to the car park. Note that the bus does not run on Sundays. • The nearest train station is located 1.75 miles (2.8km) away at Llanfairpwllgwyngyllgogerychwyrndrobwllllantysiliogogogoch, once the longest train station name in the world, now the second. • Should you wish to extend your birding experience, then it is possible to walk the Menai Strait from Bangor to Plas Newydd along the scenic estuary and woodlands (5 miles/8km). The same route on the roads can also be cycled.

Access and conditions: The gardens are open 10:00–16:00 every day during winter hours, and 09:30–17:00 during summer. The Plas Newydd House is only open during the summer months. For up-to-date information, visit the National Trust website. There is a fee to enter the property. • There is an adapted property leaflet produced by the National Trust which is focused on their accessible routes and available to download from their website.

There are accessible paths throughout the grounds and an accessible toilet and baby-changing facilities located at the Old Dairy near the house entrance. Should you require further assistance, there is a volunteer-run buggy service, which will drop you at various points throughout the property.

•• Consisting of 16 hectares of beautiful gardens and 52 hectares of woodland, as well as a Grade I Listed House, Plas Newydd is the perfect place to unwind and enjoy a gentle stroll. As well as its listed main house, there are also two prehistoric scheduled monuments that you may stumble across during your walk around. These were among the first monuments to be granted legal protection under the Ancient Monuments Protection Act 1882. The Plas Newydd Burial Chambers are two adjoining stone chambers of a Neolithic burial cairn, located on the private lawns in front of the house. The second monument is a little walk away from the house, located on the edge of 'Garden Wood'. The Bryn-yr-Hen-Bobl Burial Chamber ('hill of the old people') is a large mound with a stone chamber within. Finds have included bones and pottery from the Neolithic period and it is thought that it was the location of a settlement prior to it becoming a burial site. The wildflower meadows on top of the settlements are home to various butterflies feeding on the flowers such as peacock, small tortoiseshell, speckled wood and brimstone. You may also spot six-spot burnet moths nestled among the vegetation.

The standout attraction at Plas Newydd are the red squirrels. Six individuals were brought here in October 2008 and held in

an enclosure within the woodland for a few weeks before their release into the wider deciduous woodland. Thanks to the efforts of the Anglesey Red Squirrel Project, they went on to breed successfully and the site now has a thriving population. There are feeding stations around the wood where you stand a good chance of spotting these shy animals. The best place to start your red squirrel mission is Church Bank Wood, which is located on the very edge of the Menai Strait and is where you will see the feeding stations. On your walk around the rest of the gardens, you can head towards the estuary where kingfishers, herons and red-breasted mergansers are seen throughout the year and winter brings in flocks of knots, oystercatchers and curlews using the sandbanks to locate prey.

CEMLYN BAY

Cemlyn Nature Reserve, Cemaes, Anglesey LL67 0EA • OS Explorer Map 262 • Grid ref SH329936 • What3Words: slip.strictest.greet

How to get there: The nearest train station to Cemlyn Bay is at Holyhead which is 12 miles (19.3km) away. The trains are regular from Bangor train station with the journey taking 30 minutes. From Holyhead station, take the 61 bus service to Amlwch, disembarking at Cemaes after around an hour and then walk northeast on Lon Penrallt for 1.5 miles (2.5km), following the signs to Cemlyn Bay. During this walk you pass through farm fields and coastal tracks filled with birds and butterflies during the summer months. • The National Cycle Network Route 566 passes close to the bay. The route begins at Holyhead and is a circular network around Anglesey ending at Menai Bridge, passing through Cemlyn Bay. The section from Holyhead to Cemlyn Bay is 15 miles (24km).

Access and conditions: The best visiting experience is during the summer months for the breeding terns, or winter for visiting wildfowl and waders. • The terrain is difficult as the majority of the site is shingle ridge, making it unsuitable for wheelchairs and those with difficulty walking on uneven surfaces. It is possible to park in the nearby car park and view with a scope from there. • There are no toilet facilities at this site.

•• The infamous ridge known as 'Esgair Cemlyn' is vital habitat for plant species such as sea kale, sea campion and yellow horned-poppy, all of which thrive here. It was not so well thought of in the past, as the rocky shoreline was the cause of many shipwrecks. The area was once home to a mill, a medieval church and Anglesey's first lifeboat before becoming a designated National Landscape, National Nature Reserve and Site of Special Scientific Interest (SSSI). Since 1981, it has been monitored by a warden, which has provided a unique overview of the changes that this picturesque shingle ridge has undergone.

What makes Cemlyn Bay Nature Reserve such a special place to visit is the sheer number of terns that breed here. In the past few years, there has been a whopping 1,500 pairs counted on the lagoon and ridges, and watching this swirling sky of white birds is an absolute delight. Among them are internationally important numbers of Sandwich terns, which return at the beginning of April and continue their stay through to July when the young fledge and depart the ridge. There are also common and Arctic terns breeding and the possibility of roseate terns.

Don't forget to take a peek offshore as the bay itself is home to plenty of wildlife, with grey seals and harbour porpoises being notable species to look out for. Listen out for oystercatchers, redshanks and curlews using the rocks to feed, and look out for gannets diving for fish. Divers and grebes are also frequent visitors, particularly during the autumn and winter months.

Sandwich tern.

RSPB CORS DDYGA

RSPB Cors Ddyga, Tai'r Gors, Gaerwen, Anglesey LL60 6LB • OS Explorer Map 262 • Grid ref SH46377257 • What3Words: cello.shall.friends

How to get there: The nearest bus stop is located on the A5 in Pentre Berw, which you can reach on the 4A service from Bangor bus station to Llangefni, disembarking at Pentre Berw after around 90 minutes. From the bus stop, walk down the hill and turn into Lon Coliar; after 100m, turn right and continue for 500m to the start of the RSPB visitor trail. • The nearest train station is Llanfairpwllgwyngyllgogerychwyrndrobwllllantysiliogogogoch, which is 4 miles (6.4km) from the reserve. While it is possible to walk or cycle from here, you can also get the 543 bus from the train station to Pentre Berw, which takes around 15 minutes.

Access and conditions: There are no toilets on site and the nearest public toilets are in Llangefni, around 3.5 miles (5.6km) away. However, there is a gorgeous farm shop called Holland Arms Garden Centre just off the road to Cors Ddyga (around 0.7 miles/1km from the reserve), which has facilities for customers as well as delicious cakes. • Most of the pathways on this site are stone track and grass-covered clay. There are, however, accessible pathways on some parts of the site, which travel from the Berw Colliery Scheduled Ancient Monument alongside the fields over the bridge. This pathway is completely tarmacked and suitable for wheelchairs and pushchairs.

•• A jewel in the middle of one of the largest lowland wetlands in Wales, Cors Ddyga is made up of 273 hectares of lakes, ponds, ditches and reedbeds, all adorned with grasslands, making this one of the best spots for wetland-related species.

During the summer months, the reserve is home to breeding populations of lapwings, which nest among the grasslands and overfly the fields giving cartoonish calls and performing acrobatic display tumbles. The songs of skylarks pour down from overhead while reed buntings and reed warblers sing from the extensive reedbed systems around the site, and the distant calls of cuckoos are often heard. There are also more than 30 scarce wetland plants to observe, with the bright purple heads of orchids towering above the rest. Plant species around the site include devil's-bit scabious, where marsh fritillary butterflies may also be lurking, bog myrtle, purple moor-grass and bladderwort.

Winter is also a brilliant time to explore. Starling murmurations are a common sight, the massed birds creating beautiful shapes in the sky before they drop down into their nightly roost. Hen harriers, marsh harriers and buzzards glide above the ponds and grasslands, seeking their prey. You may even see the eerie shapes of short-eared owls and barn owls along the reedbeds.

Keep your eyes and ears open for water voles, otters or the odd weasel running across the pathways. These can be seen throughout the year, but otters are somewhat easier to spot in the winter months.

RSPB SOUTH STACK

South Stack, Holyhead, Anglesey LL65 1YH • OS Explorer Map 262 • Grid ref SH21098188 • What3Words: startles.boggles.bitter

How to get there: The only way to get to South Stack by public transport is via train to Holyhead station. There are regular trains from Bangor, which take about 30 minutes. There are no buses from Holyhead station to South Stack, so from here, it's a 4-mile (6.4km) walk along scenic cliffs. It's a very enjoyable journey, where you can watch fulmars gliding on the cliffs and listen to the sounds of choughs filling the sky. Pause to look for harbour porpoises and common dolphins in the sea below. • Alternatively, you can cycle from Holyhead to South Stack along South Stack Road for 3.5 miles (5.6km). • There are seven Blue Badge spaces, found at the Ellin's Tower and Visitor Centre car parks.

Access and conditions: Toilets, including accessible toilets and baby-changing facilities, can be found within the visitor centre and are open seven days a week between 10:00 and 17:00. There are no toilets at Ellin's Tower. • It is possible to enjoy South Stack by wheelchair by using the access paths running from the Ellin's Tower car park down to the viewpoint. The route down to Ellin's Tower involves climbing down a set of 25 uneven steps. The terrain on the coastal route is more rugged and difficult to walk.

•• South Stack is a wonderfully diverse site for British wildlife watching with cliffs, sea, farmland, heathland and rocky faces surrounding you on all sides. The viewpoint at Ellin's Tower is ideal for looking out to sea and taking in the spectacular scenery and the birds gliding above the waves. The tower was originally built in 1878 as part of the lighthouse system with the tower designed to house the signal station, the lighthouse keeper's family and other staff. It's thought to have got its name from the wife of the lighthouse keeper at the time. The lighthouse became automated in 1984 and the tower fell into disrepair before restoration work in the 1990s transformed it into a viewpoint.

The heathland and farmland surrounding the site are part of the largest area of maritime heath in North Wales, supporting endemic plants such as the

South Stack or spatulate fleawort, a subspecies of field fleawort, as well as butterflies such as silver-studded blue. Among the wild thyme, heather and clifftops you can also spot migratory butterflies such as painted ladies, or listen out for the gentle wing flaps of hummingbird hawkmoths, which have been observed feeding on the surrounding plants. You may even be lucky enough to spot adders or common lizards basking in the sunshine.

Each spring, puffins return to the cliffs to breed, delighting visitors with their distinctive appearance and behaviour. The reserve offers various vantage points to observe the 100 or so pairs of puffins, which contribute to the rich seabird diversity of South Stack. From Ellin's Tower, look out towards the lighthouse to search for these charismatic birds. Visitors can also enjoy guided walks and talks to learn more about the different bird species that breed and visit here. Other notable bird species include peregrine falcons, kestrels, and migratory birds such as willow warblers, European storm petrels and Manx shearwaters. The spring and autumn can result in some unusual birds such as red-throated pipit, Pallas's warbler and yellow-browed warbler using the area as a feeding stop-off during migration.

Guillemots.

WREXHAM

Wrexham offers an abundance of opportunities to experience nature up close, whether you're birdwatching, exploring tranquil woodlands or discovering wildlife along rivers. With a well-connected public transport network, visitors can easily access some of the region's best wildlife spots, including Alyn Waters Country Park (page 172), World's End (page 167) and the nearby Dee Estuary (page 173). Alyn Waters, located just outside Wrexham, is a particularly popular spot and is easily accessible by bus from the city centre. The park spans more than 80 hectares of woodland, meadows and wetlands, and is home to a wide range of species. The trails within the park are perfect for walking and cycling, offering a peaceful setting for wildlife observation especially if you are looking for a gentle meander around a central location. Venture further afield for the exciting experience of watching black grouse lekking in the morning light at World's End, where your walking day will be filled with upland delights such as short-eared owls, hen harriers and merlins, before listening out for the wing pumping of the black grouse and spotting the peering heads of red grouse looking for a mate. A walk through the former working quarry of Minera (page 168) will provide nocturnal wonders as bats emerge from the stones and surrounding trees.

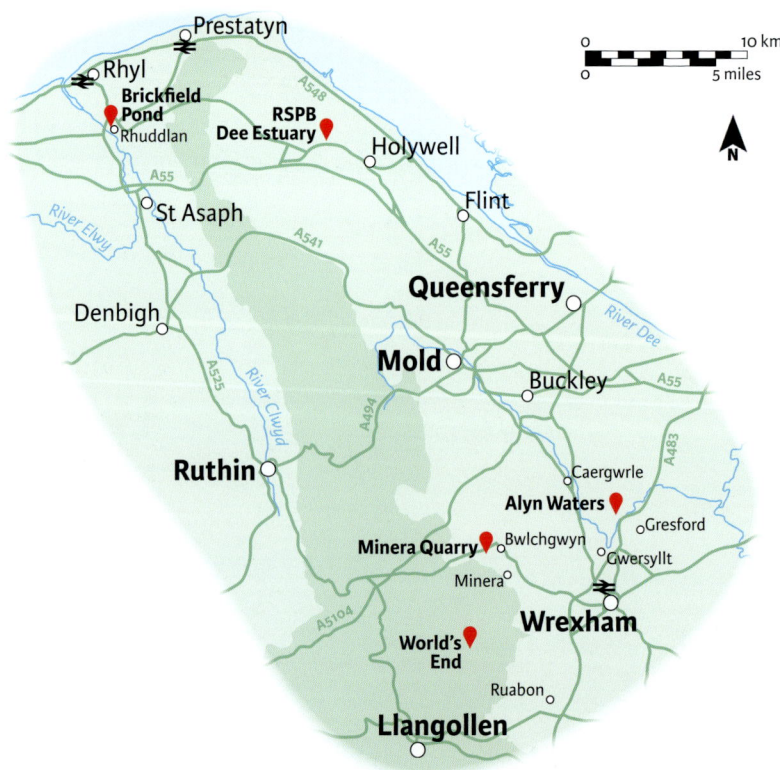

WORLD'S END

World's End, Coedpoeth, Minera, Wrexham LL11 3DE • OS Explorer Map 256 • Grid ref SJ236477 • What3Words: barbarian.chuck.harp

How to get there: World's End is a treasure of the Welsh hillside, but public transport is very limited. There are regular buses that run from Wrexham city centre to the nearest town of Minera, including the 11A and X51, which take around 15 minutes and drop you off in the town centre. The earliest bus is at 06:05 and the latest is 18:10. From here, World's End is a 4-mile (6.4km) walk through beautiful heathers, with a chance to spot pipits and larks. Alternatively, you can get the bus to Llangollen and walk the same distance to the location. • There is also the possibility of cycling to World's End for 5 miles (8km) along the B5101, which increases in incline as you ascend to the World's End site. • For those unable to walk or cycle, it is possible to park by the side of the road at the top of the hillside.

Access and conditions: There are no toilets at this site as this is a natural heathland with very few amenities. The nearest toilets can be found in the towns of Llangollen or Minera. • Access to the World's End hillside is mixed with tarmacked roads allowing you to walk a comfortable journey. • To help protect the local black grouse, there are conservation initiatives in place to attempt to reduce the number of off-road bikes using the various tracks.

Black grouse.

•• Surrounded by a blissful soundscape of skylarks and meadow pipits, the area around World's End is a great place to visit if you are looking for a walk on the wild side just off the edge of a city centre. Part of the Ruabon Moors, World's End offers an excellent vantage point for observing black grouse, the standout species here. The area is a mix of heathland and moorland, providing an ideal environment for these birds. Early morning, especially during the breeding season from late March to early April, is the best time to witness the lekking behaviour. These leks are conducted by the male birds during spring and summer, when they gather to perform an elaborate courtship display in an attempt to attract females. The males puff out their chests, inflate their neck sacs and perform a distinctive drumming sound by rapidly flapping their wings and parading around. To ensure you are in place to witness this spectacle, take your position on the roadside on the top to observe the species from a distance and look for clearings in the vegetation where the males will congregate. It is advisable to arrive before dawn (transport allowing) to observe the full display. Black grouse populations across the UK and Europe have declined due to habitat loss and fragmentation; conservation initiatives in the area focus on habitat restoration and management to support these birds. As well as black grouse, you can often hear and see red grouse among the heather too.

Other species of note here include tree pipits, meadow pipits and stonechats. If you do visit in the early morning, you may see short-eared owls or barn owls hunting the moors. The odd hen harrier can also be observed. Step carefully and look out for adders, peeping out from the heather while enjoying their bask in the sunshine.

MINERA QUARRY NATURE RESERVE

Minera Quarry Nature Reserve, Maes y Ffynnon Road, Minera, Wrexham LL11 3DE • OS Explorer Map 256 • Grid ref SJ258519 • What3Words: alike.moats.managers

How to get there: Bus is the only public transport option to reach Minera Quarry Nature Reserve from Wrexham. Take the Arriva bus service 11 from Wrexham bus station and disembark at Minera Post Office. The service operates Monday to Saturday (excluding bank holidays) and takes 15 minutes on average. From the bus stop, the quarry is approximately a 0.8-mile (1.1km) walk up Church Road; look out for the nature reserve sign signalling your arrival at the quarry.
Access and conditions: The reserve features a mix of terrains, including woodlands, open grasslands, and rocky quarry areas. Paths throughout the reserve are generally well maintained, but some areas, especially the quarry's rocky and uneven grounds, can be challenging for those with mobility difficulties. Visitors can enjoy bat watching from the perimeter without needing to enter the most rugged parts of the site. • The nearest facilities are in the town of Minera.

•• Minera Quarry is a remarkable blend of nature and history, with a fascinating industrial past stretching back over 400 years. A thriving lead mine and limestone quarry until it closed in 1994, the site has transformed into a wildlife haven. It is as culturally significant as it is ecologically rich, with the old quarry workings, including remnants of industrial buildings and machinery, providing an insight into the area's history as well as vital habitat for a variety of species.

Minera Quarry is also a renowned geological area as the site of a seabed dating back 440 million years. Keep your eyes peeled for fossils scattered throughout the landscape. Just a short walk from the entrance, you can spot ancient boulders that tell the story of Earth's deep past.

The air is filled with the songs of spotted flycatchers, redstarts and blackcaps as you explore the woodlands, while in the evenings you'll be serenaded by the fluting hoots of tawny owls. As you wander across the reserve, you may find rare invertebrates such as the mountain bumblebee, grayling butterfly and the elusive six-belted clearwing moth among the grasslands and gravelly terrain. Whilst the site is exciting for birds, the bats are the real stars of the show here. Lesser horseshoe bats roost in the kilns and caves within the reserve, along with Natterer's and brown long-eared bats. While bats are primarily nocturnal, dusk and dawn are optimal times for observing their activity, and taking your position in the centre of the quarry with your bat detector or thermal imager will really allow you to see the quarry come to life.

There are various different routes you can take throughout the site, but one of the most popular routes it to walk the 4-mile (6.4km) route from the quarry car park up towards Minera Mountain, which offers gorgeous scenic views of the former industrial site. There are some areas of incline as you ascend the mountain but the wildlife and views are well worth it. Should you be itching for some more wildlife, you can extend your visit by taking the pleasant 6-mile (9.7km) walking route to Llangollen Canal. Look out for kingfishers, goosanders and herons hunting the waters, with the possibility of otters fishing too.

BRICKFIELD POND

Brickfield Pond, Ffordd Derwen Rhyl, Wales LL18 2RN • OS Explorer Map 264 • Grid ref SJ014803 • What3Words: congratulations.spin.dock

How to get there: To travel to Brickfield Pond from Wrexham, take the Arriva X51 bus from Wrexham bus station to Rhyl via St Asaph. The journey takes approximately 90 minutes. The nearest bus stop to Brickfield Pond is Ascot Drive, approximately a 3-minute walk from the pond. • You can also get the train from Wrexham General to Rhyl, which takes 55 minutes. From Rhyl train station, take the 38A service (a journey of about 7 minutes) or walk to the ponds down Ernest Street and Kingsley Avenue (0.8 miles/1.3km).

Access and conditions: The Brickfield site features a 0.6-mile (1km) circular path around the pond. The terrain is primarily tarmac and suitable for wheelchair users. • There are no toilets on the site itself, but there are plenty of nearby cafés and public toilets that you can visit on your route back to the bus stop.

•• This former clay pit has been transformed into a haven for various waterfowl, providing great respite from the busy town nearby. With its rich variety of flora and fauna, Brickfield Pond is a thriving habitat for both beginner and experienced wildlife enthusiasts to explore. Whether you're watching the birds, observing insect activity or simply soaking up the peaceful surroundings, there is always something to appreciate.

Emperor dragonfly.

The site boasts typical inner-city wildlife species such as coots, moorhens, mute swans and various ducks. Great crested grebes build their nests on the central island, allowing great views as you walk the circular paths. Kingfishers are also occasionally seen using the reedbeds around the edge of the site, their blue plumage shining in the spring and summer sun. The spring and summer are brought to life with passing migrants such as chiffchaffs, blackcaps and willow warblers bursting into song in the towering trees and willow surrounding the pond and its nearby green areas.

The pond itself has played home to rarities such as yellow-browed warblers and greater scaup, which has delighted local wildlife watchers as it shows that their quiet nature space in the middle of town has flourished enough to allow vagrant species to also see its potential. As well as birds, the pond is also home to a variety of aquatic insects, most noticeably dragonflies and damselflies, especially in the warmer months. Species such as common blue damselfly and emperor dragonfly are often seen darting over the water.

The surrounding area has been transformed to help increase the biodiversity in the town and is a great area to wander through after your walk around the pond. The meadows and grassland areas attract butterflies such as the gatekeeper and small tortoiseshell. If you're still exploring at twilight, keep your eyes open for pipistrelles and Daubenton's bats, using the water as a feeding hotspot. During the evenings, it is also possible to hear tawny owls hooting from the neighbouring trees, or the scuffle of feet as hedgehogs, wood mice and voles emerge from their daytime hiding spots ready to feed around the pathways.

Great crested grebe.

ALYN WATERS COUNTRY PARK

Alyn Waters Country Park, Mold Road, Gwersyllt, Wrexham, LL11 4AG
• OS Explorer Map 256 • Grid ref SJ319546 • What3Words: koala.loses.respected

How to get there: While public transport directly to Alyn Waters is limited, bus services 27, 29 and 33 all run from Wrexham bus station to the nearby Gwersyllt, taking on average 30 minutes. From this point, it's a 1.2-mile (1.9km) walk north along Mold Road to reach the entrance of Alyn Waters Country Park.

Access and conditions: The park has well-maintained paths and many of the woodland, riverside and grassland trails are paved or compacted, making them wheelchair accessible. However, more rugged areas, especially along the riverbanks, have rougher terrain that may not be suitable for everyone. • There are accessible toilets and baby-changing facilities on site.

•• Nestled in the stunning Alyn Valley, Alyn Waters is the largest country park in the Wrexham area and is nothing short of a paradise for outdoor enthusiasts. With its Green Flag Award accreditation, this beautiful park offers an unforgettable escape into nature. Explore woodland trails, wander through vibrant grasslands and follow the winding path along the serene riverside, soaking up the peaceful sounds of the River Alyn. Whether you're an avid walker, birdwatcher, or simply seeking a tranquil retreat, the park's diverse landscapes have something for everyone; it is the perfect place to get lost in nature.

Alyn Waters is split into two distinct areas on either side of the River Alyn, each offering unique experiences and scenic views. The site provides a range of habitats including woodlands, grasslands and riverside areas. The woodlands are

home to a variety of bird species including blue tits, great tits, robins, wrens and blackcaps. You might also spot nuthatches, woodpeckers and the occasional treecreeper. The edges of the River Alyn are lined with reeds, rushes and water forget-me-nots, providing excellent habitat for aquatic life such as common toads, common frogs and smooth newts. The park's grasslands are teeming with wildflowers, including marsh orchids, common spotted orchids and buttercups, as well as meadow grasses, which attract a host of pollinators. Cattle and sheep are used as conservation grazers on the meadows. Butterflies are a notable sight during the spring and summer months with species including peacock, red admiral and comma. The colder months bring migratory birds, such as redwings and fieldfares, while the resident woodland birds prepare for the chill. You may also see badgers and foxes as they forage for food.

RSPB DEE ESTUARY, POINT OF AYR

> **RSPB Dee Estuary Nature Reserve, Station Road, Talacre, Flintshire CH8 9RD**
> • OS Explorer Map 265 • Grid ref SJ12468484 • What3Words: described.income.dabble
>
> **How to get there:** To reach the RSPB Dee Estuary side of the nature reserve, take the Prestatyn train from Wrexham General (around 45 minutes). From Prestatyn, you can take either the F18, 11C, 11M or 18 bus to Talacre Beach, which takes around 15 minutes. It is then a scenic 0.7-mile (1.1km) walk from the beach to the reserve. • Alternatively, it is possible to cycle from Prestatyn to Point of Ayr (3.5 miles/5.6km) by joining the A548 from Station Road outside of the Prestatyn station and following the signs for Talacre Beach and Dee Estuary.
>
> **Access and conditions:** The nearest toilets are found in Talacre, around 480m away. There are some walking paths within the reserve, but due to the nature of the landscape, some trails may be uneven and parts of the reserve may be difficult to access by wheelchair or with pushchairs. Visitors should prepare for a more rugged terrain when walking around the reserve. There are some designated areas for birdwatching along the coastline, but these may involve walking over uneven ground. The reserve's paths can become muddy or slippery during wet weather.

•• The Dee Estuary, a designated Special Protection Area (SPA) and Site of Special Scientific Interest (SSSI), is a haven for a rich variety of wildlife. Its diverse habitats, including mudflats, saltmarshes, reedbeds and estuarine waters, make it a prime location for both resident and migratory species. The mudflats and sandbanks provide habitat for large numbers of waders, especially during the winter months. Look out for redshanks, sanderlings, dunlins and oystercatchers feeding along the shoreline. The estuary is also a vital wintering ground for migratory waterfowl, with pink-footed geese, brent geese, wigeons, teals and shovelers all commonly spotted. Listen out for the eerie calls of curlews filling the air and the thundering wing claps of geese prior to their take-off. Other species of note include marsh harriers and hen harriers, which are frequently seen hunting in the reedbeds and saltmarshes, and peregrine falcons can be spotted hunting along the estuary.

In summer, the coastal grasslands and reedbeds host various species of butterflies, such as meadow brown, red admiral and small tortoiseshell. Moths like the belted beauty may also be spotted. The marshy areas and ponds within the reserve may also house amphibians such as common frogs and smooth newts. Mammals are also on the reserve and there are ample opportunities to look out to sea or search the ground for tracks to see what you can find. The estuary is one of the best places in North Wales to see common seals and grey seals. They haul out on the sandbanks, especially during the summer

months, and can often be seen basking in the sun or swimming in the waters. Although elusive, otters are known to frequent the reedbeds and saltmarshes, particularly during dawn or dusk, and their tracks can sometimes be seen along the riverbanks.

The RSPB part of the estuary is carefully managed while allowing the natural coastal processes to do their own thing. Practical conservation efforts are in place especially when it comes to species who rely upon the area. During the summer months, the shingle ridge has an electric fence erected to give the breeding birds such as little terns, ringed plovers and oystercatchers the best chance to nest away from disturbances. In the autumn and winter months, this area is roped off to allow roosting waders to rest peacefully without being disturbed. The volunteer wardens conduct patrols during high tides to ensure the birds are carefully monitored and cared for.

SCOTLAND

EDINBURGH

When it comes to Scottish wildlife, stags standing on moorland hilltops or pine martens peering above heather in secluded forests might spring to mind. However, it's not essential to hike through miles of isolated terrain to watch wildlife. With luck and good timing, it's possible to see a diverse mix of species in the middle of Scotland's capital city. The Water of Leith (page 182) passes diagonally through Edinburgh and has an unbroken pathway, suitable for walkers and cyclists, along its entire length. Rivers are vital channels for urban wildlife, often making it easy to spot a range of species along even the narrowest of waterways through built-up areas. One of the tucked-away places to explore along the Water of Leith is Warriston Cemetery (page 184) – an unassuming sanctuary where dozens of bird and insect species can be found.

Elsewhere around the city, nature reserves provide tranquillity away from the crowds. Hermitage of Braid (page 180) and Corstorphine Hill (page 186) offer chances for a leg stretch as buzzards wheel overhead and treecreepers hop up tree trunks. The grayling butterfly is a rewarding species to find in the stony grassland of Holyrood Park (page 178), where clusters of moss-coated rock offer shelter.

Lothian bus day tickets are ideal for hopping on and off all over the city. Edinburgh Waverley and Haymarket train stations provide links to many mainline stations across Britain, including Glasgow, Aberdeen and London.

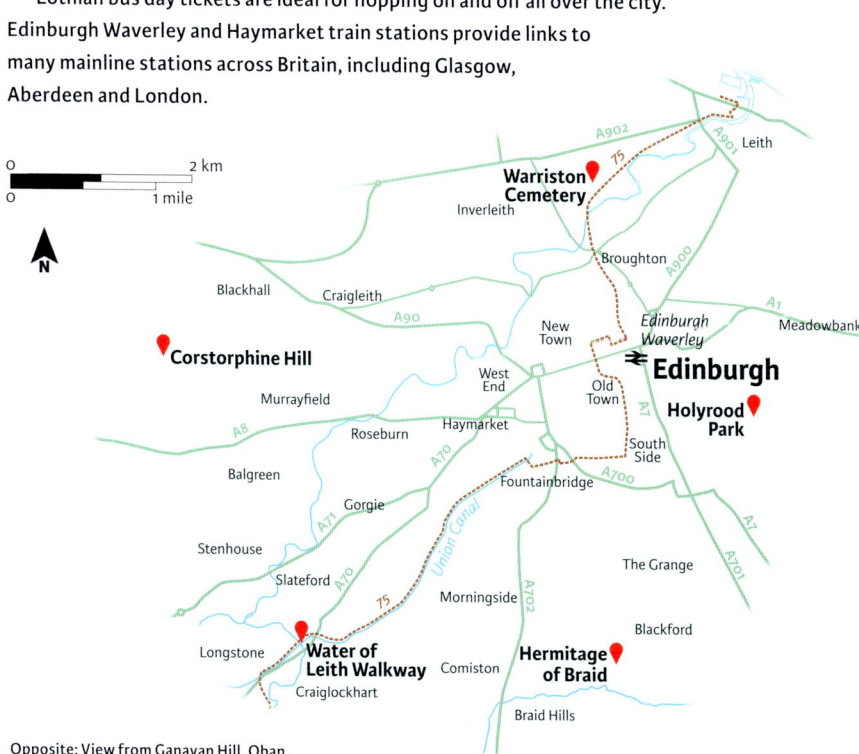

Opposite: View from Ganavan Hill, Oban.

HOLYROOD PARK

Queen's Drive, Edinburgh EH8 8HG • OS Explorer Map 350 • Grid ref NT270737 • What3Words: slot.pipe.paused (Palace of Holyroodhouse entrance)

How to get there: There are footpaths into Holyrood Park at many points around its circumference. The most popular starting point for a range of main routes, including the trail leading to Arthur's Seat, begins off Queen's Drive at the northern end. Buses do not reach any of the pedestrian entrances off Queen's Drive, but there is a small car park at this northern point for easy access. Here you'll also find an information kiosk with free map leaflets. • Alternatively, it's a 1-mile (1.6km) walk from Waverley station; the route northeast along Canongate passes Palace of Holyroodhouse and the striking Scottish Parliament Building on the way.

Access and conditions: The tarmac paths beside Queen's Drive are smooth for those with less mobility and have fine views of Holyrood's rocky hills. It's possible to see birds and butterflies in the grass and trees lining this road without venturing further. Paths inside the park, heading towards the hills, follow undulating trails of compacted earth that frequently become rocky and uneven. Sturdy shoes with good grip are recommended here, especially if you're ascending Arthur's Seat. Take care with steep drops and rough ground. • Toilets are available daily in the Holyrood Park Education Centre, located across the green from St Margaret's Loch at the northern end of the site. Exact opening times for these toilets change throughout the year – check Historic Environment Scotland for more information. All roads are closed to vehicles during the day on weekends. • Cycling is permitted on the roads and marked cycle paths only.

•• Holyrood Park contains grassland, crags, lochs and patches of bog. It's not a typical city park by any means; despite being in the centre of Edinburgh, it provides opportunities to hike or look for butterflies in an open landscape where the sounds of traffic are dulled.

At 263 hectares, this is the largest green space in the city and gets busy at the weekends and during school holidays. On spring and summer days in particular, a morning visit is best for peaceful wildlife spotting, especially if you're keen to avoid the crowds heading for the top of Arthur's Seat. This inactive volcano, standing 251m high, is what the majority of visitors to the park make a beeline for. It is topped with jagged, rusty red rocks and forms the main peak of a cluster of rocky hills within the park, offering a bird's-eye view of the city on a clear day.

Holyrood is considered one of the best spots for butterflies in central Scotland, making summer the optimal season to visit. On a sunny July day, stroll along the strip of long grass, nettles and clover fringing the northern boundary and you'll probably spot several small skippers. Despite its small size, this butterfly draws the eye with its bright orange wings, especially when perched on tall thistle heads. Unlike most butterflies, its forewings are angled above its hind wings when perched, giving it an unusual shape.

With a keen eye and lots of patience, you can also find the elusive grayling butterfly at Holyrood. These butterflies show a flash of orange in flight, but their mottled grey underwings blend seamlessly into lichen-coated rocks, which this park has in abundance. Butterfly Conservation hosts volunteer work parties to clear encroaching shrubs and keep the ground open for these expertly camouflaged pollinators. If you're interested in taking part, visit their website for information about any events or work parties planned.

Beyond Arthur's Seat, hidden behind Crow's Hill on the less-trodden southern half of the park, is Duddingston Loch. Rocks around the summit make way for gorse, blackberry bushes and the occasional rowan tree, where wrens can be heard singing. Once you reach the road – Queen's Drive again – aim for a shallow gravel staircase at the southeastern corner. This leads downhill to a set of stone and gravel steps beneath an avenue of trees, finishing at the loch.

Relatively few visitors venture down this side of Arthur's Seat, meaning Duddingston Loch is a tucked-away treat for peaceful waterside birdwatching. Usually, the first birds to pop up will be a mixture of mute swans, Canada geese, mallards and coots. However, explore the dense clumps of nettles and brambles surrounding the water and you'll find robins, wrens and chaffinches all year round, with the occasional blackcap during summer. Also during the warmer seasons, you might spot blue-tailed,

common blue and large red damselflies resting on flat leaves. Common ragwort dots the paths, clearly visible with its tall stems and bunches of yellow flower heads. Take a closer look at these in July and August and you might see cinnabar moth caterpillars among the petals. They have vibrant yellow and black stripes, indicating to birds that they are poisonous and best avoided.

HERMITAGE OF BRAID

Blackford Hill, Edinburgh EH9 3HJ • OS Explorer Map 350 • Grid ref NT255709 • What3Words: brick.chew.tens (Charterhall Road entrance)

How to get there: Take the Lothian 9 bus departing from The Mound stop MD (just off Princes Street) and disembark at Blackford Avenue after 18 minutes. Walk west down Charterhall Road for 460m until you reach the reserve on the left. There are several entrances, but this is the most direct route if arriving by bus from the city centre.
• For quicker access to the western side, including the Braid Burn path, take the Lothian 11 bus departing from Princes Street stop PV. After 20 minutes, disembark at South Morningside Primary School then turn left onto Greenbank Place and left again onto Braidburn Terrace. Bend right round the corner onto Braid Road and take the first left to enter the nature reserve.
Access and conditions: Some paths have steep inclines and steps, so those with reduced mobility would struggle to access the higher points of the reserve. However, there are several more accessible flat sections around Blackford Pond, from the Royal Observatory car park to the radio mast beside Blackford Hill, and a stretch following the Braid Burn from Braid Road to the Scout Bridge. • Toilets are available near Hermitage House, located around 0.25 miles (0.4km) from the Braid Road entrance.

•• A peaceful pocket of green, this Local Nature Reserve lies just over 2 miles (3.2km) from Waverley station. It is an undulating site, with tree-studded mounds and staircases embedded in the earth curving upwards past walls of volcanic rock in clearly defined layers.

Perhaps the best feature of the reserve is its habitat variety. Within its boundaries lie patches of mixed woodland, wetland, paddock, wildflower meadow and a pond dotted with ducks and swans. Its trees are also varied, in particular the broad-leaved species; look out for oak, ash, elm, beech, sycamore and horse chestnut, to name but a few.

Whiny whistles in the trees beside gravel footpaths draw a birdwatcher's eye to foraging coal tits, but visitors should also look down in case frogs or toads might be crossing underfoot. Although present in the reserve all year round, these amphibians are more likely to appear during spring and summer. This is when they emerge from hibernation and travel to the pond at the northern end of the reserve to breed. Frogs lay clumps of frogspawn, whereas toad spawn is produced in long strings.

The cat-like mews of buzzards sound

overhead as they circle the rocky tops of gorse-coated hills across the site, where flocks of long-tailed tits and goldfinches can also be found. In summer, speckled wood butterflies drift through scruffy bramble clearings with intermittent sunlight streaking through. Peacock and ringlet butterflies can also be seen in grassier, more open areas.

It's possible to follow the red waymarked route around the burn, the longer blue waymarked trail around the pond and Blackford Hill, or a combination of other paths throughout the reserve. There are plenty of spots to sit for a picnic or birdwatch.

The highest point of the reserve is the windswept grassy knoll of Blackford Hill (164m), located beside a radio mast. Clamber to the top to enjoy open views across the city. From here, dip back down into shady dells to reach the chattering Braid Burn that runs along the reserve's southern boundary – this is an ideal stretch for hot days when the canopy provides cool shade. The path weaves itself across the burn, switching from one side to the other via small footbridges. This is a great place to perch on the bank and look for a fishing heron, speeding dipper or grey wagtail bobbing on top of splashed pebbles. Towering walls of rock along this section transform it into a jungle-like gorge with an abundance of bracken and soggy moss.

Anyone who would like to get involved with activities and events taking place at the reserve can follow 'Friends of the Hermitage of Braid & Blackford Hill' on Facebook, or keep an eye out for notices posted on the reserve boards. One of the key maintenance tasks carried out here is the removal of invasive plants to help native species thrive.

WATER OF LEITH WALKWAY

Visitor Centre: Lanark Rd, Edinburgh EH14 1TQ • OS Explorer Map 350 • Grid ref NT221707 • What3Words: going.cook.friday

How to get there: The Water of Leith Walkway Visitor Centre is 4 miles (6.4km) west of Edinburgh's city centre, just off the A70. Both the Lothian 34 bus (departing from Princes Street stop PP) and the 44 bus (departing from Waterloo Place stop ZJ) arrive just outside it. • It is possible to cycle the entire Walkway route, with much of it overlapping National Cycle Network Route 75. • For those looking to walk or cycle one way, the tram service connects Edinburgh Airport with the Port of Leith, covering much of the walkway route.
Access and conditions: Because it stretches across the entire city, the Water of Leith Walkway can be reached via many different access points. A few have stone steps leading down from main roads, but the visitor centre is accessible for all. The centre is also dog-friendly and has toilets and baby-changing facilities. The path terrain varies depending on the section, but is well maintained and clearly signposted throughout.
• The sections accessible for wheelchair users are colour-coded in full on the map, available to purchase in the visitor centre (open 10:00–16:00 daily) or online.

Dean Village.

•• Stretching from the village of Balerno to the port district of Leith, the Water of Leith cuts a diagonal line across the entirety of Edinburgh. More than 80 bird species have been recorded here, with resident species including dippers, kingfishers, goosanders and grey herons. Wildflowers and diverse tree types, including patches of ancient woodland, line the wooded banks either side of the water. Although they are trickier to spot, the river itself thrums with fish including brown trout and bullhead, hunted by the occasional otter.

Established in 2002, the 13-mile (20.9km) Water of Leith Walkway trail has brown signs dotted along the route for visitors to follow. This enables walkers, cyclists and even horse riders on some sections to remain close to the river all the way through the city. There is the occasional detour across busy roads, but much of the walkway drifts away from main thoroughfares so it often feels like you are not in a city at all. The speed of the river constantly changes, sometimes rushing over pebbles and other times flowing serenely enough to cast perfect reflections of houses on the opposite bank. Along these slower stretches is a hushed soundscape of woodpigeons and hidden wrens.

One of the best features of the walkway is its variety; it is possible to admire both tumbling weirs and flat-calm meandering channels in just a short stretch. Because there are so many crossings from one side of the river to the other, the walkway passes over and beneath a diverse range of bridges. A particularly photogenic example is the Coltbridge Viaduct, a vast triple-arched bridge around 3 miles (4.8km) downstream of the visitor centre. With its abundance of smooth rocks jutting out of the water, the stretch of river within the viaduct's shadow is ideal for watching dippers foraging in the shallows.

With so much distance available to cover, a good place to start your exploration is the visitor centre, a renovated schoolhouse situated roughly halfway along the route. Open daily, the centre has information about the trail and the river's history and wildlife. In addition, there is a free exhibition, an interactive zone for children, a gift shop and a community café (closed over the Christmas period).

An established volunteer team is involved with maintaining the walkway and its wild landscape, with tasks carried out in all seasons including river cleanups,

invasive plant removal, tree planting and path repairs. Those interested in taking part are invited to fill out an application form on the website.

WARRISTON CEMETERY

Easter Warriston, Edinburgh EH7 4QY • OS Explorer Map 350 • Grid ref NT251757 • What3Words: curvy.lowest.barks

How to get there: Take the Lothian 9 bus departing from The Mound stop MB. Disembark at Royal Botanic Garden after 10 minutes – from here, it's a 0.5-mile (0.8km) walk northwest on the B901 to the cemetery entrance. Turn right onto Warriston Gardens; at the end of this road, cross a small bridge and bend right into the cemetery.
• Two cycle paths follow the western and southeastern boundaries of the cemetery, Goldenacre Path and Warriston Path, the latter doubling up as National Cycle Network Route 75 that cuts through most of the city centre. Because of these paths' layout around several footbridges, the only official way to join them is from the same access point for the cemetery mentioned above.
Access and conditions: Established footpaths can be found throughout, although some are narrower than others and may be muddy after heavy rain, so take care on any slippery ground. • There are no facilities on site.

•• Across the road from Edinburgh's Botanic Garden is a more secluded green space that is easy to miss if you are not looking for it. Warriston Cemetery lies 2 miles (3.2km) north of Waverley station and is close to the Water of Leith, with narrow winding gravel footpaths between nettle patches, log piles and blackberry clumps all full of wildlife on a small scale. Discoloured headstones stand at jaunty angles or lie flat altogether, camouflaged by lichen and skirts of ivy.

The cemetery is split into an open, more modern section near the entrance off Warriston Gardens, and a far more interesting corner dating back to the nineteenth century on the other side. With little uniformity and plenty of greenery, this older part gives birds and insects free rein to take over.

At first, you'll likely see magpies perching on the heads of stone sculptures or grey squirrels bending the branches above, but stay a while and more diverse wildlife might appear. Within just a few patches of thistles, foxgloves, rosebay willowherb and buddleia, you may encounter long-tailed tits, goldcrests, great spotted woodpeckers, blackcaps, wrens, bullfinches and the occasional kestrel drifting through a rare gap in the canopy. When the light fades, the calls of tawny owls can also be heard. Visit in spring for daffodils and bluebells that add pops of colour to the greenery.

An intriguing find here is a large gathering of orange ladybirds. Often found near sycamore and ash woodland, these insects overwinter in Warriston Cemetery. If you've got keen eyes, you might spot clusters of them in the shady nooks of the headstones.

Because parts of this site are so wild and dense, it is easy to lose your sense of direction and you could

Orange ladybird

thread your way between the jumble of gravestones for hours. This gives the place a real 'secret garden' feel. There is very little management, meaning leaf litter and deadwood are left as food and shelter for a variety of wildlife. A towering stone wall encloses the cemetery on all four sides, so you can wander freely, reassured that you can't get lost for long.

The smooth tarmac of the Goldenacre and Warriston cycle paths pass beneath dense tree cover including some magnificent mature birches. The stone walls on either side are only just visible through a thick coating of ivy. All this dense foliage is good habitat for great tits, blue tits and treecreepers, the last of which may take a while to locate despite their persistent calls.

The cemetery only covers some 5.6 hectares, but with so many looping and overlapping trails, it's easy to spend several hours here if you are keen to hunt for insects or small birds.

CORSTORPHINE HILL

> Corstorphine Rd, Edinburgh EH12 6UD • OS Explorer Map 350 • Grid ref NT214730 • What3Words: quarrel.match.circle (Corstorphine Road entrance)
>
> **How to get there:** The most direct access is via a subtle pedestrian entrance shaded by trees at the bustling junction of Western Terrace, Balgreen Road and Corstorphine Road, towards the western side of the city. Several buses pass this access point including the Lothian 25, departing from Princes Street Scott Monument stop PS and stopping at Balgreen Road after 22 minutes. It is also possible to enter from the northern side of the site via the single-lane road that branches off Ravelston Dykes Road, near Murrayfield Golf Club.
>
> **Access and conditions:** The hill is open 24/7 year-round; Clermiston Tower is open to the public 14:00–16:00 on Sundays, May to September. • The terrain is undulating with a few steep sections with staircases built into the earth in places. • There are no toilets on site.

•• Corstorphine Hill is Edinburgh's largest public woodland and stands on the city's western side, 3.5 miles (5.6km) from Waverley station. At a height of 161m, it is not overly high, but still has elevated views over the nearby suburbs of Balgreen, Blackhall, Murrayfield and Corstorphine. Through breaks in the trees, views of other prominent city landmarks can be admired, including Arthur's Seat and the port district of Leith, overlooking the vast Firth of Forth. The hill is a designated Local Nature Reserve.

The site is crossed by the John Muir Way – a walking and cycling route spanning 134 miles (216km) from Scotland's west to east coasts. The woodland contains a mix of tree types including oak, ash, beech, and a particular abundance of elm and sycamore. All of this dense canopy is good cover for exploring on both rainy and hot days.

From the southern entrance point on Corstorphine Road, follow the footpath

Clermiston Tower.

Speckled wood.

uphill into alternating patches of shaded woodland and scrubby grassland, where chaffinches rummage through gorse bushes and buzzards, sparrowhawks and kestrels hunt on the wing. Depending on the season, you might hear the sharp *pik* call and echoed drumming of great spotted woodpeckers, or glimpse the soft tail of a red squirrel in the canopy. During summer, the air is full of the sounds of bumblebees wafting around the yellow flowers of common ragwort, and many speckled wood butterflies rest in nettle patches, representing their name well by choosing spots that are dappled with sunlight. Flora enthusiasts should keep their eyes peeled for rare species such as lords-and-ladies, small balsam and common spotted orchid.

Corstorphine Hill is located right next to Edinburgh Zoo. While submerged under the trees, it's easy to forget how close you are to this attraction until you catch a surprising glimpse of zebras through the fence line on the western side.

As well as sheltering plenty of wildlife,

Corstorphine Hill is also protected because of its geological and historical significance. Some of the exposed rocks found here bear cup marks that were carved some 3,000 years ago.

Corstorphine Hill is a considerable expanse from end to end, but even a stroll would be enough to sample both its wooded and open habitats. One of the key features shown on a map of the site is Clermiston Tower, which can be found near several masts at the southern end of the woods. It was constructed in 1871 to celebrate the centenary of Sir Walter Scott's birth and was presented to the city in 1932, marking 100 years since the poet and playwright's death. Visitors can climb the tower during summer (see opening times above) and reach an even higher vantage point over the city and the Firth of Forth. The tower is run by volunteers, who also host guided walks covering the history, geology and wildlife of the reserve. Check the Facebook page – Friends of Corstorphine Hill – to find out what's going on.

Another, more concealed, feature of the reserve is a small walled garden, close to Clermiston Road on the western side of the site. The area once stood neglected and overgrown, but was restored by volunteers in 2001 and is now open to the public daily. With benches tucked beneath curling branches of buddleia and tiny footbridges over a miniature patch of marshy wetland, it's a peaceful and secluded spot to rest partway along your walk through the reserve.

DUNDEE

Pockets of wildlife can be found all over the city of Dundee, from great spotted woodpeckers in the canopy of Templeton Woods (page 195), to wheatears scurrying along grass verges in Riverside Nature Park (page 191) and roe deer peering through bulrushes in Trottick Mill Ponds (page 197). Rescued from dereliction, a section of old railway line known as the Miley (page 194) is now a 1-mile (1.6km) wildlife channel with goldfinches and rosebay willowherb flashing pink in the sun. Den o' Mains (page 199), in the centre of Caird Park, provides a place to rest amid grey herons, bullfinches and pond skaters. Across the River Tay is the sprawling expanse of Tentsmuir (page 200), offering sandy beaches and chances to see lapwings, eiders and grayling butterflies.

Cyclists are well cared for in Dundee. The Esplanade path, following the southern edge overlooking the River Tay, overlaps with National Cycle Network Route 1. On the western side of the Tay Road Bridge, this swaps to National Cycle Network Route 77.

The Dundee Green Circular path loops for 25 miles (40.2km) around the city and connects Riverside Nature Park, Trottick Mill Ponds and many other attractions. Some of the route follows main roads, but much of it occupies shared-use paths with varying terrain. A Dundee Cycle Map is available for free online, showing the Green Circular route and other trails to follow.

Trains to Dundee arrive from all over Scotland, including services from Edinburgh and Aberdeen.

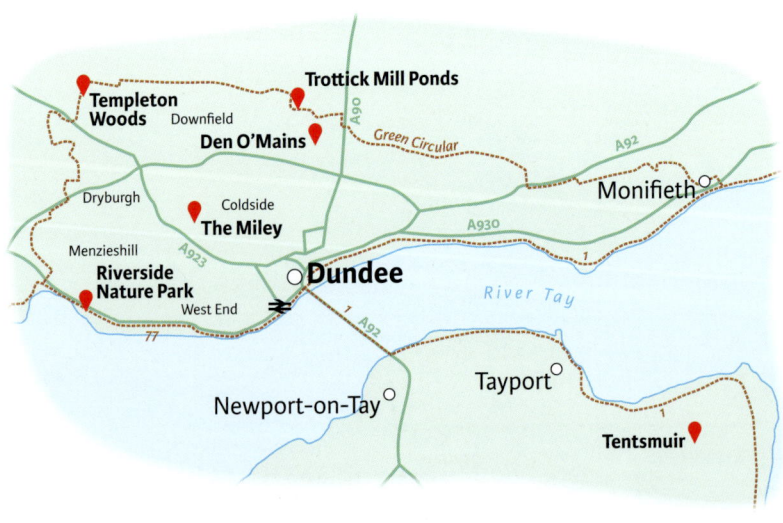

RIVERSIDE NATURE PARK

Wright Avenue, Dundee DD2 1QE • OS Explorer Map 380 • Grid ref NO359296
• What3Words: branching.poetic.sweat

How to get there: Take the Stagecoach 16 bus departing from Whitehall Street stop 3. After 14 minutes, disembark at Riverside Place and it's a 0.5-mile (0.8km) walk south across the A85 into the Riverside Recycling Centre. Follow the driveway around the corner to the right to reach the nature park entrance. • National Cycle Network Route 77 runs straight past the entrance to the park on the A85.
Access and conditions: There are firm gravel paths throughout, which are accessible for all, including cyclists. Most of the site covers flat ground with only gentle inclines. • There are no toilets available on site. • Dundee City Council states that dogs must be kept on leads in the reserve from April to the start of August, to protect ground-nesting birds during their breeding season.

Riverside Nature Park lies 3.5 miles (5.6km) west of Dundee station, overlooking the River Tay and the adjacent Tay Estuary. It offers a surprising amount of variety for its small size, with several habitats mingling over a short walk.

After leaving the car park behind, follow a corridor of gorse, buddleia and long grass that's transformed into a butterfly thoroughfare in summer. Along this short stretch alone, it doesn't require much effort to see small tortoiseshell,

Comma.

meadow brown, comma and large white flitting around at once.

One of the paths leads up to a viewpoint overlooking the River Tay, with the small village of Invergowrie visible to the west. The information boards at the viewpoint can act as a handy perch for wheatears. These insect-eaters are summer visitors to Britain and spend much of their foraging time close to the ground, standing upright and showing an obvious white rump in flight.

North of this viewpoint lies a meadow, attracting other summer birds such as common whitethroats, as well as resident goldfinches and blue tits. The unmistakable spring serenade of the skylark can be heard well here. These birds ascend until they become hovering specks in the sky, their wings fluttering rapidly.

From March to September, keep an eye out for ospreys on the reserve. If they're not mobbed by gulls, they might be gliding over the meadow on their way to hunt on the estuary. From the screen acting as a bird hide in the far northwestern corner of the site, overlooking Invergowrie Bay, visitors with binoculars can look for grey herons and a range of waders including redshanks and lapwings. Depending on the tide, they might be feeding on the mudflats or resting further up.

Several ponds and a lochan in the Highland cow grazing fields beside Riverside Avenue are worth investigating for dragonflies, damselflies and amphibians – frogs, toads and smooth newts have all been recorded here.

THE MILEY

Balfield Rd, Dundee DD3 6AH • OS Explorer Map 380 • Grid ref NO383314 • What3Words: lows.safely.gazed (Old King's Cross Road entrance)

How to get there: The southern access point for the Miley is a 2-mile (3.2km) walk from Dundee station. You can reduce walking time by catching one of several buses, including the Xplore Dundee 17 service from Nethergate stop 1. Disembark at Ancrum Road. From here, take the first right onto Loon's Road, then turn left onto Old King's Cross Road. This becomes the footpath for the Miley shortly afterwards. • The reserve can also be accessed from the northern entrance point off Clepington Road, or halfway along via a descending staircase off Harefield Road.

Access and conditions: The Miley consists of a single footpath following even gravel terrain from end to end, which is suitable for cyclists. • There are no facilities on site.

•• A wonderfully random urban nature reserve in linear miniature, the Miley is a single footpath dissecting an industrial estate in the northern end of Dundee's city centre. Managed by the Scottish Wildlife Trust, this unassuming site has dense tree cover featuring birch, hawthorn and rowan, hedgerows and low-lying green shrubbery either side of the path.

Despite being surrounded by busy roads, the avenue of trees lining the Miley does an excellent job of muffling the traffic, often making birdsong the loudest sound. It's a good location for hot days,

when the canopy shelters the path from strong sunlight. Despite its dappled ground, during summer its bed of nettles and flowers attracts butterflies such as peacocks and large whites.

Long-tailed tits, dunnocks and chaffinches are commonly seen, with the occasional greenfinch blending into the tree cover. Goldfinches forage at the treetops, using their specialised bills to tweeze seeds from birch, alder and thistles.

You might glimpse a bullfinch, whose quiet call can be tricky to hear if you don't pick out its vibrant plumage first – pinkish for males and mushroom brown for females. Extra colour can be found on the tall, pink blooms of rosebay willowherb, known for its ability to thrive on unforgiving terrain including burned ground. This inspired another of its common names: fireweed.

The Miley follows the route of an old railway line, used by both freight and passenger trains until 1967. Telegraph poles from this period are still visible, now half-submerged and used as posts for nest boxes. Today, the reserve is a short and sweet refuge for wildlife and walkers, but it used to be a derelict dumping ground. The Scottish Wildlife Trust began transforming the space in 1992 – after extensive input from volunteers, rubbish was replaced by trees, wildflowers and shrubs.

A male (left) and female bullfinch.

TEMPLETON WOODS

> Coupar Angus Rd, Dundee DD3 0QG • OS Explorer Map 380 • Grid ref NO359334
> • What3Words: once.noon.order (Green Circular access point)
>
> **How to get there.** Take either the Stagecoach bus 57 or 59, both departing from Overgate Shopping Centre. Disembark at Birkhill Inn after 19 minutes and return southeast down the A923 for 640m until you reach the Green Circular cycle path (see page 190) on the left. This cuts into the southern end of Templeton Woods and soon joins the pink waymarked trail.
> **Access and conditions:** There are established footpaths of varying smoothness and width that may be muddy after heavy rain, but are suitable for both walkers and cyclists.
> • A small building near the car park has toilets, which are open 09:00–16:30.

•• With decent walking boots, Templeton Woods is ideal for rainy day walks. The site is located 4.5 miles (7.2km) northwest of the train station. Despite being muddy in places, the pattering canopy shelters visitors from the worst of the rain, and the greens of the leaves, moss and bracken zing even brighter when wet. Also best appreciated on soggy days is the abundance of lying deadwood. This enables fungi to sprout, so take the time to peer at stumps and overgrown logs for fascinating formations.

A chain-link pattern of looping footpaths branches off in different directions. There are three main colour-coded trails: pink and blue cover the eastern side of the forest, while the yellow trail spreads north. Each trail threads through an assortment of oak, beech and spruce trees, with wooden footbridges crossing the occasional shallow ditch. Foxgloves flower in summer, with wild raspberries following close behind.

Amongst all the lush greenery, keep an eye out for a flash of orange as a red squirrel skirts up a trunk, bushy tail twitching. There are feeders dotted throughout, but these inquisitive animals can show up anywhere, so watch for telltale rustling or perch on a bench to wait for them.

You'll hear plenty of birds, although it's tricky to actually spot them between the branches. The calls of blue tits and coal tits filter through the canopy, as do the sharp sounds of great spotted woodpeckers, crisp whistles of goldcrests, and cries of buzzards overhead.

For those looking to explore the site at a quicker pace, the Templeton Tangle bike trails situated at the northeastern end of the woods have a range of tracks of varying difficulty to follow.

TROTTICK MILL PONDS

Claverhouse Rd, Dundee DD4 9DD • OS Explorer Map 380 • Grid ref NO407336 • What3Words: took.notes.stud (Claverhouse Old Road entrance)

How to get there: There are four pedestrian entry points to the reserve, branching off Claverhouse Old Road, Mansion Drive, William Fitzgerald Way and Millburn Gardens. All of these join the Dundee Green Circular cycle route (see page 190) that passes through the reserve on its 25-mile (40.2km) route around the city. • The Xplore Dundee 18 bus departs from Albert Square stop 3 in the city centre and stops at Trottick Mains on Claverhouse Road after 23 minutes. Turn north and the reserve is directly in front of you from here.

Access and conditions: The smooth tarmac surface of the Green Circular cycle route makes the paths around Trottick Ponds accessible for all. • Dogs must be kept under control to avoid disturbing wildlife. • There are no toilets on site.

•• About 3 miles (4.8km) north of the train station, Trottick Mill Ponds Local Nature Reserve has a path looping between the fast-flowing Dighty Burn on the outside and two ponds on the inside. Those arriving from the southern access point will pass over the burn first. The trickle of water over clusters of pebbles is a soothing soundscape. While crossing the small footbridge, be sure to peer down at these rocks through the low-hanging canopy, as a dipper or a grey wagtail might be perching on them.

In addition to the burn and ponds, the reserve has dense vegetation and a mix of mature trees, which chirp with hidden great spotted woodpeckers. Roe deer sometimes appear in the field just north of the ponds at dawn and dusk. Thistles, brambles and blackberry bushes grow in a meadow patch in the centre of the site, attracting butterflies in summer and sheltering mice, voles and shrews, which you may glimpse if you are lucky. Beside the meadow, a forest of butterbur sprouts in summer. This low-lying plant has huge leaves resembling rhubarb, and was named after its historic purpose of wrapping butter. In winter the leaves die back.

Mute swans, coots and moorhens are present all year, making this a popular reserve for families looking to see them up close. Tufted ducks and goosanders appear in winter, while swallows and pipistrelle bats snatch flies off the water in summer. Frogs, toads and newts make their homes in the ponds too.

The loop around both ponds barely covers 0.5 miles (0.8km), so it's worth staying longer to wait for a possible kingfisher sighting. Conveniently for birdwatchers, kingfishers sometimes announce their presence with a sharp, high-pitched whistle before zipping past.

The site was built over two centuries ago as a water source for a local linen mill. The ponds are separated by the remains of the narrow mill lade, now topped with reeds and bulrushes. Vast sheets of material were dried in what's now the meadow area beside the ponds. Because it was kept short for this purpose, a range of wildflowers have been able to grow here. The Dighty Burn was used to power a water wheel, and remains of the mill works are still visible, including old sluice gates and water channels dug to divert the flow.

The 14-mile (22.5km) Dighty was once an essential component in Dundee industry, providing water for more than 30 mills. In the past it was highly polluted, but today its improved condition is proven by the range of wildlife that can be found along and within it.

Volunteers take part in many activities at this site, including path maintenance and wildlife surveys. Those interested in getting involved should check the reserve's Facebook page for any upcoming work parties.

DEN O' MAINS

Caird Park, Dundee DD4 9BX • OS Explorer Map 380 • Grid ref NO410330
• What3Words: garden.future.game

How to get there: Take the Stagecoach 21 bus from Forum Centre stop 3. Disembark at Claverhouse Road and walk west for 0.5 miles (0.8km) through Caird Park. Follow a tarmac single-track road to the car park beside Mains Castle. A footpath runs beside the Gelly Burn to the pond. A traffic-free cycle path loops around Caird Park including the Den o' Mains section.
Access and conditions: Well-established footpaths link the main roads cutting through Caird Park with the pond itself, following even terrain. There is the occasional slope into the forested areas, but most of the tracks lie flat. • There are no public toilets available near Den o' Mains.

•• Caird Park lies 3 miles (4.8km) north of Dundee station and less than 1 mile (1.6km) south of Trottick Mill Ponds (page 197). Many of its 111 hectares are taken up by a golf course, football pitch and Mains Castle (a sixteenth-century structure now used for weddings), but nevertheless plenty of wildlife can still be found here. The best place to explore is the Gelly Burn, cutting horizontally through the park. This narrow water channel feeds the larger Dighty Burn that runs along Caird Park's northern boundary, beside Claverhouse Road. Within Caird Park, in a section known as Den o' Mains, the Gelly slows to form a pond that's cinched in the middle with a miniature island at each end, looking like a 'Zorro' mask when viewed on a map.

Despite running parallel between two major roads, it's easy to lose all sense of

Treecreeper.

them along the string of forest paths here. A mix of trees including rowan, birch and horse chestnut creates a dense canopy. Combined with equally mixed and condensed vegetation closer to the ground, the place has a closed-in feel that muffles city sounds. Patches of long grass provide plenty of dense habitat for roe deer to shelter. The leisurely burn tumbles over rocks, inviting grey wagtails to perch. Moorhens thread through them, their chicken-like clucks often giving them away before they emerge. Shyer water birds here include grey herons, often standing motionless at the edge of the water, and kingfishers. Pond skaters and water boatmen skim the surface of the pond, waiting for vibrations before pouncing on their prey. Dragonflies, damselflies and tadpoles show up throughout spring and summer – keep an eye on your feet for any passing frogs or toads.

Forest paths loop around the pond edges and also climb up slightly, staying parallel to the burn but offering a higher vantage point. Scan the trees here and listen for more elusive birds such as bullfinches. Within the shadows of the trees, you may glimpse a treecreeper sidling up trunks in short hops. Their flecked brown backs enable them to vanish against the bark, but their white bellies may give them away. Stay still a while and keep your eyes peeled for movement, and there's usually a treecreeper nearby, living up to its name.

Although the Gelly is the best place to look for most wildlife in Caird Park, the old cemetery is also worth visiting. Situated beside the castle across the tarmac from Den o' Mains, it's a good spot to watch pipistrelle bats on summer evenings.

TENTSMUIR NATIONAL NATURE RESERVE

Tayport DD6 9YB • OS Explorer Map 371 • Grid ref NO467278 • What3Words: crossing.crouching.saved (Kinshaldy car park)

How to get there: From Dundee station, take the Stagecoach 42A bus and disembark at Shanwell Road South in Tayport after 25 minutes. Be aware that not all services pass this stop throughout the day so be sure to check before you travel. At Shanwell Road South, the estuary will appear directly ahead. From here, it's approximately 2 miles (3.2km) to Tentsmuir Point at the northeastern edge of the reserve. National Cycle Network Route 1 wraps around this corner before turning south into the forest. • For those with limited mobility, the Kinshaldy car park at the southern side lies just a few hundred metres away from a fine sandy beach with tufts of marram grass. There are no bus links to this part of the reserve.

> **Access and conditions:** A network of flat, firm trails makes this site suitable for cyclists and wheelchair users. • Toilets are available in Tayport and at the Tentsmuir car park at Kinshaldy Beach, although note that this is at the southern end of the site so several miles from the bus link in Tayport.

•• This vast coastal reserve lies on the opposite side of the River Tay from Dundee, just southeast of the town of Tayport. Visitors could spend several days exploring Tentsmuir. It's a place for sitting as well as walking, with a constantly changing landscape of open grassland, swathes of meadow, shifting sand dunes and a fringe of mudflats beside the Tay Estuary. Amongst these are wedges of layered woodland, where orange-tinged pines, short birches and the occasional bunch of bell heather take turns in drawing the eye.

There are opportunities for wildlife watching at Tentsmuir throughout the year, but its impressive insect list makes it notable as a summer site. Recorded species include 18 butterflies, 270 moths and more than 460 beetles.

At the northern boundary near Tayport, a range of birds forage along sandbars revealed as the tide drifts out. Visit in spring and summer for lapwings and a stream of swallows and house martins, as well as resident grey herons and curlews.

Occasionally during summer, the gulls all lift at once, often a convenient warning to birdwatchers that an osprey has arrived. In the flurry, look for a pair of longer, proportionately slimmer wings and you might spot this fish-eating raptor hunting in the estuary. It is often worth looking for ospreys on a rising tide as the fish are drawn in. They also land on the mud at low tide, tearing into their catches.

At the northeastern corner of the reserve is Tentsmuir Point, where grey and common seals haul out on the beach to rest. You'll often hear their melancholy singing before spotting them. As always

with seals, keep your distance to avoid disturbing them and watch using binoculars or a spotting scope if possible. During winter, a variety of wading birds probe the foreshore here, including grey plovers and bar-tailed godwits. Scan the waves further out for eiders and long-tailed ducks.

From Tentsmuir Point, you can walk south into mixed woodland habitat. After 2.5 miles (4km), you'll reach the Kinshaldy entrance mentioned earlier. During summer, the open tracks here attract speckled wood and ringlet butterflies, basking on bracken leaves. Submerged within the forest are the crumbled remains of a nineteenth-century ice house, once used to store freshly caught salmon. Butterfly enthusiasts will want to gather here in particular. In and around a patch of wildflowers including bright yellow ragwort, there might be common blue, small heath, meadow brown and perhaps a dark green fritillary if you don't blink and miss it.

Between the woodland and the beach is a broad strip of grassland, where swifts and swallows soar and swoop. Below them, expertly camouflaged in the lichen, you might find a grayling butterfly. Another good place to look for graylings is Edinburgh's Holyrood Park (page 178).

There are frequent events at Tentsmuir, including guided walks and volunteering opportunities. To find out more, contact the reserve manager by visiting the NatureScot website.

Common seals.

Grayling.

DUMFRIES

The market town of Dumfries lies close to the Solway Firth, an inlet dividing the Dumfries and Galloway council area from Cumbria. Within the town itself, a walk or cycle beside the River Nith (page 204) may bring sightings of a kingfisher, grey heron or otter. When temperatures cool and days shorten into autumn, the honks of droves of geese arriving in Scotland to overwinter fill the air. Most commonly seen are pink-footed and greylag geese, but it is the large flocks of barnacle geese visiting RSPB Mersehead (page 208) that give the reserve its internationally important status. At sunrise, these monochromatic birds fly inland from their nightly roost on the sandflats to forage in the fields. Many migratory ducks also arrive here, with wigeons being particularly numerous.

Just outside Dumfries at Lockerbie, you may share woodland clearings with red squirrels at Eskrigg Nature Reserve (page 212). At nearby Castle Loch (page 210), sprays of vibrant autumnal foliage are reflected in the water, while great crested grebes perform their courtship dances in spring. The broad sandy plains of Carsethorn and Southerness beaches (page 207) are some of the best locations for wintering wading birds on the Solway Firth. Not far from here is Kirkconnell Flow (page 205), a special place with highly threatened ancient raised bog habitat.

Buses from Dumfries connect neighbouring settlements such as Lockerbie, Carsethorn and Southerness. Trains at Dumfries station arrive regularly from Carlisle and Glasgow.

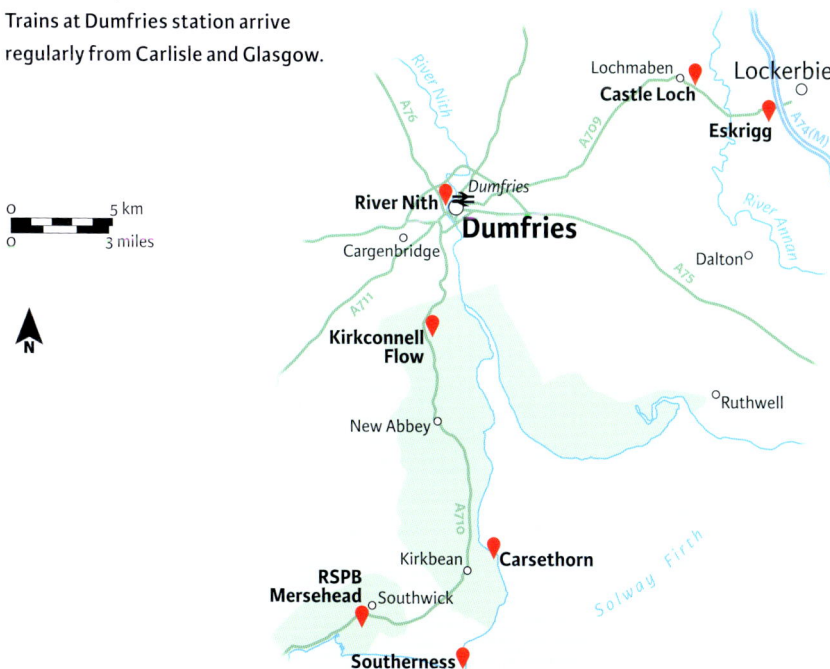

RIVER NITH

White Sands, Dumfries DG1 2RS • OS Explorer Map 313 • Grid ref NX969760 • What3Words: keyboards.echo.country (Devorgilla Bridge)

How to get there: The River Nith winds around the entire western side of the town of Dumfries, but the popular section at the White Sands car park is just 0.5 miles (0.8km) from the train station. Get there by heading southwest, following St Mary's Street, English Street and Bank Street, until the water appears just beyond the A781.
Access and conditions: At White Sands, the pavement beside the road serves as a walk and cycle path for the river, following all-access tarmac at the water's edge that also overlaps with National Cycle Network Route 7. • Toilets are available in Dumfries.

•• For urban wildlife watching in the centre of Dumfries, all a visitor needs to do is amble along the River Nith. Stretching 70 miles (113km) from East Ayrshire to the Solway Firth, the Nith is Scotland's seventh longest river.

A good place to start your explorations is a tumbling weir known as the Caul, located beside the White Sands car park. The Caul is overlooked by the pedestrianised Devorgilla Bridge, its stone arches casting a striking reflection.

One of the first birds you'll likely spot on the Caul is a grey heron standing with its feet submerged in the white water surging down the weir. Wintering goosanders and goldeneyes also dive for fish and crustaceans here. Dabbling mallards are easy spots, but treecreepers and wrens are more challenging as they forage in the avenue of scrub pressed against the stone wall lining the river. Look up at the right time and a kingfisher might be speeding by, its sharp, high-pitched call audible even above the rushing water. Grey wagtails flutter in and out of the waterlogged grass screening the sandy banks. Salmon leap up the Caul during October and November.

Perhaps surprisingly for such an urban

stretch of river, otter sightings are frequent along the Nith. These typically elusive mustelids aren't nearly as shy in Dumfries as they are elsewhere, and can sometimes be seen right by the path. If they're not diving underwater for fish, they might be porpoising out of it with energetic curved leaps. When the river floods, they feed on washed-up eels, attracting the attention of nearby herons which perch on the wall above, hoping to snag the otters' catch. Although they glance up at human spectators watching from the walkways, the otters here may forage confidently close, spinning in the shallows with a flick of the tail.

KIRKCONNELL FLOW NATURE RESERVE

Dumfries DG2 8HD • OS Explorer Map 313 • Grid ref NX961700 • What3Words: airbrush.spilled.footpath

How to get there: Take the Houston Coaches 372 bus departing from Dumfries Loreburne Centre and disembark at Mabie Forest after 12 minutes. From here, it's a 0.5-mile (0.8km) walk to the car park at Kirkconnell Flow. Head south on the A710, then branch left downhill at the brown reserve sign.
Access and conditions: Although short, the terrain of the woodland trail is tricky in places. It mostly follows a compacted earth track in the forest, but has thick roots over some sections as well as steps up onto the boardwalks covering muddier ground. • There are no toilets available on site.

•• This unassuming reserve, 5 miles (8 km) south of Dumfries, is managed by NatureScot. It is dominated by ancient raised bog, one of the world's most threatened habitats. A small circular trail stretches barely more than 1 mile (1.6km) through deciduous woodland, but despite its short length it passes through diverse habitats. At the forest's eastern edge, walkers can view the vast expanse of bog the reserve is known for.

Before entering the woods, scan the trees around the car park for chaffinches, blue tits, coal tits, wrens, bullfinches or a solitary nuthatch, all of which can show well even on overcast autumn days. During summer, look out for wall butterflies in this spot. Named for its habit of perching on walls, this orange and brown-striped species often basks on stony surfaces.

Once on the narrow, winding footpath leading into the forest, admire oak, holly, birch and other species merging with hip-high banks of bracken and fungi

Wall butterfly.

crammed into soggy stumps. Deeper into the forest, the birches blend to pines and the bracken to heather and blaeberry.

One loop of the trail joins a boardwalk across a boggy section. In autumn, bunches of bell heather and two-toned birches of orange and purple bring fiery splashes of colour. The mixture of trees and alternating sun and shade makes this area suitable for a range of wildlife – you might see the short, branched antlers of roe bucks poking above the bracken, or glimpse an adder in the undergrowth. During spring, the trees echo with the calls of cuckoos and the drumming of great spotted woodpeckers. Also on warm days in spring and summer, look out for green hairstreak and large heath butterflies, or dragonflies hovering above boggy areas.

Roughly halfway around the circular route, the path emerges from the treeline and the raised bog comes into view. Restoration work is ongoing at the site – visitors should keep off the bog's wet ground because of the fragility of this habitat. However, it's still possible to admire green, red and purple sphagnum mosses freckled with the bobbing white tufts of cotton-grass. A variety of plant life emerges here during the warmer months, including the pale pink, bulb-like flowers of bog rosemary.

The trail fringes the bog's perimeter before returning through the forest to the start point.

SOUTHERNESS AND CARSETHORN

> **Southerness lighthouse: DG2 8AZ; Carsethorn car park: DG2 8DS • OS Explorer Map 313 • Grid refs NX977543 (Southerness), NX993598 (Carsethorn) • What3Words: playful.convinced.fattening (Southerness), pulse.unwound.masks (Carsethorn)**
>
> **How to get there:** The coastal villages of Southerness and Carsethorn are situated south of Dumfries, 16 miles (25.7km) and 13.5 miles (21.7km) respectively. Both can be reached by taking the Houston Coaches 372 bus from Dumfries Loreburne Centre. The service branches off the A710 to Carsethorn after 31 minutes, then returns to the main road for another 10 minutes before arriving in Southerness. Once you reach one of the sites, you can walk to the other via a coast path stretching some 4.25 miles (6.8km). It follows the beach at times so is not suitable for wheelchairs; be sure to check the tide before setting off, as some sections are not always accessible. • Alternatively, the cycle route follows the same roads as if approaching by car, via the A710.
>
> **Access and conditions:** The Carsethorn bus stop is within a tarmac car park, so visitors can set up a scope or watch through binoculars on the grass edge here without even walking down onto the sand. Access to the beach at Southerness requires a step down off a crumbled, rocky ramp beside the lighthouse. • Toilets are available in Southerness beside the car park just off the main road.

•• Unassuming at first, these two wedges of shoreline overlooked by small settlements are some of the best spots on the Solway Firth for wintering wading birds. As well as mudflats and rocks dotted with shallow pools, the sites also contain maritime heath, reedbeds and sand dunes. It's better to visit both locations on a low or rising tide, when kelp-coated rocks emerge and birds are drawn in to forage.

It might take a while for wildlife to appear at Southerness beach – with so many crevices for them to hide in – but scan the beach long enough and you might find curlews, grey herons, redshanks or oystercatchers, with red-breasted mergansers swimming close to shore. Little egrets are the easiest to spot with their snowy white plumage. Keener eyes might also pick out bar-tailed godwits, dunlins, knots, purple sandpipers and golden plovers. Cast your binocular gaze further out to sea for scoters and other sea ducks, auks and divers.

A lighthouse dominates the beach – it was built in the mid-eighteenth century but is no longer operational. It opens sporadically during summer.

Nearby Carsethorn has a similar landscape, with stretches of gravelly shingle best admired at low tide. This is a popular gathering place for winter migrants – Carsethorn is described as one of the few places in the UK to see decent numbers of scaup in particular.

Birds gather on slim sandbars further into the water channel known as the Carse Gut. Given the distance, binoculars are a must here. A spotting scope would be even better, as most of the birds forage far out on the sandflats and may be difficult to make out. Look for redshanks, turnstones, oystercatchers, curlews and wigeons.

As with other sites in Dumfries and Galloway, Carsethorn is a popular roosting place for geese throughout autumn and winter. The abundance of wintering wildfowl makes these seasons the best time to visit, although migrating whimbrels may visit in spring. Whimbrels look similar to the far more common curlew, but are smaller (around oystercatcher size) with shorter bills and a striped face pattern – their call is also quite different (a seven-note whistle rather than a plaintive *coor-lee*).

RSPB MERSEHEAD

Southwick DG2 8AH • OS Explorer Map 313 • Grid ref NX925562 • What3Words: fulfilled.bank.outbid (visitor centre)

How to get there: Take the Houston Coaches 372 bus departing from Dumfries Loreburne Centre and disembark at Southwick after just under an hour. From here, it's a walk of around 0.7 miles (1.2km) to the reserve, heading east along the A710 for 160m before turning right at the RSPB sign, which leads to the visitor centre. • If you're travelling by bus and intend to visit Mersehead for either sunrise or sunset, it's worth checking when the first service of the day departs from Dumfries Loreburne Centre (Monday–Saturday) and departs from Southwick. If you visit during early autumn when the days are slightly longer and plan to be at Mersehead for dawn or dusk, this may be too late or too early when factoring in the walk from the bus stop to the reserve and then another mile (1.6km) to the beach. Fortunately, even if you miss the geese travelling to and from the roost site, they forage in the open fields throughout the day and small gaggles pass overhead frequently.

Access and conditions: Reserve open 24/7 year-round; visitor centre open 10:00–16:00 daily. Access to the reserve is free, but there is a parking charge for non-RSPB members. • Facilities including toilets and baby changing, as well as a self-service refreshment station and viewing area, are available in the visitor centre.• A 2-mile (3.2km) wheelchair-accessible wetland trail connects two bird hides with step-free, ramped access, and a 2.5-mile (4km) coastal circular route follows gravel terrain to the dunes if you want to venture further out. • When ground-nesting birds are breeding from April to August, please keep dogs close, preferably on short leads.

Southerness beach.

Barnacle geese.

•• RSPB Mersehead lies 16.5 miles (26.6km) south of Dumfries, overlooking the Solway Firth. It is a treat for birdwatchers no matter the season, with a mix of wetland, sand dunes, saltmarsh and sandflats at its edges and arable grassland and woodland in the centre. From late September, the reserve is inundated with so many barnacle geese that it's considered an internationally important site for the species. The exact number varies each year, but regularly reaches the thousands at the height of the season. Throughout autumn and winter, skeins of geese shuttle from their roost site on the mudflats to inland grazing grounds.

Aside from barnacle geese, there's a chance of pink-footed geese, whooper swans, lapwings, curlews, wigeons, shelducks, pintails, shovelers and teals from either of the two hides at Mersehead. Both of these face northeast over waterlogged plains. Raptors including buzzards, peregrine falcons, hen harriers, merlins and red kites have all made appearances, with reed warblers and the elusive water rail also having colonised the reserve. The straight section connecting the two hides is lined with berry bushes, attracting starlings, song thrushes and redwings during winter.

The bird list alone is impressive, but otters, natterjack toads and porpoises in the Firth can also be seen. During summer, a range of butterflies fly along the grassy verges and the wetlands draw in dragonflies and other insects. These in turn attract swallows and house martins.

A visit to the sandy beach is rewarding, especially for an autumn sunrise. The white rumps of retreating roe deer bob in the gloom of first light and bats swirl overhead in the brightening sky. A coastal path leads through scrubby grassland, with wrens, chaffinches, dunnocks and linnets, and a chance of stonechats once you reach the dunes.

The sprawling beach blends to muddy sandflats, and it's out there that you'll hear the distant chattering of the geese before they fly inland and graze for the day.

CASTLE LOCH

> **Lochmaben, DG11 1LP • OS Explorer Map 322 • Grid ref NY089819 • What3Words: blazed.luxury.cosmic (car park)**
>
> **How to get there:** Take the Stagecoach 81 bus departing from Dumfries train station and disembark in the high street of Lochmaben, a small town 8 miles (12.9km) northeast of Dumfries, after 20 minutes. From Lochmaben, it's a 0.25-mile (0.4km) walk to the northern edge of Castle Loch. You can follow a 3-mile (4.8km) circular footpath around the loch's perimeter in either direction; at the fork, either head southeast towards Lockerbie on the A709 or south on the B7020, passing a bowling club on the left.
> **Access and conditions:** There is an established but slightly uneven footpath with alternating terrain of gravel, forest floor and a boardwalk section near the southern hide. • Public toilets can be found on Castle Street. • The loch has narrow pathways rather than open spaces so isn't the most suitable for dogs to run freely, and it's worth noting that the road is nearby on several occasions.

•• Even on overcast days, the mix of tree types makes Castle Loch an autumn highlight, with leaves burning ochre and copper. These hues are mirrored in the loch's reflection, bringing colour to the watery landscape.

Castle Loch is a large freshwater loch in Dumfriesshire. Internationally important numbers of pink-footed geese roost here, as do large numbers of greylag geese and goosanders, with barnacle geese occasionally flying over. The best times to see geese here are dawn and dusk, as they move between the surrounding fields by day and the loch by night.

Binoculars or a spotting scope would come in handy to find the smaller visitors on this loch, such as wigeon, pochard, goldeneye, teal and tufted duck. Even sharper eyes may spot a resident kingfisher or a grey heron waiting for its next meal. Great crested grebes perform breeding displays in early spring and summer.

Less common birds on Castle Loch include pochard, gadwall and smew. Rare

Male smew.

winter visitors to Britain, smews are small diving ducks, the drakes sporting smart black and white colouring.

Fringing the loch is a mixture of woodland and grazed marshland, adding terrestrial birds to the mix. Birch leaves rustle with flocks of long-tailed tits, chaffinches and great tits, with the occasional reed warbler appearing in summer. The patches of mixed forest have both spindly saplings and mature, twisted trunks covered in mossy coats and bracket fungi jutting out at every angle. Dominated by birch, alder and willow, the ground here is often flooded and poorly drained, making it a rare wet woodland habitat. A unique combination of dead and rotting wood and damp conditions supports a range of insects, mosses, liverworts and plants such as marsh marigolds and yellow irises. Look and listen out for the rare willow tit here too.

More trees were planted in 2022 by Lochmaben residents, as part of the Queen's Green Canopy Project to mark Queen Elizabeth II's Platinum Jubilee.

While walking the footpaths around the loch's circumference, you can rest at several birdwatching hides, each offering a different vantage point over the water.

South of the car park on the eastern side of the loch, a small wooden footbridge crosses the Innerfield Burn before continuing into an open grassy patch. Look for goldfinches and stonechats foraging around teasels and grassy seed heads. In time, the trees give way to open fields and the path presses close to an intermittent hedgerow, where redwings, the UK's smallest thrush, perch on hawthorn sprigs during autumn and winter.

Continue following the path onto a boardwalk winding through the trees, soon reaching a small hide on the loch's southern edge. This overlooks a stretch of tall reeds, where you may hear the pig-like squeal of an elusive water rail. Tucked as it is amongst trees, there are chances of smaller woodland bird sightings from the side windows here too.

ESKRIGG NATURE RESERVE

Lockerbie DG11 1HY • OS Explorer Map 322 • Grid ref NY129806 • What3Words: cookery.songbird.paces (car park)

How to get there: Despite their stations being just 12 miles (19.3km) apart, there isn't a train link between Dumfries and Lockerbie. However, the Stagecoach 81 bus provides access and departs from Dumfries train station. There is no need to travel into the centre of Lockerbie for Eskrigg; disembark at Vallance Drive after 29 minutes and walk down this minor road, following a sign for the reserve down the first right turn. Continue on the narrow farm track for some 270m until you reach the car park, then follow an established gravel footpath heading right between open fields to the reserve.

Access and conditions: The reserve is open 24/7 year-round. The Eskrigg Centre and compost toilet are open from 08:00 to 17:00 March–October and 09:00–16:00 November–February. • Paths connecting the hides and leading into the woodland are mostly gravel, but there may be the occasional muddy section after rain. • Dogs must be kept on leads to avoid disturbing the wildlife.

•• With pockets of wetland, heathland, coniferous woodland, reedbeds, grassland and a freshwater pond, Eskrigg Nature Reserve offers a concentrated dose of wildlife within its 2.8-hectare area. There's the occasional rumble of a train from Lockerbie, 1.25 miles (2km) northeast, but the reserve is tucked away and peaceful enough that the sound of woodpigeons bursting into flight will make you jump.

Eskrigg lies on the site of a former curling pond and was established as a nature reserve in 1988, with help from the local community. Following the entrance path from the car park, you'll pass an assortment of trees: hazel, oak, crab apple, rowan, Scots pine and beech, all painted zingy green with fine mosses. Each tree species has been labelled by volunteers, with interpretation boards giving further insight into the reserve's flora.

Glance up and you might see a sparrowhawk spiralling above the needled points of the evergreen trees, or a great spotted woodpecker speeding from one trunk to another. During autumn and winter, the woodpeckers' calls are joined by the chattering of passing fieldfares. These grey and chestnut thrushes only visit the UK during their winter migration from Scandinavia, where they feed on berries alongside redwings, another migratory thrush with distinctive cream eyebrows. Keep an eye out for redwings in the holly trees at Eskrigg, looking festive as they gobble the crimson berries. Just past the compost toilet, several gravel footpaths lead into denser woodland, where you might hear screeching jays or glimpse a goldcrest foraging amongst the pine needles.

The main place to gather at Eskrigg is the pond. This is mostly inhabited by mallards, but, in the past, rarities such as mandarin ducks have turned up, so it's always worth a look. Wrens often flit between the trees lining the water and the tall scrub standing on the central island.

Visitors can view the pond in comfort whatever the weather from two different vantage points. The Eskrigg Centre is a multi-purpose building used as a birdwatching hide, research lab, classroom and office. The centre has wheelchair access and large windows facing feeders buzzing with coal tits, siskins, chaffinches and more. Check the board for sightings of the day. There's also a smaller hide at the opposite end of the pond for a different perspective.

Something seen here and not often elsewhere in Scotland is the nuthatch, drawing the eye with its chestnut belly, blue-grey back and black eye stripe. These robust little birds move in a similar way to treecreepers, but instead of only hopping up the trunk, nuthatches often descend headfirst.

Nuthatch.

A third hide is dedicated to watching red squirrels, and chances are good that you'll have several of them bounding and snuffling mere feet away from you before long. They come for the peanut and seed feeders hanging from the branches, but if you're looking for more natural photos, they also hop onto log piles and fungi-studded tree stumps scattered throughout the clearing.

OBAN

The landscape in and around Oban ranges from windswept grassland to temperate rainforest, with a mix of lochs, streams and the coast adding more variety.

A star spring visitor to Corran Esplanade (page 215) on Oban's shorefront is the black guillemot. Although it is found in scattered locations all along the British coastline, here on Scotland's west coast this red-legged auk can be seen by the side of the road.

Overlooking the harbour is Dunollie Wood (page 216), a rare example of temperate rainforest with such a rich selection of mosses and lichens that it is considered internationally important. Not far beyond this lies Ganavan Hill (page 218), best visited in summer for its impressive range of butterflies including the chequered skipper, for which Scotland is one of the few strongholds. Also found here is the marsh fritillary, which usually rests with its stained-glass wings held open. Both of these west coast specialists can also be seen during early summer visits to Glasdrum Wood (page 222), a small but rewarding insect haven overlooking the River Ure.

Trains at Oban station link regularly to Glasgow. Within Oban itself, many of the green spaces are clustered together so can be accessed on foot – the esplanade path is suited to both walkers and cyclists. One of the numerous ferry links is to the underrated Isle of Lismore (page 220), where butterflies and bees stir along the hedgerows.

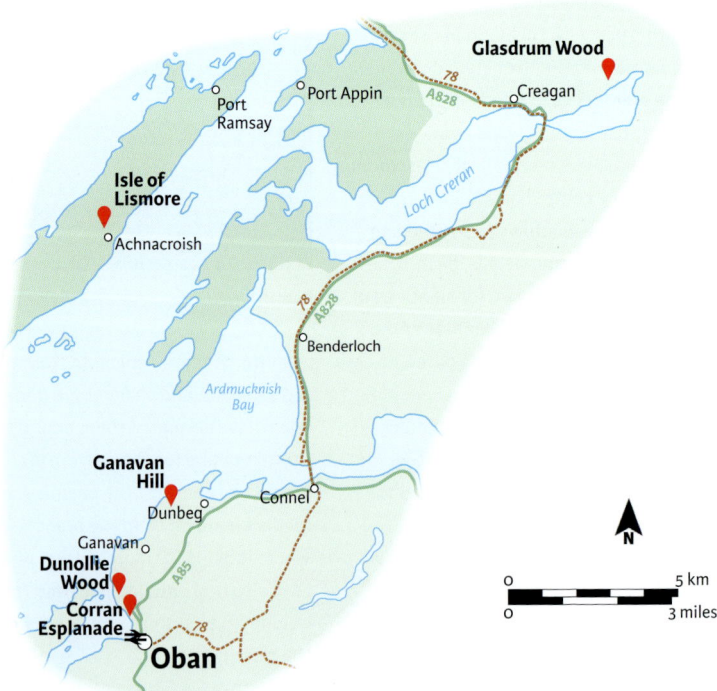

CORRAN ESPLANADE

Oban PA34 5AA • OS Explorer Map 376 • Grid ref NM856305 • What3Words: albums.nicer.shams

How to get there: You can walk at the water's edge all the way through the centre of Oban. Black guillemots are the wildlife highlight here, and they seem to show up best on the stretch just west of the small roundabout beside Corran Halls, 0.5 miles (0.8km) north of the train station. To get there, simply follow the main road (A85), keeping close to the bay.

Access and conditions: The official esplanade runs for 0.75 miles (1.2km) from just north of the North Pier ferry terminal to Oban's war memorial, near where the road becomes Ganavan Road. The esplanade has a concrete walkway so is suitable for all. • Public toilets are available at Oban North Pier (charge applies).

•• With kayaks, tour boats and ferries criss-crossing every few moments, Oban's harbour is a restless landscape. It's perhaps surprising, then, that Corran Esplanade – a road and adjacent footpath at the northern end of the bay – is a prime location for an uncommon seabird.

Unlike guillemots (larger white-bellied auks that gather in large numbers at clifftop nesting sites around the coast), black guillemots in breeding plumage have entirely black bodies, with a white patch on each wing. The inside of their mouths is fire-engine red, matching their legs. In the Scottish Isles they're known as 'tysties', believed to derive from their Norse name. In Oban, they nest in the

Black guillemot

drain pipes embedded in the stone wall encircling the bay, so it's easy to watch them up close throughout the day when they arrive for their breeding season each year, any time from January onwards.

Sightings are most frequent in the morning, and the black guillemots seem to favour a higher tide when flying into their nests. It's believed this is in case the landing doesn't go as planned and they can splash safely into the water below. Spring and summer are the best times for admiring the black guillemot's smart breeding plumage; once autumn arrives, they become speckly and then almost white.

They are relaxed around people – a steady stream of pedestrians use the esplanade path, often not even realising that these striking seabirds are directly under their feet. This provides a unique opportunity to watch black guillemots without the need for a boat trip. It's not just a flyby either – they often dive for fish and crustaceans among the wafting strands of kelp. Occasionally they burst into fluttering flight, beating their short wings to propel themselves up and into the wall's nest cavities. Fairly sedentary, they only travel short distances offshore after breeding.

In mainland Britain, black guillemots are found almost exclusively in Scotland, with the highest numbers on the west coast. Black guillemots don't gather in vast nesting colonies like most auks, but groups of a dozen or more may be seen at Corran Esplanade. This depends on their activity as they come and go all day, much like boats in the harbour.

The black guillemots are the standout wildlife highlight here, but other birds also use this sheltered bay to feed and rest. Swifts scream above the harbour noise during summer, while turnstones and eiders might appear during colder months. With a bit of luck, an otter could show up, dragging fish or even a small octopus ashore to eat.

DUNOLLIE WOOD

Oban PA34 5PN • OS Explorer Map 376 • Grid ref NM857306 • What3Words: reissued.supposed.rips (Corran Halls entrance)

How to get there: Dunollie Wood is only 0.5 miles (0.8km) from Oban's harbour, so is easily walkable from town. There are several entrances, but the natural starting point is next to Corran Halls car park. This is located just off the A85, the main road through Oban, beside two small roundabouts.

Access and conditions: An established waymarked trail runs through the forest, but this is bumpy in places and has regular inclines, including a couple of kissing gates and steep stone staircases which might be slippery after rain. The most accessible section follows a wide, flat footpath on the southwestern side of the wood, overlooking Ganavan Road. Along here you can admire towering rock walls as tall as houses and peer through gaps in the trees at the ruined Dunollie Castle, propped up on a hill a few hundred metres down the road. • Public toilets are available at Oban North Pier (charge applies).

•• Scotland's west coast encourages the development of temperate rainforest, or Atlantic woodland, because of its high levels of rainfall and mild, constant temperatures throughout the year. Dunollie Wood is a fine example of this habitat, which is even rarer than tropical rainforest. Here you will find an abundance of the kinds of lichens and mosses that make this type of rainforest environmentally important on an international scale. The circular 'Rainforest Ramble' trail, guided by white waymarkers, provides ample opportunities to admire ground-level detail of the diverse woodland flora.

For those accessing the wood from the Corran Halls entrance, a summer visit starts with a vibrant stand of foxgloves and red campion beside the map board. Bracken, honeysuckle and nettles line the path on both sides.

As well as mosses and lichens, Dunollie is known for its bluebells. Visit in May to admire the hundreds of delicate bells bringing pops of violet to the otherwise green landscape, their frilled heads bobbing beneath the weight of dewdrops.

Speaking of which, this is a forest best admired soggy – it is a rainforest, after all – as this is when the canopy drips, grass shines with dew and the moss pasted onto every silver birch flares an even brighter green. The forest floor is strewn with deadwood, its bark overwhelmed by lichen. Huge shelves of bracket fungus jut out from twisted beeches so tall they stretch out of sight. In their shadows stand stouter birches, their limbs splayed like tentacles. A particular fungus to look out for is the hazel gloves fungus, a rare specialist of the temperate rainforest habitat.

The meandering trill of willow warblers is a looping soundtrack during summer when these unassuming migrants are here in the UK. Meanwhile blackbirds, resident throughout the year, scuffle through the leaf litter while blue tits and great tits forage higher off the forest floor. Glance up when the canopy rustles and a red squirrel might be peering down at you. Other potential summer sightings in this forest include redstarts, wood warblers and chequered skipper butterflies – the last of these is also seen at Ganavan Hill (below) and Glasdrum Wood (page 222).

Dunollie Wood is draped across two hills, Barra Mor and Barr Cruinn, so walking is steep at times. However, when there's a break in the trees, gaze southwest over Oban's harbour and the Western Isles in the distance. There are patches of dense woodland where the trail curls tightly around lichen-crusted birches, then the trees part to reveal open grassy glades with more bluebells and day-flying moths flitting among them. Another floral highlight is the yellow iris, with its droopy but vivid petals that inspired its other name: flag iris. A staple of reedbeds, ponds and wet woodlands like Dunollie, yellow irises are in flower from May to August.

Volunteer groups carry out regular maintenance work at Dunollie, including path clearing, tree planting and removing invasive species such as rhododendron. Anyone interested in getting involved could check the Woodland Trust website or look for notices on site about upcoming work parties.

GANAVAN HILL

Ganavan PA34 5TB • OS Explorer Map 376 • Grid ref NM862327 • What3Words: pianists.engineers.corn (Ganavan Sands car park)

How to get there: Ganavan Hill lies between two small settlements just north of Oban: Ganavan itself and a village called Dunbeg, 2 miles (3.2km) northeast. As a result, it can be accessed via either of these, but for those based in Oban it makes sense to start from the southern end, closest to town. It is just over 2 miles (3.2km) from the centre of Oban to Ganavan Sands car park, following Ganavan Road.

Access and conditions: Terrain across this site varies widely. Some areas have uneven gravel paths with the occasional steep section that may require grappling with hands as well as feet. However, there's a stretch of tarmac path winding around the southern and southeastern edges of the hill, connecting the beach car park at Ganavan Sands to nearby Dunbeg. This section has wonderful views of open moorland without any rough terrain and is suitable for cyclists. • Toilets are available in the Ganavan Sands car park.

•• Search for 'Ganavan' online and you'll have a string of results mentioning the sandy beach overlooking Ganavan Bay. But for wildlife watchers, it's the hill northeast of the beach that's worth exploring in detail. The highest point of Ganavan Hill is only 72m, but those who hike to the top are rewarded with panoramic views of both the mainland coast and the Western Isles.

Keep your eyes peeled from the moment you arrive, as pied wagtails bob

Marsh fritillary.

their way through the beach car park and rabbits curl up right beside the footpath. Buzzards glide overhead and the occasional *kronk* calls of ravens can be heard.

With its broad span of damp grassland, hedgerow and moorland, Ganavan Hill is an underrated site for both birds and insects, including two west coast specialists. The marsh fritillary butterfly has vibrant cream and orange markings and has faced severe declines across Europe as well as in the UK. Its range in Scotland is now mostly restricted to Argyll and Lochaber, making every sighting special. It is typically on the wing from late May to early July – look for it in damp grassland and moorland edges.

Flying from early May to late June, the chequered skipper is another butterfly mostly limited to these western regions. It's small and fast, but in direct sunlight you can suddenly find one right under your nose, basking before taking off to feed. It has chocolate brown uppersides to its wings, covered in creamy yellow spots (see also Glasdrum Wood, page 222).

Those who would benefit from flat terrain are advised to take the smooth path heading east from the car park. This rises on a steep but brief incline before levelling out onto a fantastic scrubby stretch. Amble along here in summer as it is a special spot for insects, bordered by long grass and hedgerows. You might be rewarded with a golden-ringed dragonfly perched on brambles, orange-tip butterflies on nettles or common blue damselflies clinging to blades of grass. A particularly striking day-flying moth found here is the argent & sable, which has a monochromatic pattern of symmetrical inkblots across its wings. Chiffchaffs and willow warblers can be seen and heard often during summer, with wrens present all year round.

Another, more uneven, path leads

north from the car park, sticking close to the water's edge along a rock-lined trail. Craggy outcrops are covered in moss and dense bracken corridors are brightened by sprays of forget-me-nots, bluebells and pale pink orchids in summer. During this time, the mumbling song of common whitethroats can be heard even if the bird itself stays buried in the foliage. Looking northwest from this path, visitors can enjoy views across the water to the narrow island of Lismore (see below); check the low-lying rocks for oystercatchers or shags.

On this route, the path turns to a brief muddy scramble up a rocky slope before flattening out onto windswept moorland, studded with bobbing strands of cotton-grass. There are several branched paths from here – follow the highest one to crest Ganavan Hill itself before descending gently in a shallow loop back towards the village of Ganavan, with views east towards Dunbeg. In time, this rougher trail joins the established tarmac path mentioned earlier that also began at the car park, making a convenient loop back to the start point.

ISLE OF LISMORE

Achnacroish PA34 5UJ • OS Explorer Map 376 • Grid ref NM851409 • What3Words: sweeter.reworked.pots (ferry terminal)

How to get there: Caledonian MacBrayne car ferries connect Oban to Lismore each day, although the number of crossings varies depending on the time of year. The ferry arrives at the hamlet of Achnacroish in the centre of the island after approximately 1 hour. There's also a smaller pedestrian ferry to the northernmost point of the island that runs from Port Appin, but this fishing village is 20 miles (32.2km) north of Oban. Because both ferry services are affected by seasonal variations, it's best to check online for the most up-to-date details.

Access and conditions: Terrain varies widely on Lismore, from roads to established country paths to winding trails that cross streams and muddy patches. Due to the island's remoteness, even the few main roads are quiet, so there are plenty of opportunities to see wildlife along hedgerows and field fringes without straying from the tarmac. This also makes road cycling peaceful – be sure to give way to tractors, trailers and local traffic during ferry times. • Public toilets are available at the ferry terminal at Achnacroish.

•• With its spiderweb of ferry links, Oban has a range of options when it comes to island-hopping. Mull is perhaps best known, but a closer and inconspicuous alternative is the skinny island of Lismore, easily visible from the mainland.

Just 10 miles (16.1km) long and 1 mile (1.6km) wide, Lismore is the sort of place where cars are unusual. This isn't surprising, given that it has a population of fewer than 200 people. As a result, bees often dominate the soundscape, their buzzing audible even above the trickle of narrow burns behind dry stone walls. It would be challenging to walk the length of Lismore in a day, but it's easy to explore a sample between ferry crossings.

Wildlife watching might begin before you even step onto dry land, with the possibility of gannets, razorbills and other seabirds flying over or bobbing beside the ferry. As Lismore approaches, the lighthouse at the southern tip draws the eye first. It sits on its own island and dates back to 1833.

Step off the ferry into a sheltered bay. From here, enjoy secluded walking beside open grassland and patches of marsh threaded with quivering streams. Boggier areas are dotted with orchids in summer, with the occasional primrose poking through shaggy grass. Cormorants dive in the shallows surrounding the jetty, while the trees ring with redpolls, linnets, song thrushes, chaffinches, wrens and charms of goldfinches.

Head north at the car ferry terminal and turn right in front of a line of houses to join a footpath on Lismore's eastern shore. There are tiny coves here, fringed by tufts of sea thrift poking out of jagged black rocks brushed over with grass. Wheatears might appear amongst the sheep, hopping between rocks and fence posts. Otters sometimes hunt along the shoreline and red deer have been known to swim over from the mainland.

The only roads on the island are single-track with passing places. Perch on the bench outside the post office – Lismore's central hub for information and supplies – and you might see house sparrows squeezing into tiny crevices in the roof to reach their nests. The road here is lined with long grass and is a good place to look for butterflies during summer. Orange-tips and peacocks may pass by seemingly empty patches of grass as a boisterous small heath bursts up to hurry them out of its patch.

Finally, Lismore has three small lochs: Balnagown, Kilcheran and Fiart. Balnagown is the easiest to access from both the car and pedestrian ferry terminals. Its surface is dotted with geese, ducks and gulls, with the occasional grey heron standing on its banks.

Near Loch Balnagown is Tìrfuir Broch, a Pictish stone fort that perches on a rocky hilltop and dates back to the Iron Age. This and several other historical landmarks across the island, including ruined castles and lime kilns, are so old that they have almost dissolved into the green landscape.

GLASDRUM WOOD NATIONAL NATURE RESERVE

Appin PA38 4BQ • OS Explorer Map 376 • Grid ref NN001454 • What3Words: socket.renamed.nerves (car park)

How to get there: Glasdrum Wood is 16 miles (25.7km) northeast of Oban, but is still accessible on public transport and well worth the journey. The West Coast Motors 405 and 918 buses run several daily services from Oban's Station Road, arriving at the roundabout just past Creagan Bridge after 30 minutes. This stretch of road overlaps with National Cycle Network Route 78. From the roundabout, it's a 1.35-mile (2.2km) walk east along the edge of Loch Creran to the reserve entrance.

Access and conditions: Glasdrum Wood is small but steeply stacked against the side of Beinn Churalain, so there are several brief stone staircases along its established gravel paths. For less mobile visitors, there is a picnic area close to the car park with opportunities for wildlife spotting as well as superb views over Loch Creran. • Dogs must be kept under close control to avoid disturbing wildlife. • There are no toilets on site.

•• Glasdrum Wood National Nature Reserve is a remnant of the rare Scottish rainforest habitat also seen at Dunollie Wood (page 216). With its alternating pattern of densely packed woodland and south-facing open clearings, it is renowned for butterflies including several scarce species; this makes early summer the optimum time to visit. Perfect for a hot day with its abundance of shading ash and oak trees, Glasdrum also has a burn tripping down its steep slope, giving the illusion of coolness. The loop around the reserve is less than 1 mile (1.6km) long; however, a much longer visit is recommended, especially during summer

when insect diversity is impressive.

Above the sounds of water and bumblebees, you might hear a distant cuckoo calling in May, although it can be challenging to spot one. Also during this time, if the weather is warm and sunny enough, visitors will be treated to plenty of small pearl-bordered fritillaries. These butterflies have orange wings with black lace detailing, including a line of chevron-like marks around the outer edge of their wings. Their name comes from the sprinkling of white 'pearls' on the underwings. Fairly common in Scotland, small pearl-bordered fritillaries favour woodland clearings and sunlit bracken slopes – a near perfect match of the habitat at Glasdrum. They flit past or bask with wings open on bracken fronds on warm, sunny days in summer.

The rarer pearl-bordered fritillary is also found here. Difficult to distinguish from its similar and more common relative, this species has just two white pearls on its underwings and its chevrons are floating above the surrounding black border, rather than attached to it. Differences as subtle as this are challenging to observe.

Another attractive butterfly found at Glasdrum is the marsh fritillary, also found at Ganavan Hill (page 218). It can hide in plain sight among the small pearl-bordered fritillaries too, but with a bit of luck one will land and display its more diverse range of upperwing colours.

The reserve is also known for chequered skippers; during a visit in May or June, you'll undoubtedly meet photographers drawn here for a glimpse of this tiny and scarce beauty. The males need sunny yet sheltered habitat with scattered scrub, where they perch and wait

Chequered skipper.

for passing females. Cleared corridors following the route of overhead power lines are good places to look for them. Also keep an eye out for the chimney sweeper moth, which is sooty black with narrow white wingtips.

There is one major trail running around the reserve. From the car park, it zigzags upwards, speckled with alternating sun and shade. At the top of a short hill, it reaches an open glade with a picnic bench – good for sunbathing and butterfly watching. It then bends right into more covered woodland, bordered on both sides by fans of bracken, grass tussocks and hulking moss mounds that used to be rocks. Glasdrum is an important site for lichens – one example found here is the nationally scarce Norwegian specklebelly. It is covered in fine pale spots and can be found on the trunks of hazel trees.

The path continues across a wooden footbridge before sloping back towards the car park. When the trees eventually part, a broad landscape of forested hills and the nearby Loch Creran opens up beyond.

If you're keen on butterflies and interested in carrying out volunteer butterfly surveys at Glasdrum, visit the NatureScot website to contact the reserve manager about getting involved.

ELGIN

Whether it's dippers at Sanquhar Loch (page 230) or grey seals hauled out at Findhorn Bay (page 232), the area surrounding Elgin in Moray offers exciting wildlife watching opportunities. At Lossiemouth Estuary (page 226) ospreys hunt close enough to shore for the resulting splash to be clearly heard. This constantly swelling and shrinking stretch of the River Lossie (page 225) is an ideal gathering place for both birds and birdwatchers alike, with a range of ducks, waders, gulls and more appearing throughout the year.

Bottlenose dolphins are often spotted along the Moray Coast. Burghead Harbour (page 228), with its elevated viewpoint, is a prime spot to look for them. A special winter visitor to the area is the long-tailed duck, a small sea duck typically confined to northern Scotland. Flocks often gather in sheltered bays and harbours such as Burghead. Winter berries on rowan trees in Elgin attract redwings, fieldfares and occasionally waxwings.

Buses connect Elgin to most villages in the surrounding area. Trains at Elgin station link regularly between Inverness and Aberdeen. Walkers might want to explore the Moray Coast Trail, covering 50 miles (80.5km) of dramatic coastline from Forres to Cullen. It passes three sites mentioned in this section: Lossiemouth Estuary, Burghead Harbour and Findhorn Bay. In general, the route follows the easiest terrain close to coastal villages and many sections can be accessed by cyclists and horse riders as well as walkers. The trail connects an impressive selection of habitats from cliffs to sandy beaches to caves.

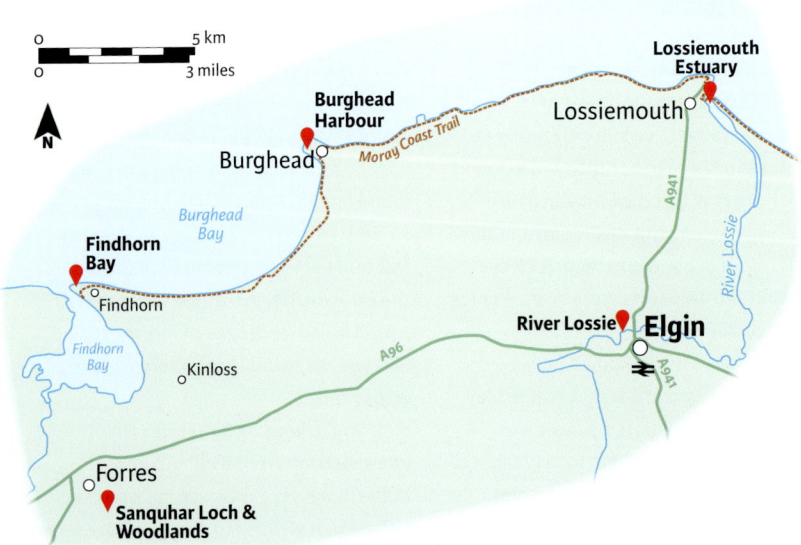

RIVER LOSSIE

Elgin IV30 1GU • OS Explorer Map 423 • Grid ref NJ216631 • What3Words: theme.dollar.scary (Cooper Park pond)

How to get there: From Elgin bus station, cross over the A96 and head east. Take the first turning on the roundabout onto the A941. Cross over again and take the first right onto Lossie Wynd North. The small Cooper Park is just up ahead, with the duck pond appearing first. The River Lossie lies at the park's northern edge, and can be followed in either direction. For your best chances of spotting wildlife, head west and cross under the A941, following the footpath all the way past the back of Moray Leisure Centre and round to Morriston Playing Fields.

Access and conditions: Established footpaths follow the river throughout, but often switch between tarmac, flat gravel and narrow earth paths. Cooper Park is well equipped for cyclists with off-road paths following the river, including a section of National Cycle Network Route 1. • Public toilets are available in Cooper Park, 180m east of Elgin Library.

•• The spaghetti-like River Lossie is a peaceful shelter for wildlife amongst an otherwise busy town. It stretches for some 30 miles (48.3km) from the hills in the centre of Moray to the sea at Lossiemouth Estuary (page 226), cutting horizontally through Elgin's northern half.

Dense thickets and path borders are left to grow as they will throughout summer, with rosebay willowherb, thistles, clover and buttercups all providing protection for hidden wrens and chaffinches.

Stroll down any of the river footpaths for chances of bullfinches feeding on catkins in early spring, chiffchaffs calling their name throughout summer, and redwings or even the occasional waxwing

passing over in winter. Elgin is a fantastic place for overwintering thrushes, with its abundance of rowan trees. The berries that grow on them are a valuable food source for both visiting and resident birds.

On the water itself, you may catch the blue flash of a kingfisher as it shoots past. Grey wagtails bob on protruding rocks and overhanging branches, while a grey heron often stands on the small weir located in the shadow of the A941 bridge just west of Cooper Park.

While some sections of the Lossie cast reflections of the trees lining its banks, others churn with rushing rapids. Dippers are common on these turbulent patches, either standing on perching pebbles or foraging in the shallows, heads bowed into the current. Dippers often sit in the open along the less-trodden section of the river path on the western side of Morriston Playing Fields.

Red squirrels sometimes dangle recklessly over the water as they forage. Keep very quiet and you might encounter a roe deer, although they usually stick to the opposite bank. Occasionally they are so submerged in the foliage that all you can make out are blinking eyes or a set of antlers among the branches.

LOSSIEMOUTH ESTUARY

Lossiemouth IV31 6GH • OS Explorer Map 423 • Grid ref NJ238701 • What3Words: giants.upsetting.laptops (caravan car park)

How to get there: Take the Stagecoach 33A bus departing from Elgin bus station and disembark at Park Place in the small town of Lossiemouth after 15 minutes. From here, continue northeast on Clifton Road then turn right onto Seatown Road when the estuary appears at the end. Follow the road round for 0.5 miles (0.8km), keeping the river on your left, until you reach the caravan car park. The line of benches along here is the best spot for wildlife watching. • The Moray Coast Trail (see page 224) passes through Lossiemouth, hugging the coastline on both the west and east beaches.
Access and conditions: The estuary has a mix of terrain including cut grass, shingle and mud, so will vary depending on the tide and weather. You can enjoy great views without venturing from the tarmac car park. • Please keep dogs under control so they do not disturb shorebirds, or head to the beach on the other side of the dunes where they can run freely; this is accessible via a footbridge on Clifton Road. • Public toilets are available close to the estuary on Seatown Road.

•• There are few places where you can watch ospreys dive for flatfish just a few metres away, but Lossiemouth Estuary, located 5.5 miles (8.9km) north of Elgin, is one of them. This narrow strip of water on the southeastern side of Lossiemouth is the very last section of the River Lossie (page 225) before it filters into the Moray Firth. Wildlife can show up anywhere along the estuary, sheltered behind hulking sand dunes, but usually you needn't venture further than 1 mile (1.6km) from the caravan park to sample an impressive variety.

The tideline varies widely here; vast borders of sand and mud vanish underwater in just a few hours. During low tide, the banks are dotted with gulls, ducks and waders. Herring gulls and black-headed gulls are the most obvious with their pale plumage, but if you perch on one of the benches overlooking the estuary and scan with binoculars, you'll likely find plenty more species. Wigeons and teals are some of the more colourful – although both small ducks, the males attract attention with warm chestnut heads on the former and a vivid green eye stripe on the latter. They are most common in winter, when numbers are boosted by migrating birds from Europe. Ringed plovers scurry across the sand and curlews probe the mud for worms. The occasional shelduck, goldeneye, little grebe or goosander drops by too.

Perhaps the highlight of a visit to Lossiemouth Estuary is the opportunity to watch ospreys at very close quarters.

Summer visitors to Britain, ospreys hunt only fish and dive to catch their prey. They appear at a few locations along the Moray Coast including Spey Bay and Findhorn Bay (page 232), but Lossiemouth is one of the more reliable spots to watch them. They can be seen from the end of March until around September; the best time to look is a few hours after low tide.

Scan the skies for the slender wings of an osprey as it follows the line of the

Osprey.

water, cruising high as it searches for a potential meal. If it spots something worth investigating, it will hover on the spot. If conditions are right, anyone watching will see it fall into a dive – slow at first, then gaining in speed until it strikes the water with wings pinned back and talons extended. A few moments and strong wing flaps later, the osprey emerges with or without a catch. Either way, it gains some height and performs a brief shimmy to shake off excess water before wheeling away to feed or try again. The spectacle is especially dramatic if you happen to be in the right place to hear the smack of the osprey hitting the water.

BURGHEAD HARBOUR

Burghead IV30 5UA • OS Explorer Map 423 • Grid ref NJ109690 • What3Words: cello.scarcely.shelter

How to get there: The Stagecoach 32 bus connects Elgin bus station to the village of Burghead. Disembark at Church Street after 26 minutes, then either continue northwest onto a vehicle track for direct access to a higher sea view vantage point, or head southwest downhill on Church Street to reach the harbour after 90m. • The Moray Coast Trail (see page 224) passes through Burghead, approaching from the south through Roseisle Forest before returning to the coastline on the northeastern side of the village.
Access and conditions: The harbour itself is completely flat, with concrete walkways beside the water. Avoid the set of steep stone steps (this is advisable for everyone during strong winds) to the headland by continuing to the very end of Grant Street, ignoring the left turn down Church Street. Aim for the visitor centre (open 12:00–16:00 daily April–end of September) up ahead and enjoy an almost 360° view of the Moray Firth shortly afterwards. • Public toilets are available at the harbour.

•• Marine vantage points, good shelter and the lure of returning fishing boats all make harbours great places to watch wildlife. The village of Burghead, 8.5 miles (13.7km) northwest of Elgin, is an excellent example, with species throughout the year including bottlenose dolphins, long-tailed ducks and basking sharks. With little light pollution, it's also a spot where the Northern Lights can show well during winter and early spring.

When fishing boats pull into the harbour with a fresh catch, grey seals are usually close behind. They appear almost daily, logging in the water and barely sparing a glance to passers-by. It's important not to approach seals when they are hauled out on beaches, but as they willingly enter the harbour here it's a privilege to watch them at ease at such close quarters. They often drift so close that their breath huffs loudly as they emerge from a dive.

As well as seals all year round, the harbour attracts exciting winter birds seeking shelter from stormy weather behind the high sea wall. Eiders show well around February and March, the piebald

males and mottled brown females drifting into the harbour to dive for molluscs and crustaceans. On other occasions, they gather in huge rafts of several hundred birds just offshore. It's worth scanning these flocks with binoculars in case there's a king eider among them.

Another winter bird that visits this site is the long-tailed duck. These sea ducks don't breed in Britain, but spend winter in parts of northern Scotland, with smaller numbers further south. The males have long tails and their winter plumage is mostly white, with patches of black and other muted colours. The short-tailed females have darker, mostly brown plumage. One of their nicknames is 'coal-and-candlelight', which supposedly sounds like the garbled phrase they repeat frequently. Harder to spot in choppy conditions when their small bodies are concealed by waves, they are best seen when they venture into the harbour itself, bobbing amongst the seals.

Keep an eye on the sea walls surrounding the harbour, where a mixture of redshanks, turnstones, grey herons, cormorants and pied wagtails perch and forage. A rarer winter visitor here is the purple sandpiper, a stocky little wader with orange legs and a downward-curving bill.

Climb the stone steps at the northwestern corner of the harbour onto a broad platform known as Rotten Rock for elevated views over the Moray Firth. Follow the stone ramp up to a grassy headland – where the small visitor centre is located – and the view expands further, revealing Hopeman to the east, the next fishing village along the coast.

This unrivalled panoramic view makes Burghead a prime location for watching whales, dolphins and porpoises (cetaceans). The bottlenose dolphins here in the Moray Firth are the largest and the most northerly in the world. Sightings peak from May to September, but they can show up at any time of year. Sometimes small pods pass through calmly, with only the occasional dorsal fin breaking the surface. At other times, they perform astonishing breaches, launching their 4m-long bodies completely out of the water.

Basking sharks are less frequent, but a few are sighted most years from late summer to early autumn. They're not as active as the dolphins, but if one drifts close enough to land, the swishing tip of its tail might be visible as well as its broad dorsal fin. Rarer cetaceans seen from Burghead include orcas, common dolphins and even the occasional humpback whale.

Marine wildlife enthusiasts might be interested in volunteering with Whale & Dolphin Conservation's Shorewatch citizen science programme. Burghead is just one of dozens of designated sites around Scotland's coastline where trained Shorewatch volunteers conduct 10-minute surveys and record any cetaceans they see.

Bottlenose dolphins.

SANQUHAR LOCH AND WOODLANDS

Forres IV36 1DG • OS Explorer Map 423 • Grid ref NJ039580 • What3Words: ballpoint.customers.machinery (loch car park)

How to get there: Take the Stagecoach 10 bus departing from Maryhill House in Elgin and disembark at Castlehill Road in Forres after 25 minutes. From here, it's a 0.5-mile (0.8km) walk to Sanquhar Loch. Head southeast on Castlehill Road, turn left onto Burdsyard Road then right onto Sanquhar Rd, following it until the loch appears on the left.
Access and conditions: There's a mix of routes through the woods following established footpaths. It's worth noting that there are numerous uphill sections with thick roots crossing the path and the occasional set of steps. However, the loch is always busy with birds, so plenty can be seen from the wide gritted paths in sight of the parking area.
• Public toilets are available in Grant Park, 1 mile (1.6km) north of the loch.

•• Tucked away on the southern side of Forres, 1 mile (1.6km) southeast of the town centre, Sanquhar Loch and Woodlands is a large enough site to offer plenty of nature and tranquillity. On arrival the prominent sound is the roar of a large weir rushing beneath the road. Wait a while on the footbridge crossing it and a dipper could burst out from beneath your feet and perch on top of the weir. The stream flowing in and out of the loch is the Burn of Mosset, which supports several of these unusual aquatic birds. During the spring, you can watch them gathering tufts of moss to line their nests. The sunken channel running parallel to the road beside the weir is an excellent spot to explore, as there's a series of perfectly placed stone perches jutting out of the water, where both dippers and grey wagtails rest between foraging trips.

The woodlands beyond Sanquhar Loch could easily take up half a day of strolling, but the range of footpaths also enable shorter circular walks. The easiest way to access the woods is to leave the weir behind and follow the footpath heading northeast from the car park. This tracks the loch's northern edge and then follows the winding trail of the Burn of Mosset. Red-breasted mergansers sometimes bob among the mallards and mute swans, while treecreepers scale the hulking oaks beside the water. Roe deer occasionally roam the steep banks during the day, peering down the slope before bounding out of sight.

The woods echo with the calls of jays and great spotted woodpeckers and contain a variety of tree types, with sections dominated alternately by oak, rowan, silver birch, Scots pine or Sitka spruce. The pine sections in particular have a striking display of heather during the summer and early autumn. After rain or heavy dew, the hanging spiderwebs strung across their lilac flowers glisten.

Foxgloves bring some colour during summer, as do the changing hues of bracken when autumn arrives. Diverse examples of fungi thrive on large deadwood logs in Sanquhar, with elaborate patterns of fans, curls and fingers as well as the more easily identifiable scarlet caps of fly agaric. Another vibrant flash could be a red squirrel high up in the canopy. Although they don't tend to linger for long, you may spot them jumping between branches.

A summer visit will usually be accompanied by diverse insect life. Orange-tip and speckled wood butterflies might emerge close to the path. The smaller lochans submerged within the woods are good places to look for dragonflies hovering above the bullrushes, or a pond skater on the water's edge.

FINDHORN BAY

Findhorn IV36 3YF • OS Explorer Map 423 • Grid ref NJ038644 • What3Words: presumes.variety.ruled

How to get there: There is no regular bus service to Findhorn from either Elgin or Forres, but it is possible to reach Findhorn by cycling the Moray Coast Trail (see page 224) from Forres (5.75 miles/9.3km) or Burghead (7.5 miles/12km). The Burghead route passes through Roseisle Forest, home to roe deer, red squirrels and crested tits – the last of which is a specialist of the Scots pine woodlands here. To reach these sections of the Moray Coast Trail, see page 228 for the bus journey from Elgin to Burghead and page 230 for the bus journey from Elgin to Forres. • For those unable to cycle, there is parking overlooking the bay on the B9011 (What3Words: slips.durations.decimals) and by the dunes in front of the beach (What3Words: pouting.tolerates.rapid). From the latter, walk west along the beach for about 0.5 miles (0.8km) and follow it around the corner into the bay.

Access and conditions: Most of the eastern side of the bay is bordered by the village of Findhorn, so you can stand at the edge of the water while remaining on concrete paths. The beach is a combination of fine sand and shingle, with the occasional steep bank. • Public toilets are available at the beach car park, just east of the mouth of the bay.

•• At the end of its 62-mile (100km) journey, the River Findhorn flows into a circular bay spanning several square miles. This is located beside a village of the same name, 5 miles (8km) north of Forres. At Findhorn, the river joins the Moray Firth and looks vastly different depending on the tide. It attracts a host of mammals, birds and insects throughout the seasons, making it a worthwhile stop-off point

whatever time of year you visit.

With regards to wildlife, the bay is perhaps best known for the impressive number of seals that gather around the mouth on most days. At high tide, only their heads emerge above the waves, but they drift close to the shore to watch passers-by. As the tide recedes to reveal longer sandbars, the seals often haul out on land. This enables visitors to watch them out of their usual environment, but always keep your distance to avoid disturbing them while at rest. On a calm day, their haunting song-like calls carry over the bay even when they are too distant to see. Both grey and common seals can be seen at Findhorn. Grey seals are larger and have sloping Roman noses and parallel nostrils. Smaller common seals have shorter, more dog-like snouts and V-shaped nostrils that meet at the bottom. The two haul out together at Findhorn, showing a mix of fur colours from dark grey to almost white.

Further into the bay, where the water is calmer and mudflats appear at low tide, a range of birds forage during all seasons.

Ospreys, spring and summer visitors to Britain, occasionally hunt here. They could be cruising past with a flatfish clutched in their talons, hovering high overhead as they scan for potential prey, or even swooping vertically down into the water to snatch it. However, osprey sightings are likelier at Lossiemouth Estuary (page 226).

During autumn and winter, Findhorn Bay is dominated by overwintering geese. Although occasional rarities such as barnacle and even snow geese have arrived during past winters, the majority are pink-footed. From September onwards, these migrating birds leave the bay each morning and return to roost each evening, with numbers reaching some 20,000 at the peak of the season. It is not uncommon to hear incessant honking as vast skeins of them pass overhead, sometimes in pitch darkness. Foraging amongst the geese are many different ducks and waders, such as wigeons, goldeneyes and teals. Less likely but still possible sightings include shovelers, scaups, gadwalls and pintails.

Waders include resident oystercatchers and curlews, frequently spotted all along the Moray Coast, but depending on the time of year there might also be sanderlings, dunlins, knots and bar-tailed godwits picking around in the mudflats at Findhorn Bay.

The butterflies you'll find vary depending on the habitat. North of the village, a patch of sand dunes attracts common blues, small heaths and the occasional grayling around the shingle. The beach car park overlooks an area of heathland, and here you could see peacock, small tortoiseshell and meadow brown butterflies. South of the bay, within the saltmarsh habitat, ringlets and Scotch argus sometimes appear.

GLOSSARY

Ancient tree A tree in the third and final stage of its life, typically exhibiting a small canopy, and a wide and hollow trunk. Though there is no set age for a tree to be classed as ancient, it is typically a couple of hundred years old.

Blue Flag Award An internationally recognised standard for good quality and well-managed beaches, marinas and sustainable boating tourism operators, administered in the UK by Keep Britain Tidy.

Endemic A species or subspecies that is naturally found only in a particular geographic area and nowhere else in the world. Such species are usually highly specialised and sometimes vulnerable to environmental change or habitat loss.

Green Flag Award An internationally recognised standard for good quality and well-managed public parks and green spaces, administered in the UK by Keep Britain Tidy.

Hemi-parasite A parasitic plant that gains some of its nutrients from a host plant, usually via the host's roots or stems, but still performs photosynthesis to generate nutrients. Mistletoe and yellow-rattle are two common hemi-parasites.

Indicator species An organism whose presence, absence or abundance reflects, and can be used to monitor, the health of a habitat. For example, certain lichen species indicate lack of air pollution, and dippers reflect good water quality.

Irruption A sudden change in a bird's population density, typically involving movement into areas outside of their typical range and usually triggered by food shortages or harsh weather.

Murmuration A mesmerising aerial display where thousands of birds (usually starlings) fly in swirling flocks, typically at dusk prior to roosting.

Odonata A taxonomic order of flying insects which consists of dragonflies (suborder: Anisoptera) and damselflies (suborder: Zygoptera).

Pleistocene A geologic epoch spanning from about 2.6 million to 11,700 years ago, characterised by repeated glacial and interglacial cycles, and often referred to as the 'Great Ice Age'.

Red List A scientific assessment of native species' conservation status, categorising them based on extinction risk, and based on the guidelines of the IUCN (International Union for Conservation of Nature) Red List of Threatened Species.

Rewilding The process of restoring natural ecosystems by allowing landscapes to regenerate and, where appropriate, reintroducing native species.

Seawatching Observing offshore seabirds from a fixed point on the coast, usually a headland.

Scheduled Ancient Monument A nationally important ancient site, given protection against change which may damage it.

Veteran tree A mature tree notable for its age, size or condition, often showing features of an ancient tree even if it has not yet reached the typical age to be classified as such.

Visible migration The seasonal movement of birds that can be observed with the naked eye, often in daylight and from prominent viewpoints, particularly during spring and autumn migrations.

ABBREVIATIONS USED IN THE TEXT

BTO British Trust for Ornithology
GiGL Greenspace Information for Greater London
LNR Local Nature Reserve
NHSN Natural History Society of Northumberland
NNR National Nature Reserve
RSPB Royal Society for the Protection of Birds
SAC Special Area of Conservation
SLINC Site of Local Importance to Nature Conservation
SNCI Site of Nature Conservation Interest
SPA Special Protection Area
SSSI Site of Special Scientific Interest
ssp. subspecies
TNSI Tree of National Special Interest
UK BAP UK Biodiversity Action Plan
WWT Wildfowl and Wetlands Trust

RESOURCES

USEFUL WEBSITES

accessable.co.uk An accessibility guide for thousands of venues across the UK

bustimes.org Timetables and fare information for services across the UK

countrysidemobility.org and **outdoormobility.org** Two organisations from which partners at visitor attractions and areas of interest can hire out all-terrain Trampers. The former is in West England and Wales, and the latter across the North of England

euansguide.com Disabled access review website where people can find and share the accessibility of venues around the UK

lowcarbonbirding.net Advocates for a climate-friendly approach to birding

ramblers.org.uk Charity dedicated to removing barriers so everyone can enjoy walking in green spaces, and to improving Britain's walking places

slowways.org A not-for-profit initiative aiming to connect all of Britain's towns, cities and national landscapes by walking routes

sustrans.org.uk Charity working to improve walking, wheeling and cycling for everyone in Britain. Custodians of the National Cycle Network

RECOMMENDED READING

Forget Me Not by Sophie Pavelle (Bloomsbury Publishing, 2022)

Local by Alastair Humphreys (Eye Books, 2024)

London in the Wild by London Wildlife Trust (Octopus, 2022)

Low-Carbon Birding by Javier Caletrío (Pelagic Publishing, 2022)

USEFUL APPS

OS maps The official Ordinance Survey app, useful for finding footpaths, bridleways, and green spaces

Outdooractive An app for finding footpaths.

Slow Ways Showing the walking routes between Britain's towns, cities and national landscapes

Wildling A relatively new app, aiming to help people find and connect with nature and green spaces

Merlin ID A very useful app for identifying birdsong

iRecord One of many apps for submitting records of wildlife.

Seek One of many apps useful for identifying wildlife

PHOTO CREDITS

Bloomsbury Publishing would like to thank the following for providing photographs and for permission to reproduce copyright material within this book. While every effort has been made to trace and acknowledge all copyright holders, we would like to apologise for any errors or omissions, and invite readers to inform us so that corrections can be made to future editions.

Key to page positions T = top; L = left; R = right; B = bottom; BL = bottom left; BR = bottom right.

Abbreviated photo agency names: AL = Alamy; Getty = Getty Images; NPL = Nature Picture Library; SS = Shutterstock. *Abbreviated author names:* DR = Dan Rouse; MS = Megan Shersby; RG = Rebecca Gibson; WI = Wild Intrigue.

1 RG; **2** WI; **6** DR **7** MS (both); **12** MS (both); **14** MS (both); **16T** MS; **16B** Ealing Beaver Project; **18** Mike_AA/SS; **20** Steven W Grant/SS; **22** MS (both); **24** MS; **25** MS; **26L** MS; **26R** Alex Cooper Photography/SS; **28** MS (both); **30** MS (both); **32** MS (both); **34** MS (both); **36** MS (both); **39–9** MS (both); **40** MS; **42–3** Erni/SS; **46** M.J Bulich/SS; **47** MS; **48** MS; **49** MS; **50** MS; **52T** Martin Fowler/SS; **52B** MS; **54** MS (both); **57** MS (both); **59T** Erni/SS; **59B** Tom Meaker/SS; **60** MS (both); **62–3** MS; **64** MS; **65** MS (both); **66** WI; **69** WI (both); **71** H Athey/SS; **73L** WI; **73R** Michal Hykel/SS; **74** MS; **75** Christine Rose Photography/Getty; **77T** WI; **77B** M N Studio/SS; **80T** Erni/SS; **80B** WI; **82** WI (both); **84** WI; **86** LFM One/SS; **87** WI; **88T** Shutterstock; **88B** WI; **90** WI; **91L** WI; **91R** Erni/SS; **92** MS; **93** WI; **94–5** WI; **96** Alex Cooper Photography/SS; **97** KPixMining/SS; **98** WI; **99** WI; **102** WI (both); **104** WI; **106** WI;

108T Wirestock Creators/SS; **108B** scullydion/SS; **109** Simon Edge/SS; **119** Mattam1005/SS; **112** WI; **113** WI; **115** WI; **117** WI (both); **119BL** Mattam1005/SS; **119BR** WI; **121** WI; **122** Matt Gibson/SS; **124L** DR; **124R** Sam Viles; **126** Jon Moorby/SS; **128** PJphotography/SS; **129** DR; **131T** Sam Viles; **131B** Tony Baggett/SS; **132** DR; **133T** Sam Viles; **133B** DR; **136–7** Mike Charles/SS; **139** DR; **140–1** Helen Hotson/SS; **141T** DR; **143L** DR; **143R** Rhian Mai Hubbart/SS; **144L** Mark Caunt/SS **144R** Marina Veder/SS; **146–7** Lukassek/SS; **149T** MaybelmaLeo/SS; **149B** Phil Kieran/SS; **150** Colin Ward/SS; **151** DR; **152–3** cktravels.com/SS; **153T** Martin Fowler/SS; **155** ET Swift/SS; **157** Sabena Jane Blackbird/AL; **159** Keith Heaton/SS; **160–1** Gail Johnson/SS; **161T** Sam Viles **163** Gail Johnson/SS **164–5B** Gail Johnson/SS; **167** Mark Caunt/SS **169** Alan Williams/NPL; **170** Helen J Davies/SS **171** Ian Redding/SS **172** Gavin Haskell/AL; **174–5** Alan Saunders photography/SS; **176** RG; **179** RG; **180** RG; **181** RG; **183** RG; **184** RG; **185T** HWall/SS; **185B** RG; **187** RG; **188–9** RG; **191** RG; **192-3** RG; **194** RG; **195** Leo Bucher/SS; **196** RG; **198** RG; **199** RG; **200** Mark Robert paton/SS; **201** RG; **202T** grafxart/SS; **202B** RG; **204** RG; **205** Sandra Stanbridge/SS; **206** dvlcom/SS; **208** RG; **209** RG; **210** Erni/SS; **211** RG; **213T** RG; **213B** Barry and Carole Bowden/SS; **215** RG (both); **217** RG; **219** RG (both); **221** RG; **222** RG; **223** RG; **225** RG; **227** RG (both); **229** RG; **230** grafxart/SS; **231** RG; **232** RG.

Front cover (clockwise from top left): WI; SAKhanPhotography/SS; MS; WI; Robert Harding Video/SS; George Baliasov/SS.

Back cover: RG.

INDEX

Usually only the first mention of a species in each reserve has been indexed.

adder 65, 72, 144, 165, 168, 206
Aira Force 76
Alyn Waters Country Park 172
anemone, wood 92
ant, narrow-headed 64
   wood 59
Arnos Vale Cemetery 49
Ashton Court 45
aster, sea 54
avocet 43, 52, 83, 100, 102, 104, 147
Aylesbeare Common (RSPB) 60

badger 50, 115, 137, 173
balsam, small 188
bat, Brandt's 37
   brown long-eared 169
   Daubenton's 16, 71, 107, 171
   Leisler's 16, 37
   lesser horseshoe 46, 154, 169
   Natterer's 169
   noctule 71, 82, 140, 154
   pipistrelle 71, 82, 93, 106, 107, 113, 140, 154, 171, 197, 200
   soprano pipistrelle 71, 140, 154
beaver 15, 16, 44
beetles 201
   cobweb 45
   dor 61
   green tiger 36, 37
   lesser stag 37
   minotaur 60, 61
   rhinoceros 37
   stag 19
   wasp 57
   whirligig 57
Berney Marshes (RSPB) 31
bittern 27, 30, 42, 75, 80, 84, 89, 91, 142, 144
black duck, American 126–7
blackcap 43, 97, 103, 105, 106, 119, 142, 151, 152, 158, 169, 170, 173, 179, 185
Blacktoft Sands (RSPB) 83
bladderwort 162
bog pimpernel 125
bog rosemary 72, 206
bogbean 30, 144
Bovey Heathfield 64
brambling 70
Brickfield Pond 170
broomrape, ivy 50
Bryn Pydew Nature Reserve 150
bullfinch 113, 121, 158, 185, 190, 195, 200, 205, 225
bunting, cirl 57, 62
   Lapland 147
   reed 25, 71, 72, 74, 82, 105, 115, 126, 147, 162
Burghead Harbour 228
bush-cricket, Roesel's 81
butterbur 197
butterflies 47, 201
   black-veined white 13
   brimstone 144, 159
   brown hairstreak 13, 16
   chalkhill blue 13
   chequered skipper 214, 218, 219, 22
   comma 97, 103, 173, 192
   common blue 58, 103, 137, 202, 233
   dark green fritillary 202
   Duke of Burgundy 14
   Essex skipper 37
   gatekeeper 106, 171
   Glanville fritillary 13, 14
   grayling 61, 149, 169, 177, 179, 190, 202, 233
   green hairstreak 13, 14, 37, 206
   holly blue 50
   large heath 73, 206
   large skipper 37
   large white 192, 195
   long-tailed blue 17
   marbled white 37, 38, 50, 58
   marsh fritillary 124, 162, 214, 219, 223
   meadow brown 58, 137, 174, 192, 202, 233
   orange-tip 41, 99, 219, 221, 231
   painted lady 165
   peacock 159, 173, 182, 195, 221, 233
   pearl-bordered fritillary 59, 223
   purple emperor 17
   red admiral 103, 106, 173, 174
   ringlet 50, 99, 182, 202, 233
   Scotch argus 233
   silver-studded blue 61, 149
   silver-washed fritillary 59, 61, 144, 192
   small blue 13, 14, 74
   small copper 37, 97, 103
   small heath 202, 221, 233
   small pearl-bordered fritillary 59, 223
   small skipper 37, 178
   small tortoiseshell 99, 137, 159, 171, 174, 191, 233
   speckled wood 103, 106, 159, 182, 188, 202, 231
   swallowtail 23, 26, 27, 29
   wall 205
   white admiral 61

buzzard 11, 38, 77, 82, 117, 144, 151, 154, 162, 177, 181, 188, 196, 209, 219

Carsethorn 207
Castle Drogo 58
Castle Loch 210
Cemlyn Bay 160
chamomile 127
chiffchaff 38, 40, 43, 52, 97, 103, 106, 119, 142, 152, 158, 171, 219, 225
chough 126, 127, 128, 133, 135, 137, 149
Chudleigh Knighton Heath 64
Clifton Downs 47
clover, hare's-foot 39
conehead, long-winged 81
Conwy (RSPB) 146
cormorant 57, 107, 113, 117, 131, 153, 221, 229
Corran Esplanade 215
Cors Ddyga (RSPB) 162
Corstorphine Hill 186
cotton-grass, hare's-tail 37
crabs 88, 125–6, 135, 141
crane, common 51, 52
cranesbill, bloody 148
crayfish, white-clawed 95
creeping jenny 144
crocus, sand 63
crossbill, common 11
cuckoo 30, 43, 51, 57, 77, 91, 125, 162, 206, 223
cuckooflower 41, 81
curlew 22, 51, 52, 53, 72, 80, 111, 113, 117, 119, 128, 138, 145, 147, 158, 160, 161, 174, 201, 207, 209, 227, 233

daffodil, wild 37
daisy, ox-eye 39, 57, 58
damselfly, blue-tailed 81, 99, 124, 143, 179
   common blue 99, 143, 171, 180, 219
   emerald 143
   large red 180
   red-eyed 99
   small red 65
   southern 60
   willow emerald 26, 81
Dawlish Warren 61
Dee Estuary (RSPB) 173
deer 18
   Chinese water 30
   fallow 17, 45, 59
   red 17, 45, 221
   roe 45, 50, 53, 59, 82, 106, 113, 115, 121, 190, 197, 200, 206, 209, 226, 231

Index

demoiselle, banded 99
Den o'Mains 199
dipper 58, 59, 68, 95, 97, 121, 154, 182, 183, 197, 224, 226, 230
divers 119, 161
   black-throated 71
   great northern 136
   red-throated 110, 136
dog violet 125
dog's mercury 158
dolphin, bottlenose 119, 224, 228, 229–30
   common 128, 135, 141, 149, 230
   white-beaked 119
dotterel 127, 149
The Downs 47
Dowrog Common 124
dragonfly, black darter 73
   black-tailed skimmer 53, 81
   broad-bodied chaser 57, 106
   common darter 57, 143
   downy emerald 65
   emperor 53, 57, 60, 81, 143, 170, 171
   golden-ringed 219
   hairy 65, 124
   migrant hawker 53, 81
   Norfolk hawker 26, 29–30, 80
   ruddy darter 57, 81
   scarce chaser 26
   southern hawker 106
   white-faced darter 73
Drumburgh Moss National Nature Reserve 72
dunlin 53, 62, 119, 152, 158, 173, 233
Dunollie Wood 216
Durdham Downs 47

eel 59, 100, 205
eelgrass 62
egret, great white 102, 134, 139, 142
   little 40, 42, 102, 139, 158, 207
eider 119, 190, 202, 216, 228–9
   king 229
Eskrigg Nature Reserve 212

Far Ings National Nature Reserve 79
fen-sedge 144
ferns 63, 120, 158
fieldfare 52, 97, 108, 173, 212, 224
Findhorn Bay 232
Fingle Woods 58
firecrest 158
Flamborough Cliffs 87
fleawort, field 165
flycatcher, pied 12, 77
   spotted 11–12, 71, 169
forget-me-not, water 173
   wood 92
fritillary, snake's-head 91
frog, common 173, 17

marsh 20
fulmar 88, 119, 128, 130, 135, 149
fungi 17, 34, 37, 39, 59, 70, 77, 92, 120, 217, 231

gadwall 53, 115, 119, 210, 233
Galeruca laticollis 26
Ganavan Hill 218
gannet 19, 88, 110, 119, 126, 131, 153, 161, 221
garlic, wild 14
Glasdrum Wood National Nature Reserve 222
glow-worm 65, 151
goat, wild 145, 148
godwit, bar-tailed 62, 102, 104, 119, 158, 202, 207, 233
   black-tailed 19, 51, 83, 102, 104, 142, 147
goldcrest 50, 107, 119, 147, 154, 185, 196, 212
goldeneye 74, 104, 115, 147, 204, 210, 227, 233
goldfinch 54, 82, 113, 182, 190, 192, 195, 211, 221
goosander 68, 74, 147, 169, 183, 197, 204, 210, 227
goose, barnacle 52, 203, 209, 210, 233
   brent 173
   Canada 179
   greylag 52, 203, 210
   Hawaiian 51
   pink-footed 78, 91, 100, 101, 173, 203, 209, 210, 233
   snow 233
   white-fronted 30, 52
Gosforth Nature Reserve 114
goshawk 154
Gowbarrow Park 76
grass of Parnassus 37
grass snake 50, 65
grasshopper, lesser marsh 81
Great Orme 148
Great Orme berry 148
grebe, black-necked 22, 89, 91
   great crested 21, 27, 28, 36, 91, 107, 115, 158, 170, 171, 203, 210
   little 74, 107, 115, 227
   red-necked 71
   Slavonian 79
greenfinch 82, 105, 113, 195
greenshank 83, 142, 147
Gronant Dunes 151
grouse, black 166, 167, 168
   red 168
guillemot 88, 128, 130, 135, 149, 156
   black 149, 215–16
gull, Bonaparte's 147
   little 104
   Mediterranean 141, 143
Gwydir Forest Park 154

Hampstead Heath 11
hare, brown 84, 102, 119
harebell 17, 39
harrier, hen 22, 102, 125, 139, 156, 162, 166, 168, 174, 209
   marsh 27, 30, 43, 80, 83, 102, 144, 162, 174
hawkweed, mouse-ear 17
heather 59, 64, 72, 124, 165, 201, 206, 231
helleborine, broad-leaved 158
   dark red 148, 150
   marsh 63
   narrow-leaved 46
Hermitage of Braid 180
Hilbre Islands 109
hobby 11, 27, 30, 60, 73, 91
Holyrood Park 178
honewort 48
honeysuckle 217
horehound, white 148
horsetail, water 41
Hutchinson's Bank 13

iris, yellow 211, 218

jay 70, 93, 107, 114, 121, 140, 212, 231
Joy's Meadow 34

kestrel 11, 54, 82, 84, 89, 91, 97, 102, 106, 113, 117, 119, 130, 137, 151, 165, 185, 188
kingfisher 15, 27, 41, 51, 57, 58, 59, 68, 79, 95, 97, 99, 106, 107, 111, 113, 158, 160, 169, 170, 183, 197, 200, 203, 204, 210, 226
Kirkconnell Flow Nature Reserve 205
Kirkstall Valley Nature Reserve 96
kite, red 95, 121, 144, 209
kittiwake 88, 128, 111, 117, 135, 141
knot 104, 138, 160, 233

ladybird, orange 185
lady's smock 91
lady's tresses, autumn 47, 63, 151
lapwing 30, 40, 52, 91, 102, 104, 117, 119, 138, 143, 145, 158, 162, 190, 193, 201, 209
lark, short-toed 127
lichens 76, 223
linnet 54, 102, 209, 221
Lismore, Isle of 220
lizard, common 72, 73, 95, 144, 165
   wall 48
Llanelli Wetland Centre (WWT) 142
Llanrhidian Saltmarsh 138
lobsters 88
long-tailed duck 136, 138, 202, 224, 228, 229
lords-and-ladies 188

Lossiemouth Estuary 226
Lower Ouseburn Valley 112
Ludwell Valley Park 56

mandarin duck 212
marigold, marsh 105, 211
Marloes 125
Marshside (RSPB) 101
marten, pine 177
martin, house 21, 52, 70, 107, 201, 209
  sand 52, 57, 68, 71, 74, 91, 111, 112, 145
meadow-rue, common 26
Meanwood Valley 93
mergansers 147
  red-breasted 158, 160, 207, 231
merlin 125, 154, 166, 209
Mersehead (RSPB) 208
Middleton Lakes (RSPB) 41
Middleton Woods 92
The Miley 194
Minera Quarry Nature Reserve 168
Moseley Bog 34
moss, Indian feather 26
moths 13, 201
  argent & sable 219
  belted beauty 174
  belted clearwing 16
  burnet companion 38
  chalk carpet 151
  chimney sweeper 223
  cinnabar 38, 180
  cistus forester 151
  double line 18
  elephant hawkmoth 106
  emperor 72
  heath rustic 151
  horehound plume 148
  hummingbird hawkmoth 103, 137, 165
  narrow-bordered five-spot burnet 38
  reddish light arches 151
  scarlet tiger 124
  silky wave 48
  silver-Y 58
  six-belted clearwing 38
  six-spot burnet 38, 58, 137, 159
  sprawler 26
  yellow-legged clearwing 26
mouse, harvest 16, 61, 82
Mumbles 139
myrtle, bog 162

newt, great crested 46, 53
  smooth 173, 174, 193
nightingale 25
nightjar 60, 65, 154
Noddle Hill Nature Reserve 81
nuthatch 50, 70, 93, 107, 114, 121, 173, 205, 213

oaks 17, 45
onion, Bristol 48
orca 230
orchid, bee 13, 37, 39, 47, 63, 103, 143, 147
  common spotted 34, 35, 46, 70, 124, 147, 173, 188
  early marsh 147
  early purple 144, 147, 150
  fragrant 124
  green-winged 37, 46, 150
  heath spotted 61
  lesser butterfly 124
  man 14
  marsh 30, 152, 173
  northern marsh 70
  pyramidal 13, 39, 144, 148, 150, 152
  southern 124
  southern marsh 25, 63, 105, 144, 147
  spotted 105
oriole, golden 127
osprey 193, 201, 224, 226, 227, 233
Otiorhynchus ligustici 38
otter 20, 30, 41, 51, 58, 69, 75, 80, 84, 97, 111, 113, 115, 133, 142, 162, 169, 175, 183, 203, 205, 209, 216, 221
owl, barn 11, 27, 43, 53, 54, 82, 84, 106, 139, 144, 156, 162, 168
  little 89, 91
  short-eared 43, 73, 85, 102, 119, 125, 139, 156, 162, 166, 168
  tawny 11, 50, 82, 140, 154, 169, 171, 185
oystercatcher 40, 62, 104, 119, 127, 138, 140, 142, 145, 153, 158, 160, 161, 173, 175, 207, 220, 233

Pant y Sais National Nature Reserve 143
Paradise Fields 15
parakeet, ring-necked 107
peregrine falcon 40, 49, 77, 84, 102, 117, 126, 128, 130, 154, 165, 174, 209
petalwort 63
phalarope, Wilson's 102
pintail 52, 84, 102, 134, 138, 209, 233
pipit, meadow 102, 137, 152, 168
  red-throated 165
  rock 119
  tree 168
  water 119
Plas Newydd 158
plover, golden 30, 52, 102, 119, 138, 207
  grey 202
  little-ringed 40, 104
  Pacific golden 138

ringed 104, 119, 152, 175, 227
pochard 52, 74, 102, 115, 210
Point of Ayr 173
poppy, yellow horned- 161
porpoise, harbour 10, 119, 126, 128, 134, 136, 149, 161, 209
Portbury Wharf Nature Reserve 53
puffin 88, 123, 128, 129, 131, 156, 165

ragwort, common 180, 188, 202
rail, water 15, 84, 105, 115, 144, 147, 158, 209, 211
Rainham Marshes (RSPB) 19
raspberry, wild 196
rattle, yellow 13
raven 36, 77, 104, 219
razorbill 88, 128, 130, 135, 149, 156, 221
redpoll 221
redshank 19, 53, 72, 104, 111, 113, 117, 119, 138, 142, 147, 161, 173, 193, 207, 229
  spotted 83
redstart 77, 103, 154, 169, 218
redwing 52, 97, 108, 113, 173, 209, 211, 212, 225
Rhosili 135
Richmond Park 17
Rickerby Park 68
Rimrose Valley Country Park 105
ring ouzel 12, 38, 149
River Lossie 225
River Nith 204
Riverside Nature Park 191
Riverside Valley Park 56
rock-cress, Bristol 48
rock-rose, common 48, 150
Rowley Hills 37
ruff 83

salmon 59, 113, 204
sanderling 119, 140, 173, 233
sandpipers 80
  buff-breasted 102
  curlew 83, 102
  purple 110, 207, 229
  spoonbilled 51
  spotted 127
Sandwell Valley (RSPB) 40
Sanquhar Loch and Woodlands 230
scabious, devil's bit 144, 162
  field 39
scaup 71, 207, 233
  greater 170
scoters 207
  common 110
  surf 136
sea campion 148, 161
sea fan, pink 125
sea holly 152
sea kale 161

Index

sea lavender 54
　rock 132
sea slug, sea fan 125
Seaforth Nature Reserve 103
seahorses 63
seal, common 10, 174, 201, 202, 233
　grey 10, 88, 100, 110, 111, 118, 126, 128, 130, 135, 136, 140, 141, 149, 161, 174, 201, 228, 233
Sefton Park 107
shag 88, 220
shark, basking 228, 230
shearwater, Manx 110, 126, 128, 129, 133, 165
shelduck 100, 102, 104, 110, 111, 117, 138, 209, 227
shoveler 74, 115, 119, 138, 142, 173, 209, 233
shrew, water 57
shrike, isabelline 127
Siddick Ponds Nature Reserve 73
siskin 113, 213
Skomer Island 127
skuas 110, 119
skylark 46, 54, 72, 102, 119, 137, 152, 162, 168, 192
Slimbridge Wetland Centre (WWT) 51
slow worm 50
smew 210
snipe 15, 27, 40, 53, 61, 72, 84, 105, 119, 143, 158
　jack 27
sorrel, sheep's 17
　wood 92
South Stack (RSPB) 164
Southerness 207
sparrowhawk 27, 38, 82, 84, 97, 106, 114, 121, 188, 212
spearmint, wild 81
spearwort, greater 105
sphagnum 12, 72, 206
spider, fen raft 30, 144
Spinnies Aberogwen Nature Reserve 157
spoonbill 32, 102, 134
Spurn National Nature Reserve 85
squill, autumn 48
squirrel, red 67, 77, 130–1, 156, 159, 188, 196, 203, 213, 218, 226, 231
St Aidan's (RSPB) 90
St Govan's 132
St John's-wort, trailing 37
St Mary's Island 118
stint, little 83, 102
stonechat 19, 36, 60, 119, 127, 132, 168, 209, 211
stork's bill, sticky 110
storm petrel 132, 165
　Leach's 100, 110
Strumpshaw Fen (RSPB) 29

sundew 72
Surlingham Church Marsh (RSPB) 27
Sutton Park 35
swallow 21, 25, 52, 70, 74, 197, 201, 202, 209
swan, Bewick's 52
　mute 36, 71, 98, 112, 126, 170, 179, 197, 231
　whooper 52, 74, 91, 126, 209
Swansea City Centre 139
Sweet Briar Marshes 24
swift 21, 22, 25, 52, 71, 86, 91, 202, 216

Talkin Tarn Country Park 70
teal 74, 84, 102, 104, 115, 126, 134, 147, 173, 209, 210, 227, 233
　green-winged 147
teasel 81, 211
Templeton Woods 195
Tenby 130
Tentsmuir National Nature Reserve 200
terns 27, 119
　Arctic 21, 153, 161
　black 21
　common 21, 22, 40, 91, 104, 110, 115, 153, 161
　little 110, 145, 152, 175
　roseate 161
　Sandwich 21, 110, 153, 161
thistle, carline 150
　creeping 26
　marsh 41
　melancholy 115
Thornley Wood 120
thrift, sea 132, 221
thrush, mistle 108, 113
　song 25, 57, 82, 113, 209, 221
thyme, wild 165
tit, bearded 20, 27, 30, 80, 84, 89, 91, 144
　marsh 114
　willow 211
toad, common 60, 173
　natterjack 110, 153, 209
treecreeper 70, 93, 107, 114, 121, 173, 177, 186, 200, 204, 231
trefoil, bird's-foot 47, 58
Trottick Mill Ponds 197
trout, brown 22, 59, 183
　rainbow 22
　sea 59
tufted duck 71, 74, 115, 119, 142, 197, 210
turnstone 119, 140, 207, 216, 229
Tyne Estuary 116

vole, Skomer 128
　water 16, 20, 21, 28, 30, 53, 84, 106, 107, 162

wagtail, grey 58, 59, 97, 112, 113, 154, 182, 197, 200, 204, 226, 231
　pied 218, 229
walrus 130
Walthamstow Wetlands 21
warbler, blackpoll 126
　Cetti's 20, 27, 43, 82, 103, 144, 147, 152
　Dartford 12, 19, 60, 126
　garden 43, 105, 151
　grasshopper 27, 30, 43, 72, 82, 103, 105, 119, 144
　Pallas's 165
　reed 27, 30, 40, 43, 52, 74, 82, 84, 105, 106, 115, 126, 144, 147, 151, 162, 209, 210
　sedge 25, 27, 30, 40, 43, 52, 82, 96, 97, 106, 115, 119, 126, 144, 147
　willow 25, 40, 43, 82, 97, 119, 142, 151, 165, 170, 217, 219
　wood 218
　yellow-browed 119, 165, 170
Warriston Cemetery 184
wasp, heath potter 65
Water of Leith Walkway 182
watermint 70
waxwing 225
weasel 82, 137, 162
whale, humpback 230
　minke 149
wheatear 62, 103, 127, 132, 152, 190, 221
Wheatfen Nature Reserve 25
whimbrel 22, 80, 208
whinchat 103
whitebeam, round-leaved 37
Whitehall Riverside Pocket Park 98
whitethroat, common 25, 40, 43, 82, 106, 119, 192, 220
　lesser 43, 82, 106
wigeon 30, 52, 53, 74, 84, 102, 115, 138, 147, 173, 203, 208, 209, 210, 227, 233
　American 102
woodcock 11, 105
woodpecker, great spotted 70, 93, 107, 114, 121, 185, 188, 190, 196, 197, 206, 212, 231
　green 38
　lesser spotted 42
World's End 167
wrasse 135
wren 113, 173, 179, 183, 204, 205, 209, 212, 219, 221, 225

yarrow, fern-leaved 81
yellowhammer 57, 82